French Politics, Society and Culture Series

General Editor: Robert Elgie, Paddy Moriarty Professor of Government and International Studies, Dublin City University

France has always fascinated outside observers. Now, the country is undergoing a period of profound transformation. France is faced with a rapidly changing international and European environment and it is having to rethink some of its most basic social, political and economic orthodoxies. As elsewhere, there is pressure to conform. And yet, while France is responding in ways that are no doubt familiar to people in other European countries, it is also managing to maintain elements of its long-standing distinctiveness. Overall, it remains a place that is not exactly *comme les autres*.

This new series examines all aspects of French politics, society and culture. In so doing it focuses on the changing nature of the French system as well as the established patterns of political, social and cultural life. Contributors to the series are encouraged to present new and innovative arguments so that the informed reader can learn and understand more about one of the most beguiling and compelling of all European countries.

Titles include:

Gill Allwood and Khursheed Wadia
GENDER AND POLICY IN FRANCE

Sylvain Brouard, Andrew M. Appleton, Amy G. Mazur *(editors)*
THE FRENCH FIFTH REPUBLIC AT FIFTY
Beyond Stereotypes

June Burnham
POLITICIANS, BUREAUCRATS AND LEADERSHIP IN ORGANIZATIONS
Lessons from Regional Planning in France

Jean K. Chalaby
THE DE GAULLE PRESIDENCY AND THE MEDIA
Statism and Public Communications

Pepper D. Culpepper, Bruno Palier and Peter A. Hall *(editors)*
CHANGING FRANCE
The Politics that Markets Make

Gordon D. Cumming
FRENCH NGOs IN THE GLOBAL ERA
France's International Development Role

David Drake
FRENCH INTELLECTUALS AND POLITICS FROM THE DREYFUS AFFAIR
TO THE OCCUPATION

David Drake
INTELLECTUALS AND POLITICS IN POST-WAR FRANCE

Graeme Hayes
ENVIRONMENTAL PROTEST AND THE STATE IN FRANCE

David J. Howarth
THE FRENCH ROAD TO EUROPEAN MONETARY UNION

Andrew Knapp
PARTIES AND THE PARTY SYSTEM IN FRANCE
A Disconnected Democracy?

Michael S. Lewis-Beck *(editor)*
THE FRENCH VOTER
Before and After the 2002 Elections

John Loughlin
SUBNATIONAL GOVERNMENT
The French Experience

Mairi Maclean and Joseph Szarka
FRANCE ON THE WORLD STAGE

Mairi Maclean, Charles Harvey and Jon Press
BUSINESS ELITES AND CORPORATE GOVERNANCE IN FRANCE AND THE UK

Susan Milner and Nick Parsons *(editors)*
REINVENTING FRANCE
State and Society in the Twenty-First Century

Gino G. Raymond
THE FRENCH COMMUNIST PARTY DURING THE FIFTH REPUBLIC
A Crisis of Leadership and Ideology

Paul Smith
THE SENATE OF THE FIFTH FRENCH REPUBLIC

Sarah Waters
SOCIAL MOVEMENTS IN FRANCE
Towards a New Citizenship

Reuben Y. Wong
THE EUROPEANIZATION OF FRENCH FOREIGN POLICY
France and the EU in East Asia

French Politics, Society and Culture
Series Standing Order ISBN 978–0–333–80440–7 hardcover
Series Standing Order ISBN 978–0–333–80441–4 paperback
(outside North America only)

You can receive future titles in this series as they are published by placing a
standing order. Please contact your bookseller or, in case of difficulty, write
to us at the address below with your name and address, the title of the series
and the ISBN quoted above.

Customer Services Department, Macmillan Distribution Ltd, Houndmills,
Basingstoke, Hampshire RG21 6XS, England

The Senate of the Fifth French Republic

Paul Smith
Senior Lecturer
The University of Nottingham, UK

First published 2009 by
PALGRAVE MACMILLAN

Palgrave Macmillan in the UK is an imprint of Macmillan Publishers Limited,
registered in England, company number 785998, of Houndmills,
Basingstoke, Hampshire RG21 6XS.

Palgrave Macmillan in the US is a division of St Martin's Press LLC,
175 Fifth Avenue, New York, NY 10010.

Palgrave Macmillan is the global academic imprint of the above companies
and has companies and representatives throughout the world.

Palgrave® and Macmillan® are registered trademarks in the United States,
the United Kingdom, Europe and other countries.

ISBN: 978–0–230–00811–3   hardback

This book is printed on paper suitable for recycling and made from
fully managed and sustained forest sources. Logging, pulping and
manufacturing processes are expected to conform to the environmental
regulations of the country of origin.

A catalogue record for this book is available from the British Library.

A catalog record for this book is available from the Library of Congress.

10 9 8 7 6 5 4 3 2 1
18 17 16 15 14 13 12 11 10 09

Printed and bound in Great Britain by
CPI Antony Rowe, Chippenham and Eastbourne

For my father

Contents

List of Tables

List of Maps

Acknowledgements

The Senate is a living assembly which continues to evolve within a political system that never ceases to change. Only last year the French parliament passed a bill making more than 30 amendments to the constitution, marking the 24th revision since 1958. And as I was writing these words (in early March 2009), former prime minister Edouard Balladur was poised to deliver his report into the reform of local government, a matter which touches the hearts of the Senate and of senators very deeply. It is quite possible, too, that in a very short time the Senate, for so long a bastion of the right, will fall to the left. Exciting times indeed for Senate-watchers. (Both of us).

The research on which this book is based has been funded by the British Academy and by my own institution, the University of Nottingham. I am naturally grateful to both. I have also received encouragement along the way from colleagues and friends too numerous to mention, but I am particularly grateful to Alain Delcamp, general-secretary of the Senate, for the support he has given my work and to Jean-Louis Hérin, director of the Senate's Service de la Séance, for sharing some insights with me and also providing a raft of statistics. Catherine Maynial and her staff in the Senate library, especially Isabel Girardot, have made various visits to the Luxembourg Palace a pure pleasure. I should also like to mention my colleagues Jean Garrigues and Jean-Marie Mayeur, whose own work, as well as their interest in mine, has been more important than they know. My thanks, too, to Robert Elgie for going with the idea of this book in the first place, and to my editor for being *very* patient. The greatest debt of gratitude is to my wife, who has seen my work progress 'avec un train de sénateur'. *Festina Lente.*

Abbreviations

AFE	Assemblée des Français de l'Étranger
CDS	Centre des Démocrates Sociaux
CMP	Commission Mixte Paritaire
CRC	Communiste, Républicain et Citoyen
CSFE	Conseil Supérieur des Français de l'Étranger
DL	Démocratie Libérale
MRG	Mouvement des Radicaux de Gauche
MRP	Mouvement Républicain Populaire
PCF	Parti Communiste Français
PRG	Parti des Radicaux de Gauche
PS	Parti Socialiste
RD(S)E	Rassemblement Démocratique (et Social) Européen
RPF	Rassemblement du Peuple Français
RPR	Rassemblement pour la Républqiue
SFIO	Section Française de l'Internationale Ouvrière
UC(DP)	Union Centriste (des Démocrates de Progrès)
UDF	Union pour la Démocratie Française
UDR	Union des Démocrates pour la République
UMP	Union pour un Mouvement Populaire
UNR	Union pour la Nouvelle République
URI	Union de Républicains et Indépendants

Introduction

There are two holy places in the Republic: school and parliament.[1]

Were it not that the gates were already locked and the Luxembourg Gardens had assumed their nocturnal calm, or that most of its incumbents were engaged elsewhere, on the evening of 6 May 2007 the innocent *promeneur* in that delightful Parisian park might have heard a collective sigh of relief issue from the palace that houses the French Senate. The confirmation, a little after eight in the evening, that Nicolas Sarkozy had seen off the challenge of Ségolène Royal, meant that the right-wing Senate majority would not have to cohabit with a Socialist President and National Assembly intent on reforming the upper house. The fact that a number of senior senators had lent their weight to the campaign of the President-elect and that he in turn was planning to name one of them prime minister, added to the satisfaction.[2] Until 2002, when Jacques Chirac chose Jean-Pierre Raffarin, no senator had been appointed to the Hôtel Matignon since Michel Debré in 1959. Sarkozy's choice of François Fillon meant that the Senate would provide a second prime minister in the space of five years.[3] It was no mere coincidence either that the only members of parliament Sarkozy invited to join him, his family and closest friends at a celebration dinner at Fouquet's that evening were both senators: Raffarin and Fillon.[4]

The appointment of two senators as prime minister in such quick succession and an invitation to dinner does not mean, by any stretch of the imagination, that the Senate, whose members are indirectly elected by universal suffrage, through departmental colleges of local

1

councillors, to 'ensure the representation of local authorities' (Article 24-3), has suddenly resumed the power and prominence of its illustrious/notorious ancestor: this is the Fifth Republic, not the Third. But it does have a symbolic importance for the upper house, reflecting its re-emergence as an assembly that is viewed by politicians as a legitimate platform on which to build, rebuild or extend their careers. It is not just a comfortable retirement home for superannuated deputies - in fact less than one senator in four is a former deputy. Nor is it purely an assembly of local notables racking up elected offices: the rate of *cumul des mandats*, the simultaneous holding of more than one elected office, has been lower in the Senate than in the National Assembly for more than a decade.

Of course, there is a grain of truth in both views. Prominent politicians have chosen to move from the noisy bustle of the lower house to the more serene surroundings of the upper since the republican Senate was first created in the 1870s. In an assembly where Jules Ferry, Georges Clemenceau and Raymond Poincaré continued their careers, so now one might cite the example of Pierre Mauroy, the former prime minister who, anticipating the rout of the left in the 1993 general election, moved to the Senate in September 1992. It would be disobliging to Mauroy, however, to describe his senatorial career as one of peaceful retirement. It is also true that the Senate can still serve as a parliamentary refuge for politicians whose luck has run out in general elections. The ecologist Dominique Voynet, the Communist Robert Hue and, most recently, poacher-turned-gamekeeper Jean-Pierre Chevènement, who as interior minister in Lionel Jospin's *gauche plurielle* government between 1997 and 2000, enjoyed some splendid exchanges with the Senate majority, have all entered the upper house.

Others have used the Senate in a different way. In 1995, Bertrand Delanoë's leadership of the left's campaign in Paris in the municipal elections was followed by a seat in the Senate for the city-department in the autumn of the same year. Six years later, when he became mayor, he resigned from the upper house. For two years, however, the mayors of France's first three cities all sat in the Senate. In 1999, another Socialist, Gérard Collomb, became senator for the Rhône, then mayor of Lyon, in 2001.[5] Unlike Delanoë, Collomb did not resign from the Senate, instead using it and Lyon city hall as a dual base to try to break into the leading circle of the Parti Socialiste (PS).

These examples have been taken from the left and for a reason. Since the 1980s, when a succession of Socialist governments ran into obstruction in the Senate, the left has cried foul of the in-built right-wing majority there. In April 1998, Jospin provided a rallying cry when he described the Senate as an anomaly because structural distortions in the system used to elect the departmental colleges meant its majority never changed.[6] Then, Jospin's government could count fewer than 100 supporters in an assembly of 321. In the intervening period, the Socialists' sense of injustice has only increased, as impressive performances in local elections (regional and departmental in 2004, municipal and departmental in 2008), gave them control of 20 of the 22 regions, 58 of the 96 departments and many of France's major cities. Their performance in municipal elections in the spring of 2008 led directly to the PS gaining more than twenty seats at the Senate *renouvellement* the following September, giving them 115 of 343 seats (compared to 151 for Sarkozy's Union pour un Mouvement Populaire - the UMP) and it is possible that in 2011 the Socialists will become the largest group in the upper chamber. Whether that will allow them to claim the presidency is another matter, but it is one of the reasons Gérard Larcher, who began his term as speaker on 1 October 2008, knew he had little time to waste if he hoped to be re-elected in 2011. Before then, the Senate will have to absorb the impact of two of the most important institutional reforms of recent years: a thoroughgoing reform of the constitution and a fundamental rethinking of the administrative map of France.

Sarkozy appointed two separate commissions to examine these areas of fundamental reform, one in July 2007, the other in October 2008, but he appointed the same man to chair both: Edouard Balladur. His conclusions and the responses to them are described below. The first commission was given a brief to rebalance the institutions of the Fifth Republic. On the one hand, it was driven by a desire to streamline the presidentialisation of the regime brought about by the reduction of the term to five years and the coincidence of the elections of the head of state and the National Assembly. On the other, Balladur was invited to examine how parliament's prerogatives could be enhanced to offset this process. Many, though not all, of Balladur's recommendations provided the basis for the law of 23 July 2008, the 24th revision of the constitution, whose conditions and those of a raft of other organic and ordinary laws introduced to implement them have already begun to have an impact on parliament.

The second reform, still under discussion as this book was being completed, will be one of the major legislative *chantiers* of parliament's 2009 spring session. It could involve a reduction to the number of regions and a major adjustment of the relationship between France's regions, departments and major cities and the creation of a Greater Paris authority (*le Grand Paris*). Given the Senate's constitutional role to ensure the representation of local government (*les collectivités territoriales*), and the stipulation under Article 39-2 that all legislation affecting local government must be presented there in the first instance, to say nothing of the central place that the interests of local *élus* and the *territoires* play in senators' idea of themselves, these changes will have (and are already having) a profound impact on the Luxembourg Palace. Perhaps that sigh of relief that mild May evening was in fact a sharp intake of breath.

* * *

The French Senate has a reputation for political and social conservatism that is not altogether deserved. It is an institution that has evolved with the regime, though not always, as we shall see, easily or happily. Just as Sarkozy's Republic is not de Gaulle's, so Gérard Larcher's Senate is not Gaston Monnerville's. The architecture outwardly looks the same, but there has been some major extension and demolition work to the edifice. The Senate's problem is that, like many second chambers in non-federal states, it has difficulty finding its place in the Republic, where the media focus is more normally on the President, government, parties, the National Assembly, or trades unions. Its contribution appears peripheral, secondary, and obscure.

And yet, paradoxically, the Senate forms the apex of a political culture to which French citizens are profoundly attached: 70 per cent voted in the 2008 municipal elections and in some small communes the rate passed the 90 per cent mark. Half-a-million citizens, one in 100, sit on municipal councils and 130,000 serve as *grands électeurs* in the departmental colleges that elect senators, though not in equal proportions. The system is far from perfect, but this perhaps crude outline gives some weight to the view of the late Yves Weber that wherever it is found 'bicameralism informs and reflects entirely the deeper nature of the political system.'[7] The story of the Senate of the French Fifth Republic is at one and the same time an exercise in constitutional and institutional history and political culture.

Pierre Mazet wrote of the Senate:

> Accused of conservatism, criticised for defects in its
> representivity, the upper chamber is permanently obliged to
> justify its place among [political] institutions [...] The place

and role of the Senate have been and always are the object of negotiation and updating.[8]

Senators are fated, then, to a Sisyphean 'travail de légitimation' and a process of reinvention in a way that deputies are not. They legitimise their place and their role by recourse to a number of ideas about themselves and their institution that Mazet calls *structures structurantes*.

These *structures* are many and varied. In the first place is the Senate's primary, legislative role. The Senate is a *chambre de contrôle* and a *chambre de réflexion*. Both houses have a mission to control the government, of course, but the Senate's is double: controlling the government but acting as a counterweight to the government and its majority. This links to the function of reflection: that the Senate, by virtue of going second (mostly, though not exclusively) or being second, and also because it is less exposed to the ebbs and flows of opinion, places a premium on the painstaking, meticulous work of its commissions in rooting out poor draughtsmanship and making good law. It is a matter of quiet satisfaction among senators that every year thousands of their amendments make their way onto the statute book. In recent years, the Senate has taken an important lead too in evaluating the application of legislation and its annual report is eagerly awaited.[9] The reflective view is reinforced by the pervasive air of calm in the Luxembourg Palace and the stability of its membership. Some would say that the serenity of the house masks the deadly truths that lie beneath. As an anonymous senator put it during the contest to elect the speaker in 1998, the Senate gives one 'time to hate'.[10] This is, after all, a Medici Palace. And one man's stability is another's stagnation. In fact, membership of the Senate turns over at a greater rate than has generally been acknowledged.

While insisting on the importance of its participation in the whole legislative process, the Senate has also, for a variety of reasons, assumed particular interest in a number of areas which provide a supplementary group of *structures*. The danger that docile majorities in the National Assembly might be too easily led by governments wanting to wield the big stick has led the Senate to claim a special concern for civil liberties, though the record is here decidedly uneven. The experience of some of its members at the hand of the state broadcasting authorities, especially over the 1962 referendum, helped senators develop a very healthy interest in control of the media: in 1986, the upper chamber rewrote the bill privatising TF1. In financial matters, the Senate inherited from the Third Republic a reputation for budgetary orthodoxy, while its concerns for the interests of French expatriates springs from its monopoly, until 2012, of representation of citizens living abroad, a monopoly that arose more by accident than design, but which has nevertheless helped to define the Senate's place. And the assembly of rye and chestnuts has always spoken for the interests of French agriculture, though usually 'big' rather than 'little' agriculture.

It is, however, in its constitutional vocation to represent the *collectivités territoriales*, the communes, departments and regions of France and especially their *élus*, as the assembly representing the territories of France and the men and women, the modern-day active citizens, elected to govern them, that the Senate has come, today, to most clearly assert its identity and difference. Léon Gambetta called the Senate the Grand Council of the Communes of France and whether that is true or not, as Jean Mastias wrote, one can hardly read 20 pages of the *Journal Officiel* without one senator or another using it.[11] In the 1960s and 1970s, representing the territories mainly involved protecting local councillors from the encroachments of the state – and in 1969 fighting off the threat of corporatism. From the 1980s, however, after the Defferre decentralisation reforms, senators came to insist on their constitutional vocation, a view confirmed in 2003, when the constitution was amended, under the Raffarin government, establishing the Senate's primacy over legislation affecting local government. How that happened, and how the changes under consideration by the Balladur commission in 2009 went straight to the heart of the Senate's concerns are explored below.

Two final *structures* emerge from studying the French upper house. It has always been and remains a viscerally Europhile assembly. 'First generation' senators were deeply embarrassed by the rhetoric of de Gaulle and the Empty Chair crisis. There successors were determined that, in 1992, after the Maastricht referendum, the Eurosceptic Charles Pasqua should not become speaker. In 2005, the Communists were the only Senate group to vote against ratifying the EU constitution.

More recently, the Senate has cast itself as a leader in the international bicameral movement. This was a particular hobby-horse of former speaker Christian Poncelet, who saw it as means of reinforcing the Senate's legitimacy. Despite the potential for such an enterprise to become an exercise in moral instruction, the process has proved to be one of real dialogue and a symbol of remarkable openness as to how ideas from elsewhere might be adopted and adapted to make the Senate more effective. A *rapport d'information* drafted by two senators, one UMP, one PS, into the functioning of six different EU parliaments produced a number of recommendations that the upper chamber has since introduced into its procedures.[12]

Just as *sénatophiles* use these *structures structurantes* to justify the Senate's particularities, so *sénatophobes* have a range of what one might call *structures déstructurantes*. To Jospin's anathematisation of the anomaly, aimed at the right's apparently impregnable grip on the upper house, one could add Jean Grangé's attack on its 'dysfonctionnement': that in fact the Senate does not act as a counterweight at all.[13] It assists right-wing governments and does its best to hinder left-wing ones. The counterbalances to government lie outside parliament, in the Constitutional Council, European law and public opinion. The way it is elected is a throwback to a France that no longer exists. For Robert Badinter, former president of the Constitutional Council and since 1995 senator for the Hauts-de-Seine (though a man who has never actually won an election by universal suffrage), the upper chamber is the most acute problem facing the Republic, and the way it is elected 'archaic and a challenge to democratic principles'.[14] The Senate may well represent the various levels of local government, but it does not do so equally. Towns of fewer than 3,500 inhabitants contribute nearly half the total number of municipal delegates to the electoral colleges, while for cities of more than 100,000 it is less than five per cent. Few left-wing critics of the Senate have gone as far, however, as Ségolène Royal did in September 2005, when she called the upper house 'an unbearable anachronism' that should be abolished.[15]

These and other arguments are explored in the present work, which assesses the Senate in two ways. Part One considers the Senate in the political life of the Fifth Republic. It begins with a brief 'pre-historic' chapter on the Senate's forerunners under the Third and Fourth Republics. Despite very important differences with the modern Senate, its ancestors and the regimes they inhabited, there is still, institutionally, a strong sense of continuity - that certain characteristics have been handed down from one upper house to another. It is also important to understand how the fundamental model for the Senate, essentially the same as that established in the 1880s, came about and how some patterns of behaviour both in the Senate and among its electors have changed very little. And the Senate of the Fifth Republic is not just the product of continuities: it bears also the marks of what the successor regimes have rejected from the past.

Chapters 2, 3 and 4 examine the Senate's protean role in the unfolding of the Fifth Republic, beginning with the restoration, then rejection of the upper house under de Gaulle, culminating in the thwarted attempt at abolition in 1969. Chapter 3 examines how the Senate coped with the normalisation of politics after de Gaulle's departure, how it fell into bipolarisation and how its right-wing majority coped with the challenges of the Mitterrand years. It concludes by looking at the institutional revival between 1992 and 1997, under the stewardship of speaker René Monory. Chapter 4 opens with Lionel Jospin's attack on the Senate in April 1998 and its consequences - the fall of Monory and the election of Christian Poncelet - and examines how the latter's agenda to make the Senate the *chambre des collectivités territoriales et de la décentralisation* brought the Senate a moment of apotheosis in 2003, before a period of hesitation and doubt returned. The chapter concludes with the unexpected challenges of the Sarkozy presidency and the election of Gérard Larcher as president.

Part Two - Senators and the Senate - focuses on the structures that underpin the the upper chamber. Chapter 5 looks at the way that senators are elected in the departments, how seats are distributed and at the electoral colleges. Chapter 6 looks at how senators are elected, their relations with their electors and at the *corps sénatorial* since 1958 from a number of different viewpoints. Chapter 7 examines how their lives are organised in the Luxembourg Palace and how the political shape of the Senate has developed since 1958, to the point that in 2008, the right is preparing itself to lose control of an institution that it has controlled for 30 years. Finally, the Conclusion assesses the future of an institution that may be on the cusp of seismic change.

Part I
The Senate in the Fifth Republic

1

Bicameralism and political culture in the French Republic

Bicameralism in France dates back to the summer of 1789, when the Monarchiens, liberal constitutional monarchists who briefly held sway over the National Assembly, put before their colleagues a proposal to give France a parliament comprising a House of Representatives and a Senate, based on the provincial assemblies. The proposal failed, however, in the face of the prevailing view that representing the one and indivisible France meant there could be only one assembly. The shortcomings of the Legislative Assembly, created in 1791, the fall of the monarchy, the still-born experiment of the Jacobin constitution and the Terror, put a second chamber back on the agenda in 1795. The Thermidorians threw away the Jacobin constitution of 1793 and drew up a bicameral one that established a body of 750 representatives split into two assemblies: a Council of Five Hundred - the 'imagination' of the Republic - and a Council of Elders – its 'good sense', as Boissy d'Anglas, one of its authors, put it. The complicity of the Elders in Bonaparte's seizure of power in 1799, however, did nothing to secure bicameralism a place in the minds of nineteenth century French republicans. That the Council of Elders successors – the Imperial Senate under Bonaparte, the Chamber of Peers under the Bourbon (1815-30) and Orléans (1830-48) monarchies and the *Sénat conservateur* of the Second Empire – all comprised royal or imperial nominees, only cemented the view that the Republic should have only one chamber. From that perspective, the presence of any second chamber at all in the modern Republic is a small miracle. But the first modern French Republic, whose institutions were devised in 1875, was the fruit of a compromise in which the Senate was, in fact, the keystone.

The constitution is the Senate[1] – 1875

The Senate of the Third Republic was built on the ruins of two abortive attempts to provide France with a constitution, one by Adolphe Thiers in 1873, the other a year later by Albert de Broglie. Thiers had been chief minister under the Orleanist King Louis-Philippe, but rallied to the Second Republic after 1848, calling it 'the regime that divides us least'. In September 1870 he was a member of the Government of National Defence of the embryonic Third Republic, but in the autumn of that year it was Léon Gambetta's star that was rising. Gambetta called for a new *levée en masse* and all out war to liberate France, but when this failed, he fell. Thiers brokered an armistice with Bismarck and in early February, a National Assembly was elected. The results were something of a paradox. Thiers' ascendancy was confirmed, but the majority in the Assembly was monarchist, not republican. In August 1871 Thiers was formally accorded the title of President, largely because the monarchists were preoccupied by competing Bourbon and Orleans pretenders and over what kind of monarchy to restore. An initial attempt at restoration in 1871 ended in failure. The following year, however, Broglie returned from his duties as ambassador in London, stiffened monarchists' resolve to bring down Thiers and launch another attempt. On the first count he succeeded, on the second he failed.

Thiers hoped to rally moderate men of both sides to form a centre bloc, but succeeded only in steeling the leaders of the right and upsetting those of the left. Neither was ready yet to concede their entrenched positions. Still, in May 1873 he left as a parting gift a draft constitutional law, which established a baseline for the negotiations over the upper house: the institutional role and prerogatives Thiers gave to his Senate were reproduced almost verbatim in 1875.

Like the Monarchiens, Thiers borrowed his terms from the United States, with a President, a Senate and a House of Representatives in a semi-presidential framework long before the term had been invented. Both chambers would be elected by universal male suffrage. Members of the House of Representatives must be aged 25 to stand and would be elected for five years in single-seat districts (*scrutin d'arrondissement*). Senators would be elected for 10 years, with one-fifth facing re-election every two years. The departments, the great success story of the Revolutionary redrawing of the French administrative map, would serve as the senatorial constituency and election would be by a list system. Seats would be distributed on an equal, quasi-federal basis: the 86 metropolitan departments that remained after the German annexation of Alsace and Moselle, would each have three senators, irrespective of size or population. Belfort, the tiny *territoire* carved out of southern Alsace as part of the Frankfurt Treaty, would receive one seat, as would each of the three Algerian departments and the colonies of Martinique, Guadeloupe and La Réunion. Eligibility to stand would be restricted to pre-determined categories of citizen, ranging from existing deputies to higher bracket taxpayers, bishops and cardinals, senior officers and so on. There would be an age qualification: senators had to be at least 35. Both chambers would have equal legislative rights and the Senate would also try cases of impeachment of either the President or ministers and concerning threats to state security, a role played by the Chamber of Peers under the Restoration and the July Monarchy.

Unlike the Second Republic, where the President had been elected by universal male suffrage, Thiers' head of state would be elected by a college comprising the two chambers and three delegates from each *conseil général*, the departmental assemblies. The presidential term would be five years, to run concurrently with the lower house, but the President was not responsible before parliament. He would have the right to dissolve the House, but only with the Senate's approval (*avis conforme*).

Thiers' attempt to create a (semi-)presidential, constitutional republic could not save him. Constitutional monarchists were not yet ready to concede restoration was beyond their grasp. Broglie engineered Thiers' fall, levered Marshal MacMahon, Duc de Magenta, into the Presidency and was then charged with forming a new government. His immediate task was to make a fresh attempt to restore the monarchy. When this failed, in the summer of 1873, attention turned instead to clarifying MacMahon's position. In November the Assembly fixed his term of office until 1880 and the *septennat*, the seven-year term abolished only in 2000, was born.

Broglie turned his mind to the constitution in the spring of 1874, when he presented a bill to create a Grand Council of Notables. The Council was a mixed, quasi-corporatist assembly. Cardinals, admirals, marshals, senior judges, would be members *ex officio*. The President would appoint 150 life members, nominated by the government from among senior judges, active and retired senior civil servants and personalities from the spiritual and intellectual worlds. Ten seats would be in his gift. A third portion would be elected by departmental colleges. Each department had one seat for the first 300,000 inhabitants, two for up to 600,000, up to a cap of three. The colleges would comprise deputies, departmental and district councillors and delegates for each commune, alongside the local clergy, senior civil servants, judges, senior lawyers and representatives of commerce, agriculture, industry and high bracket taxpayers.

The Grand Council was elaborate and outdated, but it was important for two reasons. In the first place, it was the main offer on the table at the beginning of 1875, when various pressures came to concentrate minds on resolving the constitutional question and in the second because it introduced into the debate the idea of senators elected by colleges composed of councillors from the various levels of local government within each department. Thiers had defined the Senate's rights and prerogatives, Broglie provided an electoral base that persists to this day.

The idea of an upper house elected, in part at least, by local assemblies can be traced back to the Monarchiens. Since then, liberals of various stripes had suggested introducing leaders of departmental assemblies - the *conseils généraux* - into the upper house, as active citizens with a stake in the body politic and as key intermediaries between centre and periphery. By the 1870s it was an idea whose time had come, thanks in large part to the evolution of republicanism under the Second Empire. Forced from power at the centre, republicans regrouped in the communes and moderate, bourgeois municipal republicanism was born, perhaps best summed up in the person of Jules Ferry, who believed that Frenchmen would best understand and appreciate the freedoms and responsibilities of citizenship if they first practiced them at the municipal level.[2] In November 1874, despite wholesale interference by the Broglie government, municipal elections shifted the balance of power towards the republicans. By the same token, success in the communes made it easier for republican leaders to convince their followers that a constitutional compromise could be found, based on an upper chamber that drew its authority not from the old class of local notables defined by birth, land-ownership, wealth or appointment, but from a new one, based on local *élus*, tempered in the crucible of universal suffrage.

By January 1875 most parties were ready to negotiate, but the initiative now lay with the republican Centre-Left and a small hinge group of moderate Orleanists who accepted that there would never be a restoration. Among the latter was a Catholic historian named Henri Wallon and on 30 January the Assembly adopted his amendment that 'made' the Third Republic and the Senate, by 353 votes to 352.

> The President of the Republic is elected by a majority of votes by the Senate and the Chamber of Deputies meeting as the National Assembly. He is elected for seven years. He is re-eligible.

Yet all was still not settled. The Radicals on the republican left-wing managed to force through an amendment that deputies and senators should have the same electorate. Negotiators on both sides of the argument turned this apparent obstacle to their advantage in an innovative fashion. Rather than interpret the amendment as meaning that both houses must be elected in the same way, they used it as a pretext to remove *ex officio* senators and tax qualifications either for candidates or electors. The Senate would be based on indirect universal suffrage, by making all senators subject to election by one representative body or another. The question was how.

The answer was found by Louis Cézanne, a liberal deputy who proposed a mixed assembly of 300 senators, 225 elected by departmental colleges, meeting in the *chef-lieu* or capital of each department, and comprising deputies, general and district councillors and one delegate from each commune, to elect senators for nine years, with one third elected every three years. Each department was guaranteed a minimum of two seats (Belfort one). For the remainder, instead of senators nominated by the head of state, Cézanne proposed creating 75 senators, chosen by parliament in three groups of 25, to be re-elected at the same time as their departmental colleagues. The right demanded that the nominated seats should be for life-senators appointed by the head of state. The republicans conceded life-senatorships, but would not accept appointment and suggested election by the National Assembly in the first instance and by the Senate thereafter. The right conceded. The 225 departmental seats were distributed as Cézanne proposed, with at least two per department. This accounted for 176. The other 49 were allocated to the more populous departments, so that the Seine (Paris and the districts of Sceaux and Saint-Denis) and the Nord were both given five, six others received four, 27 three seats and 51 departments with the minimum. Belfort got one seat, as did each of the Algerian departments and La Réunion, Martinique and Guadeloupe. French India would also elect a senator. Eligibility was limited to French nationals aged 40 and over.

The bill creating the Senate was the first of the constitutional laws to be passed, on 24 February 1875. (The election and composition of the Chamber of Deputies, by contrast, was regulated by ordinary legislation.) The first seven articles of the law referred to the distribution of seats. The eighth, which would later become the bone of considerable contention, established that the Senate would have legislative parity with the Chamber, except over the budget, which must pass the lower house first. The law also formally established the Senate's role as a political court in cases of impeachment and crimes against the state referred to it by the government, with the Chamber's approval.

A bill setting the Senate law into the broader institutional context was enacted the following day. The first article recognised that legislative power was exercised by the Chamber of Deputies and the Senate, the second that the Senate and the Chamber, meeting as the National Assembly, would elect the President of the Republic. The President, through the government, had the right to initiate legislation, as did members of both houses. The Chamber could only be dissolved with the Senate's approval of a presidential writ. Revision of the constitutional laws could be raised in either house, but no finalised, formal text was necessary. One or other chamber need only decide that there was cause to revise the constitution to trigger a joint meeting of the houses, sitting as Congress. Revision looked very easy, but Congress met only four times between 1879 and 1940.

A third law, of 16 July 1876, finalised the relationship between the institutions. Meetings of the National Assembly, either to elect a new President or sitting as Congress to revise the constitution, would be chaired by the president or speaker of the Senate, though unlike the Fifth Republic, they were not designated as interim President: that task fell to the government collectively and it was expected that if there were a sudden vacancy, the National Assembly would meet with all speed to elect a new head of state. (Even after parliament had returned to Paris such meetings took place at Versailles, as meetings of Congress still do.) The law also established that the presidents of both chambers and their executive officers (the *bureau* of vice-presidents, secretaries and *questeurs*) would be elected at the beginning of the parliamentary session every January.

The Senate of 300 partnered a Chamber of Deputies, which in 1876 numbered 533, elected for just four years for single-member constituencies using a two-round majority-plurality system known as *scrutin d'arrondissement*. A department-wide list system was used in 1885 before a switch back in 1889. A profoundly gerrymandered system was introduced in 1919, principally to prevent the Socialists winning power. This was retained in 1924, but the old system was restored for the last three elections of the regime – in 1928, 1932 and 1936. The Fourth Republic introduced PR for the National Assembly and lengthened the term to five years. De Gaulle and Debré kept the five-year term, but revived *scrutin d'arrondissement* and it has been used in every general election bar one (1986) since.

The Senate was conservative in several ways. It was, of course, intended to preserve the government from a single assembly elected by universal male suffrage, though it also protected the lower house, since dissolution was conditional on Senate approval. In the second, it was intended to protect vested interests by recourse to an electorate of committed, engaged, active citizens – the local councillors who comprised the colleges. Thirdly, the nine-year term of office was the longest of any in the Republic: local councillors enjoyed a four-year term until 1929, when the six-year cycle was introduced. What was more, once the first elections had taken place, the Senate would never by wholly re-elected, settling instead into a rhythm of three-yearly *renouvellements*, as Senate elections are known. With the allocation of a minimum of two seats to each department, rural senators hugely outnumbered urban ones. In 1876, each of the five senators for the Seine represented 482,000 inhabitants. In the Hautes-Alpes the rate was 1:59,000. And with just one delegate per commune in the colleges, the large urban centres were swamped.

Not all republicans accepted the Senate immediately. For the Radicals, rejection of the compromise for 1875, demands for a 'real' constituent assembly and abolition of the Senate separated them from fellow republicans for the next two decades. But if the majority of republicans were not instinctive bicameralists, most were willing to acquiesce in Gambetta's description of the new Senate as a Grand Council of the French Communes, the 'guts' of French democracy.[3]

With a nine-year term dangling in front of them, it is hardly surprising that a very large number of the men who had guided France in the first half of the 1870s took up residence in the Senate: 136 of the 225 (60 per cent) of the seats elected in January 1876 went to former members of the Assembly. The presence of many of the leaders of the most moderate republican faction, the Centre-Left, in the upper chamber, led President MacMahon to call on senators, not deputies, to head government: from August 1876 to September 1880, with an interval of only a few days in 1877, each *président du conseil* was a senator. In an era of small cabinets – between ten and twelve ministers – senators took half the portfolios. The tension between conservatives and the more progressive republican majority in the Chamber became too much, however, and in 1877 provoked a crisis that would prevent the emergence of strong government for the next 80 years.

In May 1877 MacMahon became infuriated with the failure of premier Jules Simon, a Centre-Left life-senator, to take a firm line with the Chamber. Simon resigned and MacMahon responded by reappointing Broglie, but his attempt to recreated the coalition of centres that had passed the constitutional laws in 1875, in fact only consolidated the republican bloc. MacMahon had no choice but to ask the Senate to approve a writ of dissolution, which passed only because a small hinge group of liberal monarchists voted to let the constitution take its course. October's elections went badly for the government. Broglie clung on, but the turning point came when the speaker of the Senate, the Duc d'Audiffret-Pasquier, informed MacMahon that a second dissolution would find no majority in the upper chamber.

The crisis was a watershed. Parliament asserted its primacy and the institutional balance of 1875, which gave the the head of state considerable potential power, was shattered. MacMahon hobbled on until January 1879, but when the first *renouvellement* gave the left a majority in the Senate, he resigned. His successor, Jules Grévy, announced that no republican President should ever seek to dissolve a Chamber elected by universal suffrage and in the process established a rule that would not be broken until 1956. The only President to attempt to break away from the *constitution Grévy*, Alexandre Millerand, was overthrown in 1924 as a consequence - by the Senate.

1884

Republican victory in the Senate in 1879 was a certainty, following municipal elections the previous year dubbed 'the town hall revolution', such was the scale of their triumph. With majorities in both houses, the republicans set about implementing a vigorous programme of reform that laid the foundations of the modern Republic, including the introduction of free, compulsory and secular education, freedom of association, more permissive press laws and the confirmation of the status and organisation of France's 37,000 communes. Constitutional revision was also on the cards and in 1884 Jules Ferry piloted limited changes through Congress.

Despite continued calls from the left for the abolition of the Senate, Ferry had no intention of doing so: he knew it was far too important for government to have at its disposal a counterweight in negotiations with the Chamber. Thus, when Congress met at Versailles in August 1884, Ferry went to great lengths to ensure the Radicals did not turn the session into a constituent assembly by proxy. Congress agreed to a series of minor revisions, including the 'de-constitutionalisation' of the sections of the law concerning the election of senators. It was then left to senators themselves to devise a new arrangement. The subsequent law of 10 December 1884 introduced changes that have provided the electoral foundation for the upper house ever since.

The life-senatorships were abolished, with the seats to be redistributed to the departments, but only as the incumbents died. As a consequence, the last two only became available in 1920. Redistribution followed a very loose demographic logic. The priority was to ensure that as many departments as possible benefited from the windfall and all but ten got an extra seat. The most important and lasting characteristic of the reform was the reorganisation of the electoral colleges. Henceforth, instead of each commune having just one delegate, a sliding scale was introduced, linked indirectly to the population of a commune, through the size of municipal councils. This was in line with a law passed in April 1884, which established the size of councils according to broad demographic bands. The effect of the new system was to shift the overall balance within the colleges from the small communes towards France's medium-sized market towns, which in fairness, in 1884, were where most people lived. The total number of *grands électeurs*, as members of the Senate colleges came to be known rose from 43,000 to 76,000. In the Seine the college expanded from 216 electors to 713, but the most impressive increase was in Finistère in Brittany, where the college tripled in size from 392 to 1244, a reflection less of demographic size and more of the ancient patterns of communal settlement in the Breton peninsula.

A republican Grand Council of Notables

The mildness of the reform reflected both the speed and the success with which the Senate had become embedded in political culture, fostered by the unique way in which the interface between local and national politics evolved in France. During the 1880s, legislation established a series of ineligibilities between elected and official posts. It was not explicitly prohibited, however, for members of parliament to hold local and national office at the same time. There is nothing unusual about local politics acting as the nursery for budding parliamentarians of course, but in France it became both common and acceptable to be a senator or deputy and also be chairman of the *conseil général* and a mayor of one of the key towns in one's department. In the Senate in fact it became almost *de rigueur*. Defenders of this *cumul des mandats*, the vertical accumulation of offices, argued that it acted as a necessary palliative to the overbearing centralising tendencies of the state. Senators were, therefore, not only elected by local colleges, but were key actors within them and naturally cultivated and perpetuated their positions.

It was also perfectly natural that local councillors, *les élus*, came to see themselves as a special group and senators as the representatives of their corporate interests in a way that deputies could not be. The intimacy of the relationship was confirmed by the election itself, held on one day with electors converging on the departmental capital to cast their votes in what amounted to a celebration by the political elite of itself. For electors, the vote was compulsory and absence without *bona fide* reasons subject to a financial penalty. Such cases were rare: being a *grand électeur* was a mark of prestige and important business might be transacted at the election.

Renouvellements used a three-round majority-majority-plurality system. There were no thresholds to disbar candidates progressing from one to the next. Voting in the first round opened at eight in the morning, so delegates from outlying communes and districts often arrived the night before, allowing for more socialising, networking and bargaining. The results of the first round would be announced just before lunch, which then became either a moment of celebration, commiseration, or hard talking if a run-off were necessary. Quite commonplace in the early years of the regime, run-offs became the exception in later years. Candidates and their agents had usually calculated where the votes would fall and cut whatever deals were necessary well in advance with the most important electors (mayors of larger communes, the president or vice-presidents of the departmental assembly), who would in turn deliver blocs of reliable delegate votes.

It was not a hard-and-fast rule for all senators in all departments throughout the Third Republic, but it is clear that the colleges tried to balance the various interests and, for want of a better term, identities of their departments, whether these were social, cultural or economic. In some this was easier to manage than others. In the Nord, for example, with eight seats, all the *arrondissements* (the administrative subdivision of a department) could be represented. In the Basses-Pyrénées, as Pyrénées-Atlantiques was then known, it was unthinkable that among the three senators there would not be at least one representing the Béarn east and another Basque west of the department. Smaller departments did not have this luxury. In those with only two seats, for example, it was not so easy to ensure the interests of three different sectors were represented, but it was very unusual for all senators to come from one or other locale within a department. Such issues still weigh heavily today. Senators, then, became the *les élus des élus* and their assembly both a republican Chamber of Peers and a Grand Council of the Notables *not* of the communes, but of the *arrondissements* of France.

As far as moderates were concerned, 1884 drew a line under Senate reform. Radicals continued to call for abolition until the end of the decade, when Georges Boulanger, whose demagogic blend of Bonapartism, radicalism, nationalism and socialism, mostly paid for by the royalist party, appeared to offer a serious threat to the regime. A few Radicals rallied to Boulanger's call for a constituent assembly, revision and abolition, but most saw through the adventure and consequently cast revision aside. The Senate's prestige was confirmed in August 1889, when the government chose to try Boulanger and his co-conspirators before the upper chamber.

The trial of the Boulangists marked the beginning of a decade of recovery for an institution that had spent much of the 1880s in the shadows. In 1893, the Senate elected Jules Ferry to the speaker's chair, a step interpreted by his many opponents as the platform from which he would launch an attempt on the Elysée. The hypothesis was never tested. Ferry died suddenly and unexpectedly only a month later. Another six years would elapse before the Third Republic was ready to elect the speaker to the Elysée Palace. That honour fell to Emile Loubet, a senator who guided the upper house through a major test, in 1896, when it brought down a Radical government led by Léon Bourgeois.

'Senatophobic' historiography has tended to see the downfall of Bourgeois as the opening chapter in the long struggle between progressive, reformist governments and the entrenched, conservative Senate, alongside the fall of Edouard Herriot in 1925 and Léon Blum in 1937 and 1938. It was to these examples that Lionel Jospin was referring when he likened the Senate in 1998 to the Senate of a bygone age. The reality is at the same time more prosaic and more complex.

The Chamber elected in 1893 had had great difficulty finding its political centre and in 1896 President Félix Faure decided to give their head to the Radicals, who had done a great deal to undermine the various administrations that had come and gone. Faure knew that the Radical's plans for an income tax would meet formidable opposition in the Senate, despite Bourgeois having an apparently comfortable majority on paper in the Chamber. The Senate had no constitutional mechanism at its disposal to express no confidence in a ministry, but senators had developed various forms of vote through the *Règlement* (standing orders) that amounted to the same thing. A series of adverse votes there saw the government's majority in the Chamber evaporate and by April 1896 deputies abandoned the government to its fate. Bourgeois attempted to mount a counter-offensive, but his only real support was on the far-left and among the small numbers of demonstrators prepared to turn out on the street to protest. Bourgeois was no rabble-rouser and he resigned.

The crisis highlighted one of the critical tensions between the assemblies under the Third Republic. Article 8 of the Senate law stated that the upper house had the same legislative rights as the Chamber, except with regard to the budget, which had to be presented to and voted on by the lower house first. There was considerable ambiguity over whether this meant that the Senate was permitted to make amendments, but from the very outset senators had insisted on that right and were more often than not supported by governments keen to rein in public spending. There had been some support in 1884 for giving the Chamber the final word on legislation, but the Senate refused and Ferry had not been prepared to jeopardise the whole reform. The budget was habitually thrashed out by the government and the two finance commissions: if a budget was not voted in time, the state functioned on temporary, monthly *douzièmes* until it was.

Bourgeois was replaced by Jules Méline, who, in outlining his government's programme, made reference to the Chamber's 'preponderance' in the legislative process, without making it clear quite what he meant by this and neither he nor his successors returned to the theme with any enthusiasm. Méline remained in office for more than two years, surviving a general election in February 1898, only to be brought down four months later by the Dreyfus Affair.

The details of the Affair need not concern us here, but an unexpected side-effect was to usher in a new era for the Senate. One of the sticking points to a swift resolution was Faure's steadfast refusal to pardon Alfred Dreyfus. Providence intervened in February 1899 and struck down Faure. The way was now open to elect a President inclined to issue a pardon. The man chosen was Emile Loubet, speaker of the Senate, whose election set an unexpected trend: four of the seven men to follow him into the Elysée arrived directly from the Petit Luxembourg, the speaker's official residence, while a fifth, Raymond Poincaré, was elected in 1913 in an all-Senate contest. (Paradoxically Poincaré was the Chamber's candidate, against senator Jules Pams.) Only Paul Deschanel, President from January to November 1920 and his successor Alexandre Millerand, who lasted until May 1924, were elected from the Chamber. Given the role of the speaker as chair of the National Assembly and as heir more-or-less apparent to the Elysée between 1899 and 1940, it does not seem so strange that the position became known as the *deuxième magistrat de la République*, and it may in part be this tradition that de Gaulle had in mind when he elevated the speaker to interim President in 1958.

One of his first acts as President, in June 1899, saw Loubet call upon a fellow senator, René Waldeck-Rousseau to form a government to restore order and liquidate the Dreyfus Affair. There was nothing unusual in asking a senator to head the government. Senators had led eight of the 28 governments since 1879, though no senator had served as premier since Loubet himself in 1892. Senators were called upon usually as caretakers, a temporary expedient while the lower house found its majority, but Waldeck was no stop-gap. He remained in power for nearly three years, until the 1902 general election returned a majority in which there were too many Radicals for his liking. He resigned, recommending that Loubet appoint another senator, Emile Combes, as his successor. For all but six months of the ten years between the appointment of Waldeck and the fall of Clemenceau in July 1909, senators led the government.

The presence in the upper chamber of Clemenceau (from 1902) or of Léon Bourgeois (1905) certainly has a ring of irony. More significantly, their presence underlined the importance the Senate had reclaimed in the political process and they were by no means isolated cases. The new century saw a raft of heavyweights move to the Senate and not always as a comfortable retirement after long service. Clemenceau and Bourgeois still had twenty years at the forefront of French politics ahead of them, while Poincaré was only 43 when he moved there in 1903 and would go on to serve five spells as prime minister and a full Presidential term. The effect of this migration was to underline to lesser men that entering the Senate need not signal an end to one's ambitions and many prominent figures took the road to the Luxembourg Palace sooner rather than later.

Clemenceau's first stint as prime minister did not, however, result in the Senate playing a leading role in the legislative process. Indeed, so docile had the upper house become under Clemenceau that Maurice Rouvier exclaimed that there was no longer a Senate.[4] Aristide Briand, who succeeded Clemenceau in July 1909, roused the upper chamber from its torpor. In outlining his government's programme he made three direct references to the upper chamber in a speech applauded in the Chamber, but greeted with glacial silence in the Luxembourg Palace. Briand's wake-up call was intended to alert both houses that none of the promises made when Clemenceau came to power in 1906 had been fulfilled and that failure to move forward with legislation on worker's rights and pensions would only drive the proletariat into the arms of the Socialists. The message was particularly directed at the Senate, where many of the reforms lay mouldering in the *cartons* of its various commissions. Herein lay another of the problems of the regime. With no fixed number of readings, no last word, and ministries vulnerable in both houses, it was easy to stifle legislation through inertia. The Senate was undeniably the worst culprit, but both houses could smother legislation and governments were not always energetic. Briand's warning did not go unheeded, however, and moderate social legislation was at last enacted in the years before the First World War.

Absolute bicameralism

The war caused the suspension of all elections until late 1919. Then France experienced a burst of activity, beginning with a general election in November, municipal and departmental elections in December, two postponed Senate *renouvellements* and a large number of outstanding by-elections at the beginning of January 1920 and the election of a new President of the Republic two weeks later. The principal concern among republican leaders of all colours was to prevent the Socialists, and particularly their pro-Bolshevik factions, winning power in the general election. To that end, they chose to introduce an electoral system of quite breathtaking iniquity.[5] To capitalise fully required the pooling of resources and a number of politicians whose reputations had taken a battering during the war launched an electoral alliance called the Bloc National. Led by Alexandre Millerand, the alliance was intended to gather the parties who had finished the war supporting Clemenceau. In practice, the Bloc National only functioned fully in a handful of departments, but the results surprised all concerned. France had its most conservative majority since 1871 and a Chamber filled, moreover, with new and inexperienced deputies. The Socialists lost heavily, despite raising their share of the national vote, but the Radicals, who had come to consider themselves the natural party of government, were decimated. Fortunately for them, local elections and renewal of rather more than two-thirds of the Senate provided continuity. Millerand, the new premier, was delighted to have an inexperienced, impressionable and essentially reformist Chamber at his disposal. His rivals were aghast, and counted on the Senate to balance this new *chambre introuvable*. In so doing, they raised the upper chamber to an unprecedented level of intervention that continued to grow throughout the interwar period, to the upper chamber's cost at the Liberation.

In September 1920 Millerand was elected to the Elysée. The new President had already upset moderates and Radicals by suggesting that, once the task of national reconstruction was underway, parliament should turn its thoughts to constitutional reform: in short Millerand attempted to reassert the prerogatives of his office that Grévy had cast aside. In October 1923, as the legislature wound to the end of its term, Millerand broke with all precedent in a speech at Evreux in which he attempted to frame the forthcoming election campaign by attacking the *régime parlementaire* and called for the strengthening of the power of the executive. His opponents in the Cartel des Gauches denounced the speech as evidence of dictatorial tendencies, while even those on his side of the fence, most noticeably prime minister Poincaré (back in the Senate since 1920), refused their support. The victory of the left set up a power the Senate was obliged to settle.

The Cartel's leaders hoped Millerand would spare them a fight and resign, but he refused to go and when they responded by refusing to form a government, the President appointed a conservative senator, Frédéric François-Marsal. He had no majority in the Chamber, and instead of presenting his government to deputies, went instead to the Senate. Although the Radical Gauche Démocratique had a narrow majority there, Millerand knew that many of its members were uneasy with the Cartel. His hope lay in detaching enough waverers to vote for the new government, which would also indicate if there was a majority likely to vote for dissolution. Senators friendly to the government tabled what amounted to a vote of confidence, but opponents countered with a guillotine motion. The crucial decision lay with the speaker, Gaston Doumergue, as to which vote would be taken first. Though Doumergue was the most moderate of Radicals and no friend of the Cartel, he ruled (rightly) that the closure motion had priority. The government lost the vote. As news of the result reached the Chamber, left-wing deputies stood and cried 'Vive le Sénat'. The crisis was not, however, resolved to the Cartel's entire satisfaction. When parliament met to elect a successor, it chose Doumergue rather than Paul Painlevé, speaker of the lower house. The link between Petit Luxembourg and the Elysée was renewed and would not be broken again in the life of the Third Republic.[6]

Edouard Herriot became prime minister and coaxed the Senate along by making the chairman of its finance commission, Etienne Clémentel, his finance minister. By the turn of the New Year it was clear that France was running into financial problems and that in his desire to reassure the business community by taking only very timid measures, Herriot had swept the issue under the carpet. In the spring, when the parlous state of French finances was revealed, Herriot had already decided to stage-manage his own exit, by falling 'to the left' in the upper house, over the introduction of a tax on capital. Clémentel resigned. Herriot pushed the measure through the Chamber and made the bill a question of confidence in the Senate, where, as expected, he lost.

Doumergue persisted with various combinations of more-or-less watered down varieties of the Cartel before conditions were ready, in July 1926, for the Radicals to abandon the Socialists and rally to a centre-oriented Union Nationale majority, led by senator Poincaré, who successfully negotiated the general election in the spring of 1928 before ill-health forced him to resign a year later. Poincaré had never had much time for institutional reform, but the same was not true of the men who inherited his majority, André Tardieu and Pierre Laval, both of whom willingly embraced a number of measures intended to modernise, if not radically shift the balance of French politics. These measures, known as *réforme de l'Etat,* included the introduction of single round PR for general elections, reducing the number of deputies (now more than 600) and extending the franchise to women. Tardieu aspired to creating the elusive Tory party *à la française*, by establishing the conditions for bipolarisation. The force of his arguments, some of which would be repeated in 1946 and enacted in 1958, ran, however, into the obstacle of the Senate, where the Gauche Démocratique majority cast itself as the guardian of parliamentary orthodoxy. The Millerand episode had only served to boost resolve and two governments - Tardieu in 1930, Laval in 1932 - fell in the Senate over *réforme de l'Etat*.

The 1932 general election once again brought victory to a left-wing alliance, but the *néo-cartel* proved incapable of responding to the Depression. Impotent governments came and went, while a succession of politico-financial scandals fuelled the revival of extreme right-wing anti-parliamentarianism and street violence which culminated in rioting in Paris on 6 February 1934. The government should have stood its ground, but premier Edouard Daladier resigned. President Albert Lebrun persuaded Doumergue to come out of retirement and become prime minister.

In 1924, Doumergue had stood squarely in the way of the attempt to revive the constitution of 1875, but his term as President, during which he had appointed 15 premiers, led him to conclude that change was needed: *réforme de l'Etat* became fashionable once more. The Chamber set up a commission to examine changes, which included automatic dissolution if three governments fell within the lifetime of one parliament. Doumergue knew that the stiffest opposition would come from the Senate. If he had pushed early for the changes, he might have forced some concessions, but he focussed instead on transforming the prime ministerial office into one worthy of the name. By the autumn it was clear Doumergue would not find a majority among his former colleagues: senators would neither use nor lose the *avis conforme*. Doumergue stood down, though he left his successors the Hôtel Matignon, the former Austro-Hungarian embassy, as the permanent official residence of the head of government.

Réforme de l'Etat was largely an affair of the right and during the Tardieu-Laval period and again under Doumergue, the Senate had struck an unlikely alliance with the Socialists, who generally saw institutional reform as a distraction from the serious business of social reform. A time when most of Europe had fallen to dictatorship was a time to stand behind the Republic's institutions, not undermine them. This unlikely partnership unravelled in May 1936.

The surprise was not that the Popular Front won the election, but that the Socialist SFIO was its largest component and Léon Blum was obliged to accept Lebrun's invitation to form a government. The Front did not have a majority in the Senate: probably no more than fifty senators were truly pro-Front, though the votes that saw Blum fall in June 1937 and again in April 1938 suggest a slightly higher figure. Still the Senate, led for all practical purposes by Joseph Caillaux, chair of the finance commission, would not overturn a government that had won a general election immediately after it came to power and particularly not in the face of the spontaneous wave of strikes that broke out in its support.

Blum did not repeat Herriot's mistake of proposing only moderate reforms. The Matignon agreements to end the strikes were anything but timid. But Caillaux knew that the tide of euphoria would ebb and the flight of capital from France eventually weigh against Blum. In February 1937 the prime minister announced a pause in the reform programme and in June he and finance minister Vincent Auriol asked for emergency powers to tackle France's financial and economic problems. The Chamber voted in favour and left Blum to his fate. The Popular Front limped on, under the leadership of Radical senator Camille Chautemps, and it was left to the Senate to deliver the *coup de grâce* in April 1938, by rejecting Blum's request for *pleins pouvoirs* for a second time.

The later years of the Third Republic saw the Senate achieve a level of influence in French political life it had not seen since the 1870s and for similar reasons. First, the practice among leading politicians of seeking a seat in the upper house had not abated since the First World War. Second, the number of senators in government had risen again, and third, in the absence of a strong executive, parliamentary commissions increasingly took the initiative. Caillaux was never a modest man, but there was some truth in his boast that the Senate finance commission had steered the French economy through the worst of the Depression. Part of Blum's struggle with Caillaux was also a struggle to assert government prerogatives.

By the time the Republic fell in 1940, the Senate was in bad odour with both left and right. What made matters worse was the fact that senators had posed as the defenders of the Republican status quo, a bastion of stability in a dangerous world: then, in July 1940, they capitulated. Of course, senators were not alone in voting full powers to Pétain, though it did not help that, proportionately, fewer senators said no than deputies. Nor was it in the Senate's favour that Laval was a senator and that other senior figures in the upper chamber (most notably Caillaux and Chautemps) were prominent in the pro-armistice lobby. And at the climax, it was the president of the Senate, Jules Jeanneney, who chaired the sitting of the National Assembly that surrendered power to Pétain.

The Fourth Republic - Bayeux and its consequences

The Council of the Republic, the second chamber under the Fourth Republic was, like its predecessor, the result of protracted negotiation between unlikely political partners and unconvinced bicameralists. Unlike the Senate, however, the Council was more a bolted-on extra than the keystone of the constitution. Notwithstanding, from unlikely beginnings in 1946, it carved out a space that meant its leaders were well positioned to seize the opportunities offered in 1958.

In October 1945, the Provisional Government asked French men and women if they wanted to revive the Third Republic, an offer rejected by 96 per cent of the electorate. To Communists and Socialists, who together held a narrow majority of seats in the first Constituent Assembly, this meant no upper house: 'On 25 October 1945 the French people rejected the Third Republic' exclaimed the Communist Jacques Duclos, 'and that means the Senate'.[7] They consequently drafted a constitution with a weak President, a strong, single National Assembly (a significant semantic shift in comparison to the old regime) with a reinforced internal committee structure, flanked by consultative councils representing the Empire (a Council of the French Union) and the social partners (an Economic Council). The proposals passed the Constituent Assembly in April 1946, but were rejected in a referendum in May. A second Constituent Assembly was elected on 2 June. The Christian Democratic Mouvement Républicain Populaire (MRP), which favoured a second chamber, was the largest single party in the new assembly, but the other bicameral parties did less well than expected, the Communists and Socialists better. Then Charles de Gaulle weighed into the debate.

De Gaulle had resigned as head of the Provisional Government in January, partly because he was refused permission to put his ideas to the commission charged with drafting the constitution. Since then he had observed a studied, brooding silence, which he broke finally on 16 June, at Bayeux. His theme was the need to restore the authority of the state through strong institutions, in particular the President, but de Gaulle also gave deliberate prominence to a second chamber. He acknowledged that it was right that the lower house, elected by direct universal suffrage, must have the last word over legislation, but he also insisted on the need for a counterweight. De Gaulle sketched the outline of a tripartite, mixed assembly, representing the communes and departments (the *collectivités territoriales* as they had come to be known), professional and social groups and the empire, in what he called, consciously echoing Gambetta, the Grand Council of the French Union. The idea of a semi-corporatist upper chamber was not a new one: proposals to include representatives of the nation's economic and social *forces vives* had been around since the 1890s, though they burgeoned during the crisis of representation in the 1930s. Many constitutional thinkers of the Resistance advocated a mixed second assembly combining regional representation and the social partners, including such unlikely corporatists as Vincent Auriol.[8] For would-be social ideologues of Gaullism like René Capitant and Louis Vallon, a semi-corporatist upper house became part of the 'pure' vision of the *République gaullienne* and when he returned to power in 1958 de Gaulle first spoke of a Senate in these terms. There was also of course a calculation behind the speech. Gaullism was not simply a call to form a new party but an attempt to rally or undermine others, in particular the MRP. The immediate effect, however, was to force the leaders of the MRP to show greater flexibility in negotiations with their PCF and SFIO coalition partners than they might otherwise have done. Bayeux, therefore, undermined the short-term possibility of achieving a balanced bicameral system.

The Socialists argued that the general election results implied only minor changes were needed to the April constitution and suggested a marginally more robust Council of the French Union, elected by the various local assemblies in France and *outremer*. Members would participate in electing the President, but in other respects the Council was consultative: it would examine all legislation, but would only communicate its views through the speaker or the *rapporteur* of the appropriate commission, who would be heard by the Assembly.

The MRP proposed a Council of the Republic, elected by local councillors for metropolitan France only. Legislation would receive a first reading in the National Assembly and then pass to the Council, which had three months to examine and amend. Deputies could accept amendments by simple majority, reject them by absolute majority, or ask the upper house to consider a new text. The Council was expressly forbidden to overturn governments. The party's leadership overlooked the long-held preference among the party rank-and-file for a corporatist assembly, settling instead for a Social and Economic Council, and restricted overseas representation to a separate consultative Assembly of the French Union.

The deal put to the Constituent Assembly was a hybrid of these propositions. Parliament would comprise the National Assembly and a Council of the Republic, elected by indirect suffrage by the *collectivités territoriales*, a neologism that covered all levels of local representation in *métropole* and *outremer*. Members would participate in the election of the head of state and examine and vote on all legislation after a first reading in the National Assembly. Amendments made in the upper chamber could be rejected out of hand by deputies, unless they had passed by an absolute majority, in which case they could only be rejected by an absolute majority in the lower house. There was no scope for a formal *navette*, nor did members of the upper house have the right of initiative. The constitution moreover fixed the number of councillors at between 250 and 320 seats to ensure the majority in the upper house could not join with the minority in the lower when electing the President. In a curious echo of 1875, the left insisted 50 seats should be for National Assembly nominees.

Few people were really satisfied with the arrangement. The Communists suspected that an imaginative second chamber might exploit loopholes in the constitution to its advantage. The bicameral bloc of Radicals, the Union des Démocrates et Socialistes de la Résistance (UDSR), Moderates and MRP deputies came within two votes of forcing through an amendment to establish a considerably more powerful assembly. Despite misgivings, the final draft passed in the early hours of 29 September by 440 votes to 106, forced through by a government determined to obtain a vote before de Gaulle was due to speak at Épinal later that day. To no-one's surprise, de Gaulle reiterated his commitment to a strong second chamber and an even stronger Presidency and rejected the new draft. On 13 October 1946 the French participated in their third constitutional referendum in under a year. The Socialists and MRP urged a 'yes'. A reluctant PCF offered tepid support in response to the vehemence of Gaullist opposition. Radicals and Independents stopped short of outright rejection. In the conditions it is hardly surprising the constitution passed by nine million votes to a little fewer than eight, with a further eight million abstentions.

The provisional Council of the Republic

The local assemblies were in no fit state in 1946 to elect departmental colleges. A transitional article was therefore added to the constitution, allowing for municipal elections in the spring of 1947 then renewal of the upper house in 1948. For now, the prime concern amongst the parties was to ensure that the 'provisional' Council should mirror the National Assembly as closely as possible. To this end, measures were adopted to allow the parties to intervene at various points. The number of seats was fixed at 315. The French Union and the newly created *départements d'outre-mer* were allocated 51, Algeria 14. The *métropole* was allocated up to 214, which with the 50 nominated seats would have given a total of 329. The parties could choose to allocate all 214 seats to the departments and leave 36 to be distributed by the National Assembly, or to keep all 50 for the Assembly and allocate just 200 to the departments. The decision did not have to be taken until the election results were known.

For once and once only, on 24 November 1946, the French directly elected delegates for the colleges within the cantons, the grouping of communes used to elect the *conseils généraux*. The colleges then met a fortnight later. Metropolitan seats were elected in two ways. Each department's allocation was divided into two groups, A and B, where A represented the number of members to be elected directly and B the total number of direct and 'interdepartmental' seats. Thus, in departments allocated two seats, one was elected directly, those with three directly elected two and so on. In this way, a first tranche of 127 members were elected: the 68 departments with only one councillor to elect directly used a simple majority vote, in the others a blocked-list variant of the d'Hondt highest average proportional system. Candidates were obliged to declare their party affiliation for the next part of the process and each party's national vote was added up and the remaining interdepartmental seats distributed using the d'Hondt formula. Candidates who had failed in the first ballot were ranked on their party list according to the number of votes they had received individually and seats allocated as a party took a seat. Councillors were then held to represent the department where they had stood.[9] The process was completed by the nomination of 50 members by the National Assembly, according to the size of each political group. The Assembly also opted to set aside seats to represent French nationals living outside the French Union.

The Council returned to the Luxembourg Palace and met for the first time on Christmas Eve 1946, without its overseas members. The

Communists assumed that, with Socialist support, their leader, Georges Marrane, would be elected speaker, but the MRP, Radicals, Moderates and a handful of Socialists rallied behind the Christian Democrat veteran Auguste Champetier de Ribes. When the full Council reconvened in January 1947 the result was tied, but Champetier retained the post by virtue of being the elder. He was, however, terminally ill and when he died two months later, the Communists once again demanded the presidency. The MRP and the Moderates backed Gaston Monnerville, Radical member for Guyane and vice-president of the assembly. Despite instructions to the SFIO group to support the PCF candidate, Monnerville won by 141 votes to 131 in the second round, thanks to the defection of a dozen *outremer* Socialists.[10]

The secret of Monnerville's success was threefold. In the first place, his moderate Radical politics placed him in the centre of the upper chamber. In the second, he embodied the unity of Republic and Empire.[11] Thirdly, he expressed a firm commitment to exploit every opportunity to promote the Council's rights as a parliamentary assembly.[12] Monnerville, a lawyer who had practiced with one of France's best known 'political' firms before becoming a deputy and minister before the war, knew that constitutions rarely play the way their authors anticipate or intend.

Monnerville's new post was certainly no sinecure, as government and parliament tried to work out their relationship with one another. Because all legislation had to pass the lower house first, the Council experienced long periods of inactivity, exacerbated in 1947 by deputies' passing half of all legislation under emergency procedures, which reduced the Council's time for deliberation from three months to one. This began to change, however, after May 1947 when the Communists were expelled from government. Faced with the growing challenge of organised Gaullism - the Rassemblement du Peuple Français (RPF) was created in April 1947 - a succession of Third Force governments (SFIO, MRP, Radicals and others) deployed the upper chamber as a lever in negotiations with the lower.[13] Gradually the Council found the basis for a viable relationship.

The return to 1884

The next stage in the transformation of the Council from a 'façade of bicameralism'[14] came about in September 1948, when Radical prime minister Henri Queuille – a senator for the Corrèze before the war -

took a calculated risk to revive (more or less) the electoral system of 1884, in order to head off the twin threats posed by the PCF and RPF, both of which had done well in the 1947 municipal elections, but principally in France's urban centres.

The electoral law of 1948 fixed the term of office at six years, the same as all local elected offices and set the age of eligibility at 35. After a complete re-election in 1948, the Council would be renewed by half every three years. The departmental colleges once again comprised deputies, departmental councillors and municipal delegates, though the scale employed (still linked to the size of municipal council) was altered in such a way as to favour medium sized communes, where the RPF and PCF were weakest. As a consequence, the number of *grands électeurs* rose from 89,000 in 1946 to a shade over 100,000. The nominated seats were scrapped and redistributed among the departments. Although the old Third Republic minimum of two seats per department was not revived, setting the population threshold for a second seat at 154,000 meant there were only five single-seat departments, compared to 24 in 1946. One of those to gain a second seat was the Lot - population 154,893 - where Monnerville had, at Queuille's instigation, put down roots. Departments with up to three seats used a two-round majority-plurality system, those with four or more PR.

The gamble paid off. Although the MRP, formerly the largest single group, crashed from more than 70 seats to just 18, the other coalition parties performed well. The Socialist grew from around 40 to 62, the various independent and peasant groups accounted for about the same, but the most impressive gains were for the Rassemblement de la Gauche Républicaine (Radicals and UDSR), which took 79 seats. The Communists fell from 70 seats to 21. The RPF won 56 seats and its leaders predicted that there would be a pro-Gaullist *intergroupe* of 120 in the new Council, but that simply failed to materialise.[15] Queuille called the Gaullists' bluff when he announced that he regarded Monnerville's re-election as speaker as a vote of confidence. Unable to affect the outcome, the RPF abstained and Monnerville was re-elected without serious competition. The election brought a new sense of self-confidence to the institution, most clearly expressed in amendments to the standing orders in December 1948, drafted by a new member for Indre-et-Loire by the name of Michel Debré. Symbolically, the boldest of all the changes was the revival of the title of senator.

The period between the election of the second Council of the Republic and the next general election (in June 1951), was a testing time for the upper house, whose majority was very different to the National Assembly elected in 1946. This was not necessarily a bad thing, however, because Third Force governments under pressure in the Assembly were very willing to allow senators to explore the limits of their prerogatives and used the Council's good offices themselves as a bargaining chip. Legislation nicknamed *la réformette*, passed under Pierre Mendès France in December 1954, and which included the right of initiative for senators and restored the *navette*, the legislative shuttle between assemblies, really only formalised what had been allowed to happen in practice by skilful manipulation of the standing orders. In late 1953, the election of René Coty, a vice-president of the Council, to replace Auriol at the Elysée Palace, seemed to confirm the return of the upper chamber. Later invited to look back on the Council's achievements, Monnerville described the period as a 'remontée continue', a period of sustained recovery.[16] With de Gaulle's return, recovery became restoration - for a while.

2

De Gaulle and the Senate 1958-1969

The 1958 constitution is … first and foremost the Senate.[1]

On 6 May 1953, disappointed by the performance in the municipal elections and exasperated by some of his followers' craven willingness to accept ministerial positions, de Gaulle announced his withdrawal from the RPF. A little over a year later, in June 1954, Pierre Mendès France became prime minister amid hopes that an end to the war in Indochina and a dose of constitutional reform might stabilise the regime. The first was quickly achieved, through July's Geneva Accords, but the constitutional *réformette* was only ratified in December. A month earlier, the first incidents in what was to become the Algerian war had broken out. Mendès had extricated France from one war of decolonisation, but this time drew a line.

Pious hopes that modifications to the constitution might force a change of behaviour in the National Assembly proved misplaced. At the end of November 1955, Mendès's successor Edgar Faure lost a vote of confidence by an absolute majority. Under the terms of *la réformette*, if the Assembly passed two votes of no confidence by an absolute majority within a fixed period, the premier could ask the President to dissolve parliament. Faure decided to break the 80-year taboo and bring the general election forward six months to January 1956. The result was a narrow victory for the Republican Front, an alliance of the non-Communist left and centre-left. Coty invited Guy

37

Mollet (SFIO) to form a government. Despite the rapid deterioration of the situation in Algeria and disastrous events in Suez, Mollet remained in office longer than any other Fourth Republic premier. But when he fell in May 1957, normal service was resumed, first under Maurice Bourgès-Maunoury, then Félix Gaillard. The latter resigned on 15 April 1958 and it was nearly a month before Coty (who had long admitted in private that the only person capable of resolving the imbroglio was de Gaulle) was able to find a successor in MRP president Pierre Pflimlin.

The appointment provoked an angry reaction among the Algerian *colons,* who viewed Pflimlin as soft on the rebel Front de Libération Nationale (FLN). In the meantime, de Gaulle's supporters in Algeria, in France and even in Gaillard's caretaker government (e.g. defence minister Jacques Chaban-Delmas) conspired to exploit the crisis and facilitate the General's return. On 13 May, the day Pflimlin was due to seek investiture, a Committee of Public Safety took control in Algiers. Deputies responded by endorsing Pflimlin. Two days later, addressing the crowd gathered before the Forum building in Algiers, one of the members of the Committee of Public Safety, General Raoul Salan was acclaimed when he concluded his harangue with the words 'Vive de Gaulle'. De Gaulle's return was, however, neither immediate nor inevitable and the next two weeks witnessed a protracted game of musical chairs. Pflimlin was not quite powerless: on 27 May he made his own plans for constitutional reform a question of confidence and once more won the backing of the Assembly. The very real threat of military action emanating from Algiers, and the less likely menace of Communist insurrection, saw prominent figures including Mollet, Auriol and Antoine Pinay rally to de Gaulle. On 28 May Pflimlin bowed to circumstances and resigned.

De Gaulle conducted himself throughout the crisis with studied ambiguity. For most of the time he remained in Colombey-les-Deux-Eglises, but on 19 May travelled to Paris for a carefully stage-managed press conference at the Palais d'Orsay, in the course of which he famously insisted that he was not, at the age of 67, about to embark on a career as a dictator. Throughout the crisis, de Gaulle was at great pains to avoid comparisons with the events leading to Pétain's coming to power at Vichy in July 1940. To that end, though after some hesitation on his own part, he went in person to the National Assembly on 1 June to set before parliament the conditions for his investiture. These amounted to emergency powers to restore order in Algeria and a short pre-constitutional law (later known as the law of 3

June), setting the parameters for the discussion of France's constitutional future. De Gaulle was adamant there would be no constituent assembly: the new constitution would go straight to a referendum. And although delegations from both assemblies participated in the committee stages, the government dominated the process.

The froth surrounding May 1958 sometimes obscures the fact that many of the Fourth Republic's most prominent figures had come to the conclusion that the constitution was in need of a radical overhaul. The *réformette* was a disappointment, both in its content and its results and as early as 1956 proposals to introduce automatic dissolution had been revived, along with the removal of parliament's right to raise or lower public expenditure, and even the election of the head of state by universal suffrage, after a gap of more than a century.[2] No-one, however, had suggested increasing the powers of the upper chamber.

La restauration sénatoriale - writing the Senate in 1958

It might seem a paradox to speak of the restoration of the Senate, given that the Fifth Republic turned the traditional relationship between executive and legislature on its head, but that is how contemporaries interpreted the new regime in its early days. Unlike the Third and Fourth Republics, the second chamber started out with a number of advantages. Both de Gaulle and Debré favoured a Senate whose views the government could invoke when it encountered difficulties with the Assembly. In that regard, they were the heirs of 1875. The Council emerged from the debris of the old regime with a better reputation than the lower house, while its delegates worked with far clearer purpose and cohesion than their counterparts from the Assembly.[3]

The constitution-writing took place in stages, across a number of different committees and subcommittees. Apart from the government itself, there was an Interministerial Committee including the ministers of state representing the various parties and the speakers of the two chambers - Monnerville and his rather ineffectual counterpart André Le Troquer. De Gaulle chaired this group, which met only at the beginning and end of the process. There was a Consultative Committee of 39, chaired by Paul Reynaud and composed mainly of delegations from the two houses. Finally, the La Celle Saint-Cloud group of constitutional experts and senior civil servants, chaired by Debré, handled the fine detail. The timeframe was tightly constrained:

in June the government outlined its overall plan to the Interministerial Committee. The La Celle Saint-Cloud group would then co-operate with various working groups on the draft, which would be passed on to the Consultative Committee for comments. A full draft would be ready for the Conseil d'État to discuss by 13 August. De Gaulle planned to present the new constitution to the people on 4 September, the anniversary of the declaration of the Republic in 1870, before a referendum at the end of the month.

There were 10 senators sitting alongside the 16 deputies on the Consultative Committee. They were led, in name at least, by Geoffroy de Montalembert, chair of the Universal Suffrage Commission. In reality the delegation was managed by the Senate's most senior civil servant, secretary-general François Goguel, who also acted as mediator between Monnerville and Debré.[4] The delegation approached negotiations with a very straightforward brief: to restore a fully bicameral system. This, they argued, was the promise made on 3 June: that government would be responsible to parliament, not just the National Assembly. They failed on that count, through the efforts of Mollet and Pflimlin to rescue some of the Assembly's privileges and because Debré would not allow each chamber the right to censure government. Still, the delegation could be more than satisfied with what Didier Maus described as less than 1875, but more than 1946.[5]

At Bayeux in 1946, de Gaulle had invoked a mixed, tripartite second chamber, representing local government, the empire and professional associations and interest groups. That was the opening offer now, but the corporatist element was quickly abandoned. Mollet pointed out that the 3 June law stipulated that all representative institutions would be based on universal suffrage, whether direct or indirect. The Consultative Committee was almost unanimous in agreement. Debré and de Gaulle recognised that not all the battles had to be won at once and conceded. The colonial element remained in place, however, right up until August, when overseas representatives voiced strong objections. A separate Senate of the French Community was created instead.[6] This 'African Senate' disappeared *de facto* in 1961, following independence, but was only expunged from the constitution in 1995.

The upper house emerged with both its institutional prestige and its legislative role enhanced. The revival of the title of Senate was a potent symbol itself, along with the promotion of the speaker to interim head of state, a role previously played by the speaker of the lower house. In return, the speaker and *bureau* of the National

Assembly were charged with the task of organising sittings of Congress, the joint meeting of both houses revived under Article 89 as the means for ratifying revisions to the constitution. The parity of the two speakers was underlined elsewhere in the constitution. Both would nominate three of the nine members of the new Constitutional Council, alongside the President. The President, both speakers and the prime minister would have the right to petition the Council.

Article 24-3 stated that, like its predecessors, the Senate would be elected by indirect universal suffrage. But it went considerably further, stating that the Senate ensures the representation of the *collectivités territoriales* and French expatriates. At the time this was understood as an expression of how the upper house was already composed. Nevertheless, the wording was quite different to the Fourth Republic, which had simply stated that the upper house was elected indirectly by departmental and municipal councils. Largely overlooked at the time, the wording would come to have importance later.

The Senate's share in the legislative process was also enhanced. The stipulation introduced in 1954, that bills must pass two readings in both houses, was retained, with a third reading in the National Assembly if necessary (though in practice three readings in each became the norm). The government was armed, however, with various means of short-circuiting or extending this process or of applying pressure: by declaring a bill a matter of urgency, it could restrict the length of time and number of readings: or it could resort to the *vote bloqué*, a package vote that obliged the chambers to take the legislation or leave it: finally, under Article 49-3, the government could make a bill the subject of a vote of confidence in the National Assembly (though not in the Senate).

The most prominent sign of the legislative renaissance of the upper house was the creation of the Commission Mixte Paritaire (CMP), a joint-commission where both assemblies would have equal representation, despite the fact that there were only a shade more than half as many senators as deputies, charged with trying to come up with a compromise that suited both. It had been proposed that the CMP should be automatic - perhaps after two readings in each house - but Debré insisted that government retain the right of convocation.

The Senate also enjoyed a number of specific privileges. It could not bring a government down, but under Article 49-4 it could be invited to express its approval: in the event, this mechanism was not used before 1975. The Senate could not be dissolved. There were other important guarantees too. Any organic law concerning the Senate, either directly or indirectly, had to receive the approval of the upper house. The same applied (or appeared to apply) to all constitutional reforms. Finally, the constitution stipulated that the speaker of the Senate should be re-elected only following each *renouvellement*, and not at the beginning of each annual session, as had been the case since 1876.

In all other regards, senators were treated the same as deputies. Because the new constitution declared the post of minister and member of parliament incompatible, all candidates had to name a *suppléant(e)* to take their seat if they were called into government. The only exception to this rule in the Senate was in departments using PR (the new regime raised the threshold from four seats to five), where the next unelected candidate on the list would act as replacement. Ministers were still eligible to stand for election: if successful they would have thirty days to decide whether to stay in office or take up their seat. The same applied to deputies who stood for election to the Senate - and *vice versa*. The revival of the upper chamber's prestige was further emphasised when the electoral law, passed in the autumn of 1958, reintroduced a nine-year term.

The revenge of the notables

The college created to elect the President of the new Republic was much the same as that which elected the Senate, composed for the most part of delegates from France's 36,000 municipal councils. De Gaulle and Debré expected the Senate to buttress the government in dealing with a headstrong and wilful National Assembly. At its inception, then, the Fifth Republic was conceived as a *régime des notables*.

The constitution was overwhelming endorsed on the 28 September 1958: an 83 per cent 'yes' vote on an 80 per cent turn out. The next step was to use this momentum to secure a reasonably sympathetic majority in the National Assembly. Municipal elections were due in March 1959 and rather than risk voter fatigue, it was decided to leave them there and stage a complete renewal of the Senate in April. To that end, what remained of the Council of the Republic was temporarily prorogued as the provisional Senate.

De Gaulle rejected the use of PR for the general elections, as well as Debré's preference of a single round, majority system *à l'anglaise* and had insisted on a return to the majority-plurality system of *scrutin d'arrondissement à deux tours*. He did not expect the French electorate to change its political preferences overnight and anticipated having to manage with a narrow centre-left majority. He was wrong. The pro-de Gaulle Union pour la Nouvelle République (UNR) took 206 seats, the Independents 117, the MRP and Centre Democrats 64, the SFIO 47 and the PCF just 10. It was difficult, however, to say where the majority lay. Debré, prime minister from January 1959, could not call himself the *chef de la majorité* in the way Pompidou later would. There was, furthermore, a strong sense on all sides that normal service would only resume once the Algerian imbroglio had been resolved.

While the general election of November 1958 was interpreted as a *vote sanction* against the failures of the outgoing Assembly, it was not repeated in the municipal elections, despite the introduction of an electoral system blatantly intended to maximise the benefits to the UNR and its allies. Proportional representation was retained only for the 12 French cities with populations of more than 120,000. All other communes used a majority list system over two rounds, with the possibility of combining lists after the first ballot.[7] The overall results were remarkably similar to 1953 and this showed in the election to the upper house, where the underlying trend was continuity rather than change. A few high profile *refuseniks* like Gaston Defferre, Jacques Duclos, and François Mitterrand were among the 'new' intake, but 175 of 209 (84 per cent) *sénateurs sortants* seeking re-election were returned. It was not for lack of competition - there were 1200 candidates all told – but only 29 of November's 'orphans' were successful and more than a third of departments using the majority system did not require a second ballot.

Table 2.1 - **The Senate before and after 26 April 1959 (*métropole*)**

	1958	1959
Communists	16	14+1
Socialists	53	48
Gauche Démocratique	47	51
Centre Républicain-MRP	21	29
Independents and Peasants	80	85
UNR	29	27
Total	246	255

The MRP, not the UNR, emerged with most reason to smile, as the hard work of a generation of activists in organisations such as the Jeunesses Agricoles Chrétiennes bore fruit. Their group made the largest gain of any, a result at odds with their performance in the general election and one that laid the foundation for Centrism to gradually invest the Senate, to the point that ten years later they would take the presidency. For the time being, Monnerville was firmly in control and his unopposed re-election confirmed the sense of 'business-as-usual'. In contrast, the Assembly had made a decisive break with the past, rejecting Paul Reynaud and electing Jacques Chaban-Delmas to the *perchoir*.

The results provoked a mixed response among the regime's supporters. Albin Chalandon, the general-secretary of the UNR denounced the notables' 'revenge on the masses'. Justice minister Edmond Michelet, elected senator for Paris, was more sanguine.

> The UNR needs time to settle into the rural communes and establish its organisation there before we can expect the same sort of success in the Senate as has already been achieved in the National Assembly.[8]

He was right, but it was another Corrézien, a generation later, who would finally see Gaullism triumph among the notables.

Debré insisted that by providing the government with a range of means by which to impose its will, the new constitution transformed the French Republic from a *régime parlementaire absolu* into one with a *parlement rationalisé*: eviscerated might have been a better description. Not only did government have at its disposal a selection of levers with which to force legislation through and protection against votes of confidence (with abstentions being counted for the government), but parliamentary sessions were shortened and government allowed to dictate the order of business. The constitution even went so far as to limit the chambers to six permanent standing committees each. But perhaps the aspect of the constitution that wounded senators' *amour propre* most profoundly was the obligation, under Article 61, to submit the *Règlement*, the standing orders, to scrutiny by the Constitutional Council, an act by which, as the jurist and former senator Léo Hamon put it, the absolute sovereign became just another subject.

Behind all the talk of restoration, senators knew they relied entirely on the will or the need of the government. How could they claw back some independence and assert their identity? In the past the answer had lain in the standing orders, which had always been more than simple internal rules of procedure. For the Senate to operate as the significant other in the bicameralism of the Fifth Republic, distinct in character and function, would mean adopting procedures that embodied not just its own traditions and practices but also its ability to project these beyond the Luxembourg Palace.[9] By convention dating back to before the Revolution, standing orders were the business of each assembly alone. In 1948 the upper chamber, in collusion with sympathetic governments, had strengthened its position through the *Règlement* to the point where many elements had constitutional characteristics. Debré had been the author of the changes and understood perfectly to what purpose they might be put. Now he insisted the standing orders must be ratified by the Constitutional Council.

A special commission to examine the *Règlement*, chaired by Montalembert and with Pierre Marcilhacy acting as *rapporteur*, suggested simply proroguing the Council of the Republic's practices, with articles and clauses expunged or redrafted to fit the new conditions. For the first time in the history of the modern Republic, the government made its objections known, in particular to Article 76, concerning oral questions with a debate. In the draft, the debate could be followed by a vote, but Debré was absolutely against allowing either house to develop a means of interpellation. The Senate legislation commission rejected his objections: Marcel Prélot, the eminent jurist and UNR senator for the Doubs, reported that commissioners could honestly see no cause to uphold the government's view and the standing orders were duly forwarded to the Constitutional Council. The *juge constitutionnel*, however, found 15 points in contravention of or incompatible with the constitution. Senators were furious but there was no appeal. The revised version was finally ratified in October 1960.

Ostracism

No-one believed for a moment that the constitution ratified on 28 September 1958 was the final word. In April 1961, Debré gave his approval to a series of potential reforms adopted at the UNR spring conference, including the election of the President by universal suffrage and the fusion of the Senate with the Economic and Social Council. De Gaulle too was uneasy, confiding to his close circle his belief that as soon as the Algerian problem was resolved, the *classe politique* would seek to get rid of him. 'They'll be after my hide. So, I shall attack.'[10]

In March 1962 the Evian agreements were signed and de Gaulle invoked Article 11 of the constitution to call a referendum. The result was impressive, with 90 per cent voting 'yes' to Algerian independence on a 75 per cent turn out. Debré urged the General to exploit the moment and dissolve the National Assembly to give him (Debré) a solid majority. The two men had already differed over Algeria and now Debré revealed his own views on the evolution of the Republic towards a prime ministerial regime, a view at odds with de Gaulle. On 16 April, a week after the referendum, Debré was replaced by Georges Pompidou.

As de Gaulle's former personal secretary Pompidou was a loyalist, but he was no political novice. He had returned to the General's service in June 1958 as *chef de cabinet* at the Hôtel Matignon. Though his influence had been discrete, he understood the detail as well as anyone. Pompidou might have had a ministerial portfolio under Debré, but he preferred to return to his job at the Banque Rothschild, though he accepted de Gaulle's nomination to the Constitutional Council and had also acted as negotiator with the FLN. Parliament was antagonised, however, by the appointment of a man who had never been a member of either house. The new premier responded diplomatically by asking the National Assembly for a vote of confidence at his investiture, which he won narrowly. Pompidou attempted to shore up the government by offering ministerial posts to the Radicals and the MRP. The former refused outright and the MRP ministers quit within weeks over European policy. Rumour of an early dissolution hung in the air.

De Gaulle had already said on a number of occasions that he foresaw the head of state being elected by universal suffrage at some point in the not-to-distant future and that he might seek popular approval by means of a referendum. The Evian referendum confirmed his popularity and it now felt as though it was simply question of time. An attempt on his life at Petit-Clamart on 22 August 1962 provided de Gaulle with the opportunity he needed. Waiting until France had returned from holiday, on 12 September he announced to the cabinet his intention to hold a referendum on the subject. A week later he appeared on television and radio to explain to the French people that only they could endow the future head of state with legitimate authority. They would, therefore, be called upon, at the end of October, to vote on the election of the President by universal suffrage. Using Article 11, de Gaulle put the proposal directly to the people, without consulting parliament. The *classe politique* blew a fuse.

The broadcast came as politicians were gearing up for the party conference season and the parliamentary session. Senators in departments from the Ain to the Indre were, moreover, campaigning for re-election, after which the Senate would elect its speaker for the next three years. Monnerville rose to the challenge laid at parliament's door at the Radical party conference in, of all places, Vichy. He did not mince his words. The 'plebiscite' de Gaulle was proposing represented 'a deliberate, conscious, premeditated and outrageous violation of the constitution of the Fifth Republic. If this violation is allowed to happen now, afterwards anything will be permissible.'[11] He accused both President and prime minister of abusing their authority. The effect of this last accusation, in the town where Pétain had established his regime, was explosive and neither de Gaulle nor Pompidou ever forgave it. Monnerville was deemed *persona non grata* at the Elysée, while Pompidou embarked upon a personal boycott of the Senate which lasted throughout his six years as premier. Communication between Matignon and the Petit Luxembourg was kept open through the good offices of François Goguel.

Monnerville exercised his prerogative by referring the use of Article 11 to the Constitutional Council. Could it be used for constitutional reform? As he understood it, that could only happen under Article 89, after approval by parliament. The government argued that the use of Article 11 was legitimate because it concerned reform of *les pouvoirs publics* – public authorities. On 1 October the Constitutional Council expressed misgivings regarding the means, but reserved judgement on the content of the reform. The following day the parliamentary session opened with a message from the Elysée, read to the Senate by its *doyen d'âge* Marius Moutet, in which de Gaulle asserted that the spirit of the constitution gave him the right to make a direct appeal to the people. Moutet, one of the 80 parliamentarians who had refused full powers to Pétain in 1940, challenged de Gaulle to back down. Monnerville was then re-elected unopposed in a clear gesture of defiance and offered himself as the figurehead for the 'no' campaign. Deputies were galvanised and passed a motion of censure against the government and de Gaulle carried out his threat to dissolve the Assembly.

The referendum took place on 28 October. Although the result went de Gaulle's way - 13 million to eight - only 46 per cent of the electorate had voted 'yes'. The referendum had been a success, the plebiscite less so. The general election, by contrast, went very well, with the UNR and its small left Gaullist ally, the Union Démocratique des Travailleurs (UDT), taking seats from both the MRP-Centre Démocrate and those Independents opposed to the referendum. The PCF, SFIO and Radicals all made small gains, allowing a handful of Senate refugees (e.g. Defferre and Mitterrand) to return to the National Assembly. More importantly, Pompidou had a reasonably solid majority to work with. Managing his supporters was not always an easy job, but by force of character, Pompidou imposed the rules of *le fait majoritaire*.

De Gaulle heralded the election result as the end of the 'old parties'. In contrast to the Senate, barely one-third of the National Assembly had served under the old regime and there were 167 new deputies.[12] Yet his message to parliament at the opening of the legislature was intended to defuse the tension and made no mention of institutional reform. This did not mean the matter was closed and neither Elysée nor Matignon were about to soften their attitude to the upper house or its speaker. The new government's programme was read to the Senate only by a junior minister, while the ministerial benches remained empty. The government had embarked upon a selective boycott of the upper house which continued until 1968. Senior ministers attended meetings of the commissions, but often left it to junior colleagues to handle debates. Given the centrality of commissions to the work of the Senate, this was not as great a handicap as might first seem, but the meaning was abundantly clear.

Table 2.2 - **Legislation passed 1963-6**

		Bills adopted		
	Total	*Navette*	**CMP**	**Last word**
1963	68	57 - 93%	6 of 11	5 - 7%
1964	95	84 - 94%	5 of 11	6 - 6%
1965	60	48 - 88%	5 of 12	7 - 12%
1966	116	102 - 95%	8 of 14	6 - 5%
Source: Sénat - Service de la Séance				

The first sign of a hardening attitude was the number of bills presented in the first instance to the Senate. In 1961 the figure was 41 out of a total of 106 government bills. In 1965, it was just five.[13] The *vote bloqué* became a regular feature, used 72 times between 1963 and 1966, compared to just 18 from 1958 to 1962. Senators responded by rejecting 23 government bills in the same period, compared to five during the first legislature.[14] The CMP was used more, but instead of being deployed by a beleaguered government to impress the Senate's views on the National Assembly, the reverse was the case, with a rate of agreement of below half. Pompidou used the *urgence* procedure more than Debré had: 15 per cent of legislation passed in this way in 1963, 16 per cent in 1966, but only 5 per cent in 1965. And senators were debating for longer than before: 487 hours spread over 136 days were spent in the *hémicycle* in 1963. Still, senators believed that the passivity of the lower house placed even more responsibility on them to scrutinise every last detail of legislation.

The Senate's difficulties with the government were political as well as institutional. The majorities in the two houses simply did not match: the 1962 *renouvellement* saw only a handful of new senators elected and no change to its political complexion. Moreover, while most Independent deputies followed the pro-government line of young finance minister Valéry Giscard d'Estaing, their Senate counterparts were more sceptical, even hostile. Senators rejected the 1963 budget and saw the Franco-German Elysée Treaty as a blow to the multilateral and supranational aspirations of the European idea. De Gaulle's policy towards the EEC and the 'Empty Chair' crisis, which caused a breakdown in relations with Brussels, infuriated the Europhile majority in the Luxembourg Palace. That and criticism in the upper chamber of the Fifth Plan's failure to tackle mounting social problems made 1965 a difficult year. Tension increased in the autumn, with the *renouvellement* of series B and the subsequent election of the speaker, in which Monnerville saw off the first serious challenge to his leadership from majority senators who hoped a change at the top might make the government better disposed towards the upper house. The presence of two senators, Marcilhacy and particularly the Centrist Jean Lecanuet among the candidates for the Elysée hardly improved de Gaulle's mood.

Bayeux redux

Pompidou did not much like the Senate, but he saw little value in institutional reform for its own sake and had no time for demands, especially from the left Gaullists, for change. He was much more exercised in defining a prime ministerial space and developing his role as *chef de la majorité*. De Gaulle, on the other hand, still harboured a desire to put the finishing touches to the Fifth Republic and perhaps reflecting on the serious bout of social unrest in the spring of 1963, which had seen his popularity plummet, in the autumn instructed Pompidou to choose someone to head a commission to examine ways to improve the representation of social and economic groups, to streamline the Economic and Social Council (ESC) and consider the interface with the newly developing regions. The Senate was not mentioned directly, but there was little doubt where de Gaulle's thoughts were leading.

Pompidou chose Louis Vallon, *rapporteur général* to the Assembly's finance commission, leader of the UDT and director of its journal *Notre République*. The two men appointed a commission of forty, drawn from the ESC, various experts, representatives of trades unions, employers' organisations and chambers of agriculture and industry but no members of parliament. The outcome was, however, a disappointment to Vallon. The commission rejected a direct political role for the ESC and the regionalisation of representation of interest groups within the Council, using the opportunity instead to launch a forthright demand that government improve communication between itself, parliament and the ESC, a call which influenced Pompidou's decision to bring the Fifth Plan to parliament. Vallon drew up his own conclusions, however, indicating that it was perfectly possible to envisage the future integration of regional development structures and local government within a merged, consultative Senate-ESC. De Gaulle set the report to one side.

The President's caution was in part prompted by the prospect of the election in December 1965. De Gaulle assumed his re-election as given and early opinion polls seemed to vindicate his view. After formally announcing his intention to stand on 4 November, de Gaulle made almost no further effort to campaign before the first round on 5 December. It was a serious miscalculation. Mitterrand and Lecanuet made the very best of the television broadcast time allowed them to project their relatively youthful but also capable images into the homes of the electorate. Early predictions of a 60 per cent majority for de Gaulle were whittled down to 44.7 per cent of real votes cast in the first round, as 3.7 million moderate voters (15.6 per cent) preferred Lecanuet and forced the General into a second ballot against Mitterrand (31.7 per cent). On paper, he won the second ballot with something to spare, 55.2 per cent to 44.8, but the campaign and the result had a chastening effect, while the opposition was exultant and looked forward to the general election in 1967 as 'the third round'.

If the government's enthusiasm for change was cooled, senators were perfectly willing to countenance reform, but on their own terms: the senatorial tradition of *autoréforme* was quietly restated. Monnerville understood that although the challenge to his position in September 1965 had failed, he had to respond. He therefore invited

Marcel Prélot and Edouard Bonnefous to assess the possibilities. They came up with a three-point plan. The first, clearly a response to demands of the social partners in the Vallon commission, involved amending the *Règlement* to facilitate better communications with the ESC. The other proposals aimed to overcome under-representation of urban France in the Senate by adjusting the balance in the electoral colleges in favour of larger towns, by creating 44 new seats and by redistributing others. One innovative aspect of the proposals drew together the themes of under-representation and regionalisation. Assuming that the regional map of France would remain fixed to the departmental one, Prélot and Bonnefous suggested setting aside a block of seats to be allocated to regions on a demographic basis and elected by a trans-departmental, intra-regional mechanism. However original and forward thinking these proposals might be, they could only succeed with government support and that was not forthcoming.

De Gaulle returned, instead, to the theme of a mixed upper chamber during an official visit to the Nord-Pas-de-Calais in April 1966, his first since re-election. In contrast to his usual walkabout style, he met representatives of trades unions, employers' organisations and chambers of commerce and of agriculture, and made his only public speech at the very end of the trip, to open the International Fair at Lille, his birthplace. De Gaulle underlined the absolute necessity of regional structures for economic planning and implementation, represented in a semi-corporatist upper house. Although the left Gaullist press got excited about the speech, nothing would happen until after the general election in March 1967.

Despite reasonably buoyant economic conditions and opinion poll scores, the election was a disaster for the government. Pompidou had to rely on the Giscardian Independents and only had a majority at all thanks to the results *outremer*. Rather than adopt a conciliatory line, however, he used all the weapons in his arsenal: the package vote, Article 49-3 and, under the terms of Article 7, what amounted to government by decree.[15] In August 1967 Giscard, now chair of the Assembly's finance commission, denounced 'the solitary exercise of power', and earned an angry rebuke from Pompidou. Just two years after de Gaulle's re-election, a sense of 'l'usure du pouvoir' hung over President and prime minister, who it was rumoured had wanted to leave office after securing a fresh majority. Paradoxically, May 1968 allowed Pompidou and de Gaulle to launch an all out attack on parliament: Pompidou took on the Assembly, de Gaulle the Senate.

What began as a series of student protests against university conditions in the early months of 1968 became, by May, the biggest strike wave France had seen since 1936. At first the government had treated the disturbances as a minor irritation: Pompidou was in Afghanistan and Iran from 2 to 11 May, de Gaulle in Romania from the 14th to the 18th, curtailing his trip by only a few hours on account of events at home. By then France was in a state of paralysis. De Gaulle reverted to type, appearing on television on 24 May 1968 to announce a referendum on education and industrial reform. Pompidou, however, objected that a referendum was both risky and impossible to organise within the timeframe envisaged, arguing rather for a snap election. De Gaulle wavered. Then, on 30 May, as a massive Gaullist counter-demonstration made its way up the Avenue des Champs-Elysées, he announced in a radio broadcast that he would dissolve the Assembly now and postpone the referendum. Pompidou was vindicated. The Gaullist Union des Démocrates pour la République (UDR) achieved the first single-party majority in French history. The battle against the Assembly ended in triumph.

Pompidou, however, not de Gaulle, had been the *organisateur de la victoire*. After an uncertain interlude, Pompidou was dismissed and replaced with Maurice Couve de Murville. Yet de Gaulle misjudged his man. The diplomat Couve had proved his loyalty during nearly ten years as foreign minister, but he was a naturally cautious politician. This ultimately undermined de Gaulle's plan to use the impetus of June for one last referendum to restore his personal authority and complete his institutional legacy.

1969: renovation of the Senate

The Senate majority had hardly reveled in the conditions created by the 1967 general election result, but the government's discomfort had reduced the pressure. The 1968 general election, on the other hand, was a disaster on several levels. Firstly, the Senate faced a government backed by an overwhelming majority whose morphology was very different and which posed political and institutional challenges of its own: the Senate saw it as its vocation to act as the brake on a runaway majority - the *chambre introuvable*. Secondly, it was no secret that Jean-Marcel Jeanneney, minister of state and son of the last president of the Senate of the Third Republic, had been briefed to prepare the reform that would lead to the last piece of the Bayeux puzzle being put in place.

In July 1968 Etienne Dailly, first vice-president, visited Jeanneney with an offer to co-operate over reform. De Gaulle was clear. 'Absolutely not. If we negotiate with the Senate we are lost'.[16] De Gaulle made his plans public in a broadcast on 9 September, announcing his intention to fuse the Senate and the ESC. He reiterated his view that popular election of the President rendered obsolete the Senate's role as counterpoint to the Assembly. Once again de Gaulle intended to hold the referendum under the terms of Article 11, which cannot have been within the spirit of the constitution. A referendum would be held to 'déparlementarisé' one of the chambers, without parliament having a vote on the subject. De Gaulle hoped the referendum could take place before the year's end. Progress was slowed, however, when Jeanneney filled in as justice minister in November, when René Capitant fell ill, by Couve's natural hesitancy and by the crisis over the franc, which took all the government's attention for a spell in the autumn.

The electoral colleges assembled for the *renouvellement* at the end of September 1968 had plenty to discuss. As well as the prospect of a referendum and perhaps the dissolution of the Senate, Monnerville announced that he would not seek a new term as speaker. The decline of the Radicals as a force in the upper house meant that his position was already weakening. The political axis of the Senate now ran through the Centrists, and they would provide his successor. Monnerville himself did not want to fight another referendum as president.

The contest to find his successor, however, was by no means straightforward. The Centrists André Colin and Jean Lecanuet certainly fancied the post, but neither was able to rally the Gauche Démocratique. The Independents had a candidate in Pierre Garet, senator for the Somme, who led the field in the first two rounds, but could not secure Radical votes either. At the eleventh hour Monnerville introduced Alain Poher, senator from 1946 to 1948 and since 1952, a former *rapporteur général* to the finance commission, and President of the European Parliament since 1966 to the contest and he carried the day – or rather the very small hours of the morning. In such unlikely conditions began a presidency that would last 24 years.

Poher's accession witnessed a partial thaw, but meetings with Couve and Jeanneney ended fruitlessly. Jeanneney and Olivier Guichard, who had been charged with devising regional assemblies, put their proposals to parliament in December 1968. Guichard settled for regional councils that were simply extended versions of the Commissions de Développement Economique Régional (CODER), based on groupings of the existing departments and composed of experts, interest groups, certain local *élus* and deputies. Jeanneney proposed a mixed Senate comprising 160 regional senators, 13 from the DOM-TOM and 146 representing economic, social and cultural activities of the nation, nominated from the regional councils. Four seats would be reserved to represent expatriates. The term of office was reduced to six years with renewal by half every three years. Like the Council of the Republic in 1946, all legislation would be first presented and voted in the Assembly before being passed to the Senate for an opinion. The Senate would debate a bill and pass it back, with its comments, to the lower house, which would then cast a definitive vote. If deputies amended a bill after it had returned from the Senate, it would go back to the second chamber only if the Assembly or government wished.

The debate on the proposals was something of an oddity. Parliament was presented only with an outline, and there was to be no vote at the end. The government provocatively opened the discussions in the Assembly, not the Senate, and while Couve de Murville appeared before deputies, he left the Luxembourg Palace to Guichard and Jeanneney, where the reception belied the Senate's reputation for calm and courtesy. The debate cemented the majority in opposition to the government, including exasperated Gaullists such as Montalembert and Prélot. An exhausting series of sittings eventually drew to a close in the early hours of 19 December, with Monnerville given the privilege of delivering the *coup de grâce*. His speech, which was warmly applauded by his colleagues, was marred by an unfortunate and ill-tempered exchange with Jeanneney.

Curiously, de Gaulle made no reference to the reform when he presented his good wishes to the nation at the New Year and it was not until early February 1969, during an official visit to Quimper in Brittany that he returned to the subject. The tour, his first since the general elections, had gone badly and sceptics in his own camp hoped to persuade de Gaulle to abandon his plans, but now more than ever he needed a public endorsement. The referendum was a plebiscite from the outset. The final text was published on 20 March and followed the broad outline provided by Guichard and Jeanneney. There was, however, a sting in the tail. Since the Senate was to lose its parliamentary status, it made no sense for the speaker to act as interim head of state. This role would pass to the prime minister. Sunday 27 April 1969 was chosen for the referendum.

Poher's response was rapid and forthright. The day after Quimper he offered himself as the head of the 'no' campaign. Opposition coalesced rapidly. The Independents hesitated: interior minister Raymond Marcellin was one of the few members of the cabinet who appeared really to believe in the reform, but Giscard pursued the logic of his attacks on the 'solitary exercise of power' and defended the rights of parliament. Stronger in the Senate than the Assembly, neither the Independents, nor the Centrists, nor the Radicals were likely to endorse a reform to disenfranchise their core support. Organisations representing local *élus* mobilised massively against the reform of *their* assembly, while the left, demoralised after June 1968, seized the chance to claw back some self-respect.

On 10 April de Gaulle raised the stakes: 'Obviously the country's response will determine whether I continue in office or whether I go'.[17] Two days before the referendum he made a last, desperate and unscheduled broadcast, aimed straight at moderate voters and warning of the dire consequences of a 'no' vote. But at the same time, officials were packing up his personal archives and that evening he and Mme de Gaulle departed for Colombey . Before his departure the President left a letter with Couve de Murville, to be opened if it became clear that the 'no' vote had won. Post-dated to the 28th, the note informed the world that Charles de Gaulle had resigned with effect from midday.

The electorate was asked: 'Do you approve the bill put to the French people by the President of the Republic for the creation of regions and the renovation of the Senate?' 12 million voted 'no' to 10.9 million 'yes' on an 80 per cent turn out. The result swung, in the end, on 600,000 moderate 'no' votes. Without them, France would have become a semi-presidential, unicameral Republic with a regionalised, corporatist, consultative second chamber. In Senate mythology, however, the result represented a renewal of the covenant the French people had made with their upper chamber when they voted 'no' to the neo-Jacobin constitution in May 1946. Whoever picked up the reins left trailing by de Gaulle would be constrained to take a less hostile approach to the Luxembourg Palace.

3

The parliamentary other
1969-1997

There seemed some kind of justice that de Gaulle's discourteous and abrupt departure meant that Alain Poher moved into the Elysée. This was, of course, exactly what the constitution demanded: that the speaker should take over while the country prepared to elect a new head of state. But there was an extra piquancy to the fact that the rejected reform had proposed removing that very prerogative from the speaker and that the figurehead of the 'no' campaign stepped into the breach. No-one anticipated, however, that Poher would emerge as the principal challenger to the *dauphin* Pompidou. Looking back now at the 1969 campaign, Poher looks like a 'somebody, anybody' candidate, a last hurrah for the *nostalgiques du régime parlementaire*. The echo of the Third Republic, when the Petit Luxembourg had served as the antechamber to the Elysée, was unmistakable. But this was the Fifth Republic, not the Third, and presidentialism soon restored its grip.

Poher garnered enormous goodwill for his role in the referendum campaign and became the natural choice of the non-Communist opposition once it became clear that no-one else was willing to risk all against Pompidou. Poher stood little chance and he knew it, though early opinion polls actually put him ahead. The reality was that the French had voted 'no' in April 1969 precisely because they knew that there was an alternative to de Gaulle. But it was not Poher. Though he was well beaten in the end – 58 per cent to 42 – he conducted his campaign with skill and further enhanced his personal reputation and that of the Senate, even if most people still did not really know what the upper chamber did exactly.

Normalisation[1]

Pompidou had expended a great deal of effort during his six years at the Hôtel Matignon establishing the prime ministerial rules of engagement and asserting the authority of government over parliament. Piqued by Monnerville's accusation in September 1962 of 'forfaiture', he had carried out a personal boycott of the upper chamber. Yet he had never been convinced by Senate reform, and dragooned into the referendum campaign in 1969, his contribution had been luke-warm at best: Pierre Lefranc later recalled that Pompidou appeared at only one public meeting for the 'yes' campaign and then contrived not to speak.[2] This was not altogether true, though his defence of the proposal in a television broadcast on 23 April, hardly amounted to an unreserved endorsement either and his message that all parties should guard against the 'demagoguery of the last few years' was broadly interpreted as a promise of post-referendum détente in anticipation of a 'no' vote.[3]

During the presidential campaign, Pompidou wrote to all senators to signal his recognition of the result of the referendum.[4] After his victory, hosting a reception for the Senate *bureau* at which his defeated opponent was present and perhaps mindful of the overbearingly right-wing majority in the National Assembly, Pompidou stressed the upper chamber's special role as a parliamentary counterweight. His appointment of Jacques Chaban-Delmas brought to the office of prime minister a man who had been speaker of the Assembly since 1958 and understood parliament. The Senate's first sitting under the new government had to be chaired by Etienne Dailly, because Poher was meeting Chaban. In what he intended to be an important gesture towards the upper house, Chaban created a separate minister for relations with the Senate, although the experiment was not a success - both assemblies agreed they preferred to work through one minister.[5]

The relationship with government in the Pompidou years was demonstrably more courteous than the previous decade. Chaban was replaced in July 1972 by Pierre Messmer, a more brittle Gaullist, but one who sought to maintain a reasonable working relationship with the Senate, not least because he was managing a restive Assembly preparing for a general election. The majority in the Luxembourg

Palace delighted in the opportunity to caution the *chambre introuvable*. Just one such occasion was over interior minister Raymond Marcellin's plans to reform the 1901 law on associations to strengthen police powers. Pierre Marcilhacy, now chair of the legislation commission, proposed the Senate should reject the bill outright, by voting the *question préalable*. When the government persisted, senators asked Poher to exercise his prerogative to refer the bill to the Constitutional Council, which upheld the petition, ruling part of the bill unconstitutional. In a landmark decision, the Council declared that it regarded the preamble to the constitution and therefore the 1789 and 1946 declarations of rights, to be part of the constitution proper. At the Senate's prompting, the Council had 'at a stroke... incorporated a bill of rights in to the Constitution'.[6] If the decision did not appear to shake the foundations of the regime, it opened the door to unforeseen developments in constitutional and political jurisprudence beyond the scope of this study, but which have transformed and magnified the role of the Council beyond recognition.

Relations between the houses also improved. Poher and his counterparts in the Assembly (Achille Moretti until 1973, former senator Edgar Faure from 1973 to 1978) established a framework for regular dialogue between their *bureaux,* while the Senate embarked on one of its periodic internal procedural reviews, culminating in 1973 with a tidying up of the standing orders and the creation of *missions d'information*, formal sub-committees of the permanent commissions briefed to examine the application and impact of legislation.[7]

Table 3.1 - **Legislation passed 1969-74**

	Bills adopted			
	Total	*Navette*	**CMP**	**Last word**
1969	71	63	8 of 8	0
1970	73	55	16 of 18	2
1971	92	71	17 of 21	4
1972	102	86	9 of 16	7
1973	55	45	6 of 10	4
1974	49	36	13 of 13	0
Source: Sénat - Service de la Séance				

In 1969 and again in 1974 the assemblies achieved a full rate of agreement and the yearly mean never dropped below 92 per cent, though a feverish legislative season on the eve of the 1973 general election was rather bumpy. The CMP was used more often, more positively and with considerable success, as Table 3.1 shows. And senators were busy: the three sessions between 1970 and 1972 each saw more than 400 hours of debates, to say nothing of committee work.

The hope that the Gaullian period had been a caesura and that parliament would be allowed to take on a determinant role was, however, frustrated. Although Pompidou steered away from the personalism of his predecessor, he had no intention to surrender his prerogatives and his plan to introduce the five-year Presidential term (the *quinquennat*) implied a shift towards a more presidential style, not away from it.

Cut short by his death in 1974, the Pompidou presidency witnessed a number of important political developments that would have a profound impact on the Senate. In 1971, François Mitterrand emerged as the dominant figure in the new Parti Socialiste and followed that a year later by drawing the Communists into an agreement for a future left-wing coalition based on a Common Programme. The effect on the Radicals and the Centrists was decisive. The Radicals split between those who still clung to the *mystique de gauche* and adopted the title of Radicaux de Gauche, while those who rejected alliance with the PCF and who took a more pro-government, *gestionnaire* position retained the Parti Radical label and shifted to the centre-right. For the Centrists, the Common Programme finally brought down the curtain on the aspirations of men like Jean Lecanuet who had dreamt of building a French labour party. The way had been cleared for bipolarisation to replace the vestigial Third Force politics that had clung on in the Senate.

The bipolar trap

The Common Programme yielded immediate, positive results for the left in the 1973 general election, but not enough to unseat the government. Gaullism was, nevertheless, in crisis, underlined by the contest to replace Pompidou. Chaban's announcement that he was a candidate did not meet with universal approval. Jacques Chirac and a group of 40 UDR deputies put their weight instead behind Giscard and the leader of the Independent Republicans proceeded to the run-off, with more than twice the votes cast for Chaban. Giscard shaded the decisive ballot against Mitterrand by fewer than half a million votes.

Rather than antagonise his allies by dissolving the Assembly and building a Presidential majority, Giscard opted to appoint Chirac prime minister at the head of a coalition that included Gaullists,

Independents, Centre Democrats and Radicals. The UDR, with 180 deputies, was still the largest group, but was in a state of disarray, made worse by the distribution of key government posts to the other coalition parties. In the Senate things were quite different: the Independents, with 58 seats, were the largest single group after the *renouvellement* in September 1974 and their allies, the Independent Peasants held another 15. But it was the Centrists who had the wind in their sails, rising to 54. By contrast the UDR had dropped to just 30. The balance in the upper chamber was far more to the liking of the President, who hoped to create a new, post-Gaullian, post-Pompidolian centre-right party stretching from the Radicals to the UDR, with his Independent Republicans at its axis. Giscard naturally encouraged his political allies in the Senate, therefore, to consider themselves as members of the majority, with a full contribution to make to government.

The Senate's gentle renaissance was visible in a number of ways. The number of government bills first presented in the upper chamber rose overnight - 59 in 1975 alone - while more joint commissions were convoked than ever before, especially during the premiership of Raymond Barre after August 1976. The last word was used on just seven occasions in the entire septennate. Senators were also busier than they had ever been: the streamlining measures introduced in 1973 had come not a moment too soon.

Table 3.2 - **Legislation passed 1975-80**

		Bills adopted			**Sittings**	
	Total	*Navette*	**CMP**	**Last word**	**Days**	**Hours**
1975	112	85	27	0	87	576
1976	82	59	23	1	87	512
1977	102	72	30	0	85	495
1978	59	29	29	1	97	610
1979	47	33	12	2	103	674
1980	49	33	13	3	116	778
Source: Sénat - Service de la Séance						

The Giscardian period also saw the first use of Article 49-4, whereby the government invited the Senate to express approval of its policies. Chirac used it in June 1975, paradoxically, to quell rumblings among UDR deputies over foreign policy. Barre used it twice, in a more overtly political gesture in May 1977 and May 1978, to assert his authority across the presidential majority. Giscard also enfranchised members of parliament by extending the right to petition the Constitutional Council to any group of 60 senators or deputies.

The most significant change to the Senate under Giscard was a redistribution of seats in July 1976. Apart from amendments to the standing orders to improve relations with the ESC, nothing more had been heard since late 1968 of the Prélot-Bonnefous proposals: Prélot retired in 1971 and Bonnefous became chair of the finance commission the following year. Elected on a manifesto that promised to liberalise French politics, Giscard encouraged the leaders of the Senate majority to entertain the idea of reform. The changes they came up with, discussed more fully in Chapter 5 below, were, however, a missed opportunity. New seats were created to reduce the imbalances in representation from one department to another, but other more original ideas, such as the institution of regular redistribution every two electoral cycles were rejected, not by senators, but by the government and deputies.

The Senate reform was one of Chirac's last acts as premier. In August 1976, frustrated by the limitations imposed upon him by Giscard, undermined by his own non-Gaullist senior ministers and at the suggestion of his closest advisers, he became the first and to date only prime minister of the Fifth Republic to leave office of his own volition. At the end of the year he set out to transform Gaullism, in the shape of the Rassemblement pour la République (RPR), a development that would, very shortly, also transform the Senate.

Chirac had stolen a march on Giscard's plan to build a broad right-wing party and there was worse to follow. Although cracks were beginning to appear in the Common Programme, it still yielded some very encouraging results in the municipal elections in the spring of 1977. In the capital, however, where Parisians would have a mayor of their own for the first time in over a century, an initially unwilling Chirac defeated Giscard's candidate. The President's response, setting up the Parti Républicain in May 1977, rallied only the Independents. Only the imminence of a general election constrained the non-Gaullist Moderate Right (NGMR), to use Andrew Knapp's term,[8] to collaborate in Barre's Union pour la Démocratie Française (UDF) in February 1978. In the circumstances the UDF performed remarkably well: with 123 deputies it controlled as many seats as its outgoing component parties, while the RPR won only 154, compared to 183. Chirac's new party provided the 'majority of the majority' only in the National Assembly.

The opposite was the case, and emphatically so, in the Senate, where the UDF's components retained their separate identities as Radicals (Gauche Démocratique), Centrists (Union Centriste - UC) and Independents (Union des Républicains et Indépendants - URI) and held 154 seats, compared to just 33 RPR senators. When the new parliament assembled in May, Barre invoked Article 49-4 to ask the upper house to approve his programme, just to remind the RPR that they were partners in a coalition across both houses and that he was the *chef de la majorité*, a vote that also underlined that while the Senate, whose seven different political groups still gave an outward appearance of old-fashioned Third Force politics had, in reality, entered fully into bipolarisation. The cosy relationship between Barre and the upper chamber continued for the next three years and Giscard's comfortable lead in the opinion polls at the end of 1980 led the majority to hope that state of affairs would continue for another seven. They awoke on 11 May 1981 with a headache.

Une redoutable machine de guerre[9]

Mitterrand dissolved the Assembly and the subsequent general elections saw a *vague rose* sweep into power. Politicians, journalists and analysts wondered how the regime's institutions would hold up. In the event, they proved robust enough to bear the pressures of *alternance*. What no-one could foresee, however, was that *alternance* would become a fact of life for the next 26 years, until 2007, and provide a particular challenge to the Senate. In his inaugural presidential address, Mitterrand linked his election to that, 45 years earlier, of the Popular Front. He did not mention Léon Blum's problems with the Senate, but he knew his own were about to begin.

The Senate majority was determined from the outset to make life as difficult as possible for the new administration. In the course of 1981 alone, they put down 21 *questions préalables* – a motion that there is nothing to debate. In certain circumstances this device can be used by a sympathetic majority to hurry legislation through, but this was certainly not the case now. The government responded in spades. More bills arrived with a *motion d'urgence* attached, restricting the time for consultation within the commissions. The Senate reacted by heavily amending legislation, thereby forcing the government to invoke the last word nearly 30 times a year between 1981 and 1986. In 1985 68 per cent of legislation arrived under *urgence* procedures and the last word was used on 45 occasions, for 56 per cent of legislation.

The Mauroy (1981-4) and Fabius (1984-6) governments made regular use of the CMP to present the Senate majority as retrograde and obstructive. In the circumstances it seems all the more surprising that one CMP in three in the period produced an acceptable text, while more than 20,000 amendments tabled in the upper house made their way into the legislation enacted. The Senate was obstructive, but not always just for obstruction's sake.

Looking purely at the statistics summarised in Table 3.3 below, 1982 and 1985 appear to be the most difficult years. The Mauroy government's key reforms - decentralisation, broadcasting - reached the upper chamber in 1982, while the imminence of the next election explains the tensions of 1985. It was 1984, however, that witnessed the most spectacular clashes, over education and constitutional reform.

Table 3.3 - **Legislation adopted 1980-7**

Year	Total	Ordinarily	CMP	Last word
1980	49	33	16	3
1981	33	17	16	10
1982	71	28	43	32
1983	87	48	39	26
1984	73	31	42	26
1985	81	21	60	45
1986	44	24	20	1
1987	79	52	27	0

Source: *Service de la Séance*

During the election campaign, Mitterrand promised to introduce uniformity across the education system. Anticlericals took this to mean an end to state funding for private Catholic schools and education minister Alain Savary made no effort to resist amendments to his reforms to that end. The opposition seized on this as an attack on the rights of the *école libre* and on 24 June Paris witnessed right-wing mobilisation on a scale not seen since 30 May 1968. The Senate majority promised that if the government persisted, they would use every available device to paralyse political life. Summoned to the Elysée, Poher was warned by Mitterrand that he would not bring down a second President. Poher remained unrepentant and with senior members of the majority drafted a motion calling on Mitterrand to put the Savary bill to a referendum. Mitterrand responded in true Gaullian style, by way of a television broadcast on 12 July. He withdrew the bill (without consulting the minister, who resigned) and in its place promised to present a proposals to parliament to extend the range of measures that could be put to a referendum under Article 11. Once approved by parliament, under Article 89, the reform would then itself be put to the people in September.

The announcement was an undisguised attempt to destabilise the Centrists in the Senate, many of whom favoured extending the field for referenda, to cast the opposition as opponents of greater democracy, and to offer the left the chance to regroup before the general election. To test the Senate majority, the government tabled the bill there first. Poher met Mitterrand and implored him to confine the reform to a meeting of Congress and abandon the referendum, but the President was unyielding. The Senate majority responded by adopting a *question préalable* motion on 7 August and going into recess for three weeks: what amounted to a strike. When it reassembled in September, the bill was rejected at its second reading and abandoned. The Senate had proved to be, in the words of Charles Pasqua, 'a formidable war machine'.

France had been on the beach throughout the crisis, following events at a distance and the government failed to derive any significant advantage. Despite changing the electoral system (to a department-based Hayes PR system) to limit the damage in the general election, Mitterrand was obliged to recall Chirac to lead an RPR-UDF government, as the Fifth Republic embarked upon its first experiment in cohabitation.

Cohabitation and the Senate

It was something of a gamble, with the next presidential election only two years away, but as leader of the largest party in the National Assembly, Chirac accepted becoming prime minister for a second time. On 2 April 1986 he attended the opening of the Senate session and assured his audience that 'my presence bears witness to the respect in which [the government] holds your Assembly'.[10] Very different from the young minister who, in September 1968, had ostentatiously gathered his papers and left the *hémicycle* as Monnerville began his last presidential address. The reality was that Chirac needed the Senate to bolster his position as *chef de la majorité* across both houses in his dealings with the Elysée. On 15 April Poher spoke fulsomely of the 'reactivation' of bicameralism as Chirac invoked Article 49-4 to invite the Senate to approve his programme.[11] His fellow UDF senators were rather less enthusiastic, however, when Chirac used the procedure twice more, in April and December 1987 (by which point the RPR had become the largest single group in the Senate) to assert his claim as the leading right-wing *présidentiable* in the face of a challenge from Barre.

The contrast with the preceding five years could not have been more striking. The government never had recourse to the last word, and the National Assembly endorsed 90 per cent of all amendments proposed by the Senate.[12] Chirac included three senators in his cabinet: Pasqua became interior minister, Jean Arthuis, a Centrist from the Mayenne, was appointed social affairs minister and René Monory took on education. Within the Luxembourg Palace, some senators were worried that by becoming incorporated into a large, cross-chamber bloc, they were putting their legislative role at risk. Poher put this very point to his colleagues in July 1986: 'We find ourselves between two dangers. Stagnation [...] or the desire to be as efficient as possible. Playing the role of *chambre de réflexion* must remain our permanent concern.'[13] These concerns were not misplaced. Chirac had no time to waste if his legislative programme was to carry him to victory in the presidential election. The 1986 Senate session, at 129 days and 928 hours of debate, established a benchmark as the longest in the history of the Fifth Republic and included a 43-day summer session which ended in mid-August.

Among the imposing pile of legislation was the privatisation of the French television station TF1. Control of the media was a theme that senators had taken to their hearts during the 1960s, when the government had done its best to prevent dissenting views being aired on the airwaves and television screens, in particular during the 1962 referendum and it chimed with the upper chamber's unofficial, self-appointed role of guardian of public liberties. A special commission, chaired by Jean-Pierre Fourcade, former finance minister and chair of the social affairs committee, came up with 120 key amendments, reflecting the wider feeling that the legislation was poorly drafted. It took 23 days and 182 hours to debate the bill (partly thanks to 1500 opposition amendments), but in the end the bill passed was largely 'made in the Luxembourg Palace'.[14] Senators then returned to their departments to start campaigning for the *renouvellement* in September. The election marked a turning point, as the RPR overtook the UC to become the largest single group with 77 seats.

Despite their carefully plotted triumph, the RPR were not yet in a position to challenge for the presidency: the three UDF groups would still outnumber them in a fight. Instead they settled for the chairs of two key commissions: Maurice Schumann became president of the cultural affairs commission, but more importantly, Christian Poncelet was elected to the chair of the finance commission. By the year's end, senators were relieved there was no extraordinary session at the beginning of 1987 and it was not until the spring that parliament reassembled. When it did, however, both houses were immediately asked to reaffirm their support for the government. On 7 April deputies were confronted with a vote of confidence. A week later it was the turn of the Senate. Chirac was unctuousness itself: 'I need your confidence, because my government draws its strength from the support of the parliamentary majority and without the support of the whole of Parliament, nothing that should be done can be done'.[15] Despite the Centrists' assertion of their right to constructive criticism, the result (226-84) was never in doubt.

Senators were more than mildly surprised, when, on 9 December 1987, Chirac asked them once again to vote over a general declaration of policy. The UC president, Daniel Hoeffel insisted that while his group would support the motion this should in no way be interpreted as a promise about the future, meaning the forthcoming Presidential election. In Chirac's defence, he was doing nothing more than Barre ten years before, asserting his position as *chef de la majorité* in both houses. Chirac obtained his vote (226 to 68), but it availed him little. His score of 46 per cent in the Presidential run-off against Mitterrand was a humiliation.

Renovation versus reform

Chirac's poor showing was more than a political setback for the Senate majority. There was a growing sense that the institution was in worse shape at the beginning of Mitterrand's second term than the first. From 1981 to 1986, the Senate had sometimes seemed like little more than a *chambre d'obstruction*, and then changed overnight into a *chambre d'enregistrement*. What had become of the Senate's difference? A sense of isolation set in among the more thoughtful members of the Senate majority, its would-be *rénovateurs*, who began to search for a new direction for their assembly. At the same time, the left began to talk about institutional dysfunction and the pressing need for reform.

The *rénovateurs* were an illusive, nebulous collection of senators whose misgivings reflected a wider moment of self-questioning across the French right after the defeat of 1988. Some were thrown further off-balance by Michel Rocard's *ouverture* towards the centre, an approach born partly from necessity: the PS did not have a clear majority in the new Assembly. To this end, Rocard offered cabinet posts to the Centrists and Radicals, including seven senators, an exceptional number by the standards of the Third Republic, let alone the Fifth. He used Article 49-4 to ask the Senate to approve his general policy and, in the early stages, chose to represent the government personally at the meeting of the *conférence des présidents*. Despite his efforts, the majority remained solid: the Centre in the Senate was on the right. The *rénovateurs'* questions about the role of the upper house did not go away, however, and it only made matters worse for them that Laurent Fabius, the new speaker of the Assembly, was determined to exploit the government's weakness both to reinforce the lower chamber's prerogatives and undermine Rocard.[16] If there was to be renewal in the Senate, however, it had to be something more than another burst of procedural *aggiornamento* (though that was needed too). Renovation needed a cause to drive it forward and a new man at the helm, not one who had been president for more than twenty years and who, by the time the next *renouvellement* came around in September 1989, would on his way to his 81st birthday.

Most senators assumed Poher would not seek an eighth term, so there was general surprise when, on the evening of the *renouvellement*, he summoned the chairs of the majority groups and informed them he wanted one final term. Centrist senators instructed Hoeffel to try to persuade Poher to stand down voluntarily rather than face opposition from his own group, while the Independents voted overwhelmingly not to support him. Only the RPR, under clear orders from Pasqua, came out in support. His reasons for doing so and the conduct of the election are discussed in Chapter 7.

Poher persisted and eventually won an exhausting three-round contest. He promised new initiatives, but the next three years only fulfilled reformers' fears. Fiddling with the standing orders were not quite what they had in mind. Gradually, Poher seemed to become detached from the day-to-day life of the upper chamber. A term was coined to describe the situation - *pohérisation* - and it became an accusation that both his immediate successors would have levelled at them in turn.

If the change in leadership was lacking, the *rénovateurs* found a theme around which to remould the Senate in decentralisation. Looking back, the link between the Senate's constitutional responsibility and decentralisation seems obvious, but it took the coincidence of a number of factors to convince *rénovateurs* that herein lay the key to reviving the upper chamber. After two decades struggling to ensure that decentralisation (and regionalisation) should not in practice mean greater state intervention or increasing the burden on local councillors, it was not altogether easy for majority senators to change tack. They had laboured to contain the Defferre reforms, but despite their reservations and some teething problems, the changes came, in time, to be seen as a step forward, albeit one that needed constant surveillance and refinement. In partnership with the various organisations representing the interests of municipal, departmental and regional councils - their electors - senators evolved gradually towards a more positive and creative position.

In 2003, the claim to a special vocation would lead to a revision of the constitution that imposed the presentation of all legislation affecting local government to the Senate in the first instance. But that was still some way down the line, and there were strong voices of opposition to the idea of the Senate as a *chambre de la décentralisation*, including Pasqua, who rejected the idea out of hand, while Poher remained sceptical. Still, it had among its proponents influential figures such as Hoeffel, Arthuis, Jean François-Poncet and, most significantly for the future, Monory, Poncelet and a relatively young senator for the Yvelines and mayor of Rambouillet by the name of Gérard Larcher.[17]

While senators on the right were struggling towards a cause to renew the Senate, left-wing critics argued that a much more straightforward solution lay in wholesale reform. The Senate would only rediscover its vocation through a more equitable representation of the population and thus, of political balance among the communes. Put another way, only when the left had a chance of winning a majority there, would the upper house regain its moral authority. Until such time, it would struggle on with its own *dysfonctionnement*. The term was first coined by Jean Grangé, who in the course of the 1980s used the material at his disposal working in the upper chamber's Service de la Séance, to make several contributions to the debate. His 'Attitudes et vicissitudes du Sénat' assessed the chamber's legislative record and political role on the eve of the first *alternance*, while 'L'efficacité normative du Sénat' produced the first statistical analysis of the conflict with the Mauroy government and underlined the degree to which the upper chamber had become a *chambre d'obstruction*.[18] Three years later, in a special number of *Pouvoirs* dedicated to the Senate, Grangé began to focus on the imbalances of the electoral system and therefore of the legislative process in the Senate.[19] Finally, in 'Les déformations de la représentation des collectivités territoriales et de la population au Sénat', Grangé focused on a series of imbalances in representation created at various points in the election of senators, how those imbalances impacted on the political colour of the Senate and how they might be alleviated. He did not pull his punches.

> The pendulum is unbalanced. If, when the government majority is on the left, the counterweight blocks the mechanism that it is supposed to help run smoothly and on the other hand when the majority is to the right, it reinforces the power it is supposed to restrain, then it is dysfunctional.[20]

Grangé suggested reform at a number of points: a 'classic' creation of new seats and redistribution; lowering the threshold for the use of PR; but most innovatively, a thorough reassessment of and changes to the way in which municipal delegates were elected. These proposals are examined further in Chapter 5. Grangé's work was picked up by Guy Allouche (PS, Nord), who used it as the basis for a private bill finally slated for debate on the last day of the December 1991 session. The debate never took place: Jacques Larché, URI chair of the legislation commission, took on the role of *rapporteur* himself and delivered an uncompromising attack on a bill that undermined the three fundamental pillars of the upper house: equal representation of the *collectivités* (as if that existed), representation of 'l'espace français' and authentic bicameralism. The majority groups then tabled a *question préalable* which passed by 230 votes to 86.[21]

Allouche's proposals only got so far thanks to the support of the government. Mitterrand tired of Rocard in March 1991 appointed Edith Cresson, whose connection to the President dated back to the mid-1960s and the Convention des Institutions Républicaines. Another of the *conventionnels*, as they were known, was Claude Estier, chair of the Socialist group, and it was thanks to his good offices that the government rallied to Allouche's bill. Cresson and her successor, Pierre Bérégovoy, played out the last two years of the ninth legislature in an increasingly difficult atmosphere in both chambers. Table 3.4 describes the legislative process from 1988 to 1993. Less than half of legislation passed by the normal *navette* process and the government appointed the CMP to examine 56 per cent of bills, half of which failed to find agreement.

Table 3.4 - **Legislation adopted 1988-92**

Year	All	*Navette*	CMP	Last word
1988	23	13	10	8
1989	63	29	34	20
1990	69	32	37	19
1991	58	27	31	16
1992	71	25	46	16
All	284	126	158	79

Recovery

Unlikely as it might have seemed three years earlier, it was the Assembly, not the Senate, which had reached the end of its tether by the autumn of 1992. The prospect of a new speaker added extra zest to the meetings of the electoral colleges on 27 September 1992, one week after the Maastricht referendum. Pasqua, still president of the RPR group, had been at the forefront of the Eurosceptic faction within the party campaigning 'no'. The election of a new speaker offered him, therefore, an immediate, if rather unlikely opportunity to reassert his position. After consultation with senior RPR figures, Pasqua offered the UDF groups a joint primary. A minority of Independents were in favour, but most shared the Centrists conviction that a cross-majority primary would be fatal for their chances and the two leaderships stalled for time. For once, Pasqua was outmanoeuvred, lost his patience, withdrew his offer and unilaterally announced his candidacy before another RPR pretender could emerge. The UDF groups then met to elect a single candidate. The Centrist Monory and Pierre-Etienne Taittinger (URI) went head-to-head in a run-off, with the former emerging as the narrow winner. Deeply pro-Maastricht, the UDF groups were determined that Pasqua should not pass and steeled themselves for an epic contest. For his part, Pasqua announced that if were behind any other majority candidate in the first round then he would withdraw. He gathered just 101 votes to 125 for Monory, but the senator for the Hauts-de-Seine had done enough to be certain of a call to government after the general election. Monory secured the presidency in the second ballot.

Who better to modernise the Senate than the man whose vision for a few unprepossessing beet fields near Poitiers had earned him the nickname of Monsieur Futuroscope? Monory and his senior team wasted little time. On the one hand, he insisted on the need to raise the Senate's public profile and he became a regular fixture on television and radio - and in monthly opinion polls. The doors of the

Luxembourg Palace were opened to French and foreign visitors alike: Monory insisted on his position as *deuxième personnage de la République* to ensure that the Senate was included on the itineraries of foreign dignitaries, while local *élus* found it much easier to arrange visits to the Luxembourg Palace for their constituents. The Senate became a far more active sponsor of cultural events and new technologies were embraced to speed up a whole range of services. The *bureau*, which had met infrequently, now met monthly. There was a review of the standing orders and a raft of *ad hoc missions d'information* sprouted up. But the success of the Senate's recovery lay not just in internal changes. Monory's arrival at the Petit Luxembourg coincided with the right's crushing general election victory and Mitterrand's deteriorating health and political isolation.

No-one had foreseen the scale of the RPR-UDF alliance's victory. The new majority took 484 seats, 257 for the RPR and 215 for the UDF, further broken down into 107 Parti Républicain (PR) deputies and 62 Centre des Démocrates Sociaux (CDS). Nevertheless the new prime minister, Edouard Balladur, appointed an equal number of RPR and UDF ministers to his government and also shared out the portfolios equally between the PR and the CDS. The ministerial balance looked much more like that in the Senate than the Assembly and was better received in the upper chamber than the lower.

The second *cohabitation* was far more collegial in tone than the first. Balladur was not about to surrender government prerogatives, but he preferred to take parliament with him rather than whip it along. He invoked Article 49-4 only at the beginning of his term and though he was not the first prime minister to attend the *conférence des présidents*, at which only one minister is allowed to be present, he did so more than once. He appointed a senator, Chirac's advisor Roger Romani, as the minister for parliamentary relations. Senators were also pleased to see colleagues take the portfolios for agriculture (Jean Puech) and regional development (Hoeffel). The relationship was cemented with the election to the *perchoir* of Philippe Séguin, whose ambitions to refine and redefine the role of his assembly matched Monory's.

In general, the government remained sensitive to the Senate. One minister who was not, however, was Pasqua, who had returned to the interior ministry. Pasqua never bought in to the notion of the Senate's difference or specificity beloved of so many of his colleagues and he had little time for the *rénovateurs* and their ambition to make decentralisation the central theme of the bicameral renaissance. One of the first acts of the new regime in the Senate was to appoint a heavyweight *mission d'information* to assess the impact and future direction of decentralisation. Pasqua deliberately ignored their efforts, sidelined regions minister Hoeffel and went ahead with his own plans. He then rubbed senators' noses further in the dirt by presenting his *loi cadre* for the regions to deputies first, provoking a public row with Monory, though senators later took some comfort from the fact that the proposals had to be almost completely rewritten in the committee stage in the upper house.[22]

Balladur's astute management saw him emerge in opinion polls as the leading right-wing candidate for the Elysée. He was backed by roughly one-third of the parliamentary RPR, including Pasqua and Nicolas Sarkozy, along with a very large slice of the UDF. Monory, however, was not among the latter, coming down firmly on the side of Chirac. Speaking for the first time from the Elysée Palace after his victory over Jospin, Chirac deliberately placed Monory and Séguin (who had given Chirac one of the themes for his campaign, the *fracture sociale*) just behind him, a symbol, the new President insisted, of the partnership between executive and legislative. In practice this relationship was as superficial as Chirac's willingness and ability to tackle the broken society. The constitution was tidied up, a new single session was introduced and parliament was encouraged to pursue its efforts at internal reform and streamlining, but the direction of policy shifted back to the Elysée and Matignon, guided by Dominique de Villepin in the one, Alain Juppé in the other. The return of the parliamentary Republic that some claimed they had detected under Balladur was crushed by a period of *présidence absolue*. Chirac's decision to dissolve the lower house prematurely changed all that, pitched the Senate into an unexpected and difficult cohabitation with a left-wing National Assembly, cost Monory his presidency and heralded a decade that transformed the fortunes of the upper chamber.

4

Anomaly and apotheosis
1997-2009

Chirac's decision to dissolve the Assembly was based on the calculation that an economic downturn towards the end of 1997 would create difficult conditions on the stump, that a snap election would arrest the progress Lionel Jospin was making in pulling together the *gauche plurielle* coalition of Socialists, Communists and Greens, and deliver a reduced and therefore more disciplined majority whose term of office would come to an end at the same time as his own 2002. A collateral benefit to the RPR would also be to place further pressure on the UDF, which since failing to find a candidate for the 1995 presidential elections had been rapidly disintegrating. Chirac achieved only the last of these goals. The victory of the *gauche plurielle* threw the UDF into even greater confusion, but Chirac's control over the RPR was badly shaken too. Juppé, who had retained the party presidency, was replaced by Séguin, who had expressed reservations over an early dissolution and retained the sympathy of RPR deputies who had paid the price of Chirac's gamble.

The left's victory opened a new chapter for the Fifth Republic: the third cohabitation would be longer and unlike the previous two, where the Senate majority had been used to reinforce the position of right-wing governments in their relationship with the Elysée, now a left-wing majority in the National Assembly was in the driving seat, but encumbered by an upper house that would do all it could to support the lame duck President, on occasions even going beyond what Chirac wanted. If the relationship with the government was difficult, the one with the Elysée was not always straightforward either.

Une anomalie

Jospin faced a struggle with the Senate from the outset in all aspects of policy: nearly one-third of all legislation passed in the first session had to go through on the last word. In response, in the autumn of 1997, PS general-secretary François Hollande promised that if regional elections the following spring indicated public satisfaction, then the government would think seriously about Senate reform. The PS duly increased its control from two regions to eight and bolstered by the results, in an interview with *Le Monde* to mark the opening of the spring session in parliament in April 1998, Jospin announced the next stage of his legislative programme. He made no bones about his relationship with the Senate and denounced it as 'an anomaly among our democratic institutions... a remnant of those conservative upper houses of the past', where alternation of political power was impossible.[1]

The prime minister's timing was exquisite. Though the interview was published in the issue of *Le Monde* dated 21 April, the newspaper appears from the early afternoon of the day before. His words had therefore been picked over already when he appeared at the Luxembourg Palace on the 21st to participate in a brief ceremony to commemorate the late Maurice Schumann. Monory was fuming, but his tribute to Schumann was hesitant and caused mutterings of *pohérisation* among his colleagues. He recovered his composure in the days that followed, but was disappointed that an appeal to Chirac for support was met with only a guarded response: the President was not about to allow the prime minister to steal the high ground over political modernisation and replied that while he held the Senate in great esteem, a little reform from time to time did everyone good. Monory had hoped for something more concrete and though a commission was set up, chaired by Daniel Hoeffel, the talk in the Luxembourg Palace was focussed on a challenge for the presidency come the autumn.

RPR senators had wanted to claim the presidency ever since becoming the largest group in 1986, but knew solid UDF resistance would frustrate them, as Pasqua's failure in 1992 showed. Now, however, the UDF was on the verge of collapse, divided by the rivalry between UDF president François Léotard, François Bayrou of Force

Démocrate (formerly the CDS) and Alain Madelin of Démocratie Libérale (DL - formerly the Parti Républicain). In May 1998, Léotard and Séguin launched the Alliance pour la France as an RPR-UDF confederation, without consulting Madelin and Bayrou. Madelin responded by withdrawing from the UDF and negotiating with Séguin for DL to become a full partner in the Alliance, though he made it no secret that he saw this as the prelude to a merger. The RPR saw its opportunity and soon the name of Christian Poncelet, senator for the Vosges, was circulating as the challenger.

The *renouvellement* further weakened the Monory's grip. The RPR increased to 99 seats, while the Centrists lost six and fell to 52. It was difficult to talk up Monory's case. He appealed to Chirac to repay past loyalty, but was firmly told not to embarrass the President. On paper a solid UDF vote of some 120 (including the right wing of the RDSE) would see off Poncelet's 100, but the first round ballot revealed a very different balance of forces. Monory trailed with 102 votes to 118 and withdrew. The UDF chose Hoeffel as a last-gasp candidate, but he could muster only 109 votes to 125 in the second round and Poncelet eased home in the third round.

Parity, *décumul* and Senate reform

Poncelet took the helm of an ill-tempered assembly. His task might have been easier if the majority had been allowed to direct its anger at the Jospin government, but the position was complicated by Chirac's determination to pose as a political moderniser. Despite his own track record as a *cumulard*, Chirac was now fluent in the language of *décumul* and parity.[2] Relaunching his septennate at Rennes on 4 December 1998, Chirac made a firm commitment to both reforms. It was Poncelet's task to persuade the Senate to follow.

Historically, the upper house had always been an *assemblée de cumulards*: the nature and the structure of local politics made it almost a requirement for senators to hold local office(s) simultaneously. In the National Assembly it had been less common, until decentralisation reforms in the 1980s and *alternance* made local government both an appealing prospect and a necessary refuge. By 1997, 92 per cent of deputies were *cumulards* compared to 82 per cent of senators. Despite the self-interest most deputies had in retaining the *cumul*, Jospin persisted. The government proposed an organic law to prohibit deputies and senators being MEPs, from holding more than one other elected post in local government and prohibiting them from exercising a *fonction exécutive* at local level, i. e. as president of a regional or departmental council, or mayor of a commune. An ordinary law would also limit an individual to two offices at all levels of local government, prohibit them from exercising executive office at more than one level and forbid any mayor or chair of a regional or departmental assembly from being an MEP.

The Senate majority would and could have happily vetoed the organic law, but Poncelet was mindful both of Chirac's position and on the impact opposition might have on public opinion. He therefore asked Jacques Larché, perennial chair of the legislation commission, to find a basis for negotiation. Larché retained the government's stipulation of a maximum of two elected offices, but removed all reference to incompatibility between being a member of parliament and exercising executive office in local government. He added a further qualification to the limitation, stipulating that members of parliament could hold a third office in a commune of fewer than 3,500 inhabitants. It was perfectly evident that deputies in the government's majority were in fact counting on senators to protect their prerogatives and though the arguments dragged on for two years, including an inconclusive CMP, before the Assembly finally ratified the law in March 2000, it took much the form Larché had set out. At the 2001 municipal elections many senator-mayors became ex-mayors, preferring to retain their positions in departmental assemblies. Poncelet, for example, relinquished his post as mayor of Remiremont to retain the chair of the *conseil général* for the Vosges.

The government took a two-pronged approach to parity, beginning with a revision of the constitution, then changes to the electoral code. They proposed simply adding a line to Article 3 to the effect that the law should encourage the equal access of men and women to elected offices. The Senate suggested instead altering Article 4, placing the responsibility for parity with political parties and approved its own version at the end of January 1999, scotching Chirac's hope of summoning Congress to ratify the revision on International Women's Day on 8 March. Chirac was furious and Poncelet and Henri de Raincourt (chair of the majority's unofficial *intergroupe*) were summoned to the Elysée and told to whip their troops into line. Rather than waste time on a CMP, Jospin asked the Assembly to approve the Senate's version and Congress ratified the change in June 1999. The reform of the electoral code passed, on the Assembly's last word, a year later. Majority senators petitioned the Constitutional Council over the distinction made by the law between elections using a PR list system over one round (the Senate), where the law required an alternation between candidates of the two sexes, whereas for municipal elections using PR, lists were only required to have an equal number of candidates of both sexes per group of six. The petition was rejected.

In the spring of 1999 interior minister Jean-Pierre Chevènement launched the government's direct assault on the Senate with a volley of reforms, covering three areas. The first involved an increase in the number and redistribution of seats. The second reduced the threshold for the use of PR from five seats to three. The third tackled the problem of over- and under-representation within the electoral colleges *à la Grangé*, by uncoupling the number of municipal delegates from the size of each council and instead allocating delegates per head of population. The first proposal involved an organic law and was never likely to succeed under a left-wing government. The other two, however, only involved changes to the electoral code and could go through on the last word.

The Senate simply rejected the organic law creating new seats and the government withdrew the bill. But there was some room for negotiation on the other questions. Instead of a three-seat threshold, the legislation commission argued for four and instead of one delegate per 500 inhabitants suggested by the government, offered 1:700. The government stuck to its position, and the three-seat threshold was in place in time for the 2001 *renouvellement*. The reorganisation of the colleges was not. For reasons known only to themselves and despite warnings from Chevènement of the likely consequences, majority deputies adopted a tariff of one delegate per 300 inhabitants. Senators petitioned the Constitutional Council, on the grounds that such a rate would produce an unacceptable number of co-opted delegates. The objection was upheld. If Jospin wanted to reform the 'anomaly', he would have to do so President. But four years to the day after his attack on the upper house, he was eliminated from the presidential election. Two weeks later, the Senate passed a notable milestone. Comfortably re-elected to the Elysée, Chirac chose a senator for prime minister.

Apotheosis - a senator at Matignon

Jean-Pierre Raffarin was not a senator of long vintage. He held his first elected office as municipal councillor in a small suburb of Poitiers, in the department of the Vienne, where his father had been a deputy from 1951 to 1955, but where René Monory dominated right-wing politics. Indeed, Monory won his first senatorial election in 1968 against Raffarin *père*. That, however, was in the past, and although Raffarin *fils* was a member of the Parti Républicain, he was also Monory's protégé and collaborator on the project to build Futuroscope, the high-technology amusement park and industrial estate on the outskirts of Poitiers. Raffarin built his political base as a president of the regional council for Poitou-Charentes. He was already minister for small and medium-sized businesses when he won a seat in parliament for the first time, as senator for the Vienne in 1995, though he opted to remain in government and only took up residence in the Luxembourg Palace after the 1997 dissolution. Once there, he rallied to the *rénovateurs* with enthusiasm. Politically he was a member of Démocratie Libérale and the URI, but like Monory he had long believed Chirac was the only contender around whom the right could rally in 2002 and he had worked to that end ever since entering the Senate. A shrewd political mind belied by an avuncular exterior saw him rapidly assume a role of mover and shaker within the majority.

Chirac chose Raffarin for a number of reasons. For some time before the election Chirac's supporters in- and outside the RPR (with Raffarin prominent among them) had been preparing the way for the creation of a single presidential party, though there had been a number of false starts. The inevitability of Chirac's re-election after the first round in 2002 only increased their determination to use the second and the general election to engineer such an outcome. The Union pour une Majorité Présidentielle (as the UMP was initially known) was born, but Chirac needed a non-Gaullist to head the government if it was not simply to look like an enlargement of the RPR. Raffarin was not the only candidate on those grounds, but others lacked the solid backing the Senate provided. Seen from the Luxembourg Palace, the appointment had other meanings. In the first place, it lifted an unspoken prohibition on senators becoming prime minister: he was, after all, the first senator to move to Matignon since Debré in 1959. Raffarin's elevation was also interpreted as a vote of thanks to the upper chamber for the sacrifices made during the third cohabitation. The majority had not always rallied easily, but it had reined in its natural impulses. And with the Girondin Raffarin in power, the *rénovateurs* would at last realise their aspiration to make the Senate *la chambre de la décentralisation*.

The idea that the Senate had a special claim over decentralisation and regional development really took off when Poncelet became speaker and made it the central theme of his first inaugural address. *Rapporteur* to two *missions communes d'information* in 1983 and 1984 on the impact of the Defferre reforms, Poncelet had very quickly grasped the opportunity decentralisation offered the Senate to recast itself as the *chambre des collectivités territoriales* and was therefore one of the very first *rénovateurs*. From the outset he challenged colleagues to think long and hard about the next stage - *Décentralisation Acte II* - and the Senate's role in it. He had even offered Jospin a deal whereby the government could have wide-ranging reform of the Senate in exchange for a constitutional revision stating that all legislation concerning local government must be presented to the Senate in the first instance.

At Poncelet's prompting, the Senate set up a fresh *mission d'information* in early 1999 to examine the state of decentralisation and to make suggestions on the way forward. Its findings were published in an impressive two-volume report boldly entitled *Pour une République territoriale*. It was written by Jean-Paul Delevoye, RPR senator for the Pas-de-Calais and chairman of the Association des Maires de France, and Michel Mercier (UC, Rhône). A raft of far-reaching proposals included the introduction of the principle of subsidiarity into the constitution as well as the right for local authorities to experiment with different forms of organisation. No-one could really miss the point when Raffarin made Delevoye minister for regional development and the conclusions of *Pour une République territoriale* formed the basis of the decentralisation reforms of 2003-4. The first of these, which precisely introduced subsidiarity and experimentation into the constitution, also enhanced the Senate's prerogatives by amending Article 39-2 of the constitution to give the upper chamber first view of all legislation concerning local government, decentralisation and French expatriates.[3]

Over the next two years the Senate had its work cut out, reviewing and refining a whole package of measures, as Raffarin pushed on with *Acte II*. The speed and complexity of the legislation was impressive and senators laboured to simplify its content and soften the blow to local councillors delivering change on the ground. Apart from its legislative role, the Senate stepped up its efforts as an information crossroads for government and *élus*, a role delegated by Poncelet to Alain Delcamp, the Senate's energetic director of communications. By the end of 2004, however, even the most enthusiastic Girondin recognised that some sort of stock-take was necessary. After securing a third term as speaker, Poncelet announced the formal creation of the

Observatoire de la Décentralisation with a brief to monitor and evaluate the impact of legislation, to assess the application of local government policy and to propose changes and improvements. The Observatoire comprised sixteen senators. Jean Puech took the chair, with Roger Karoutchi and Mercier among the vice-presidents. Other 'observers' included Raincourt and Arthuis, chairman of the finance commission: all of them more or less prominent *rénovateurs*.[4]

Triumph came, however, at a price. Chirac, who had been backed into a corner by Giscard in 2000 and forced to accept a reduction of the presidential office to five years, was determined that the Senate should not escape a dose of modernisation too. When the news reached Chirac that with his return to the Elysée, UMP senators felt that a reduction of their term from nine years to six would hardly be necessary, they were very quickly put straight. The upshot was the *loi Poncelet* of May 2003 which created new seats, raised the threshold for the use of PR to departments with four seats or more, reduced the age of eligibility to 30 and shortened the term to six years.

Like the Socialists 20 years earlier, Raffarin learned that decentralisation wins no votes. The UMP crashed badly in departmental and regional elections in May 2004, losing control of 12 of the 14 departments it held and leaving the PS in control of all but two of France's 22 regions. Most damaging personally for Raffarin was the defeat inflicted on the list he had supported in his Poitou-Charentes fiefdom by Ségolène Royal. As a consequence, Royal's name began to appear regularly in opinion polls and soon she was being touted as a *présidentiable*. On the eve of the 2005 *rentrée parlementaire*, Royal attacked the Senate as an 'anachronism' that should be abolished, a view shared by Jack Lang in his pamphlet *Changer*.[5] Royal's posturing did not worry right-wing senators unduly, until she won the PS nomination to run for President in November 2006. Her camp promised that if elected, Royal would make Senate reform one of a series of constitutional changes to be put to a referendum, pencilled in for September 2007. Royal's defeat was a relief to the Senate majority, as was Sarkozy's decision to make another senator, François Fillon, prime minister. Fillon's appointment did not have quite the same symbolic or institutional resonance as Raffarin's, but it confirmed that the Senate was not the graveyard of political ambitions.

Between hyperpresidentialism and parliamentary fetishism

While Sarkozy's campaign focussed principally on law and order, social reform and economic liberalisation, there was little doubt that he intended to leave his mark on the constitution too. He had outlined his views on the future development of the regime towards a more explicitly presidential style when presenting his *voeux* to journalists at the beginning of 2006. By the summer of 2007, his own style was being described as *hyperprésidentialisme* such was Sarkozy's apparent omnipresence. Premier Fillon even mused over the possibility, at some point in the future, of the disappearance of the prime ministerial office.[6] The new President was keen to leave a mark on the constitution, quickly and decisively.

Sarkozy revealed his intentions to the public on 12 July 2007 at Épinal, the town in Lorraine where de Gaulle had emphatically rejected the constitution of the Fourth Republic in September 1946. In the company of the prime minister and the speakers of both houses, Sarkozy affirmed his commitment to the Fifth Republic, by very firmly rejecting the idea of a Sixth. He also announced, however, his intention to launch the broadest review of the constitution since its inception, a review 'without taboos'. The advent of the *quinquennat* and the coincidence of the election of the President and the National Assembly had fundamentally altered the relationship between executive and legislature and changes were needed to give firmer guarantees to parliament and, pursuing his theme of *ouverture* (openness) towards the centre and left, to examine how the status of the opposition could be formally recognised. By the same token, Sarkozy expected parliament to make efforts to improve its function and its transparency. The task of leading the review to 'modernise and re-balance' the constitution needed a high profile chairman, and Sarkozy confirmed that Edouard Balladur, whom he had backed in the 1995 presidential election against Chirac, had accepted the role. Turning very deliberately towards Poncelet ('Cher Christian'), the President expressed the hope that the upper chamber would play a positive role in the process - meaning that he should make sure that it did - so that the Senate 'might better reflect French diversity which needs more than ever today to be represented in our institutions'.[7]

Balladur's Comité de Réflexion et de Proposition sur la Modernisation et le Rééquilibrage des Institutions de la Ve République comprised 12 other colleagues. They included political figures such as Jack Lang, the former minister of culture, PS deputy for Boulogne-sur-Mer and author of a bold pamphlet for political reform entitled

Changer, which had proposed the abolition of the upper house.[8] He was joined by Pierre Mazeaud, former chair of the Constitutional Council, Olivier Schrameck, head of Jospin's office when he was prime minister, and constitutional specialists including Michel Rocard's former advisor Guy Carcassonne (who had been highly critical of Sarkozy's plans in 2006) and Olivier Duhamel. The committee conducted a series of hearings with various interested parties, including representatives of the Senate, before presenting its findings to the President in the autumn.

It was difficult to interpret Balladur's appointment as a good or a bad sign for the upper house. As prime minister between 1993 and 1995 he had maintained cordial relations with the Senate and was politically closer to the majority there than in the National Assembly. But Balladur was nobody's fool and was perfectly capable of asking the sort of difficult questions that Senate leaders do not much like to be asked - and are surprisingly poor at answering. On more than one occasion during the committee's hearings, Balladur asked if departments had not had their day and if the time had come to think of a regional Senate. The replies, from the likes of Poncelet and Mercier were less than convincing, but while Balladur's final report made a number of recommendations that would impact directly and indirectly on the Senate, reforming local government was beyond its remit. That bombshell was left to another of Sarkozy's special commissions, headed by Jacques Attali.

The Balladur Commission's recommendations were thorough, even if their boldness or originality lay in the eye of the beholder: several had already been raised by reformers on both right and left.[9] Perhaps the most talked about proposal was to give the President the right to address parliament directly, a privilege removed in 1873 by monarchists who wanted to prevent Adolphe Thiers influencing the course of debate and to prepare the way for establishing a head of state who was not responsible before parliament. The address could be followed by a debate, but no vote would be permitted. The commission also introduced a form of words to Article 4, recognising the formal status of the opposition and devised a number of other changes intended to strengthen parliament's hand in relation to government, including a greater say in the timetable and longer to debate private bills. In a significant change, Balladur suggested that whichever house a government bill had been introduced into first should debate the text adopted by the relevant standing committee, not the government's original bill, as was hitherto the case.

Most of the proposals would affect both houses, but a few were directed specifically at the Senate. Under Article 24-3, the commission suggested amending the Senate's vocation to represent the *collectivités territoriales* by adding a clause stating that it did so according to their population. This, it was intended, would overcome the Constitutional Council's misgivings regarding the number of co-opted delegates and pave the way for an ordinary law restructuring the electoral colleges. Despite discussions in its hearings that the Senate might relinquish its specific role in representing French expatriates, the commission did not pursue that option. Under Article 25, the commission proposed the creation of an independent body to oversee a ten-yearly review of the electoral constituencies for both houses.

Many, though not all of the commission's recommendations were incorporated into a government bill which included a few original flourishes, the most prominent of which was the limitation on the number of consecutive Presidential terms to two.[10] The government's text made it clear that any debate following a Presidential address to parliament would take place in the absence of the head of state. With regard to the Senate, the government slightly modified the commission's wording on the electoral colleges and retained the idea of an independent body to review constituencies, though it removed the stipulation of a fixed cycle. It broke, however, with the commission over expatriate representation, amending Article 24 to state that, henceforth, French expatriates would be represented in both houses.

The government's bill was presented to the National Assembly on 23 April 2008 and with Sarkozy determined to have the reforms in place by the summer recess, the pressure was on all concerned. The tension was only increased by the realisation that, with the left determined to block the reforms, even though some Socialists agreed with some of the changes, with the Centre wavering and dissent among its own supporters, the government would be hard pushed to achieve the three-fifths majority required under Article 89 for the reform to pass Congress. The bill passed its first reading in the Assembly at the beginning of June with some key amendments. Against the government's wishes, deputies added to Article One the recognition of regional languages as part of France's national heritage. Rather less dramatically, they fixed their number at 577. It was clearly intended that the Senate should make a similar gesture. The bill passed by 315 votes to 231.[11]

The Senate legislation commission duly responded to the Assembly's invitation by setting the number of senators at 348. They broke with the lower house and the government, however, over the independent commission. In the original bill it was intended that the new body should advise on all bills dealing with boundaries and constituencies for both deputies and senators. The Senate instead adopted a wording by which the commission would only examine the constituencies for deputies and the number and distribution of seats for both deputies and senators. The distinction looked unimportant to the outsider, but it was intended by the upper chamber to signal that its constituencies, the departments, were not negotiable. Senators also proved intransigent with regard to the colleges, insisting that they must continue to be composed, for the greater part, of delegates who were members of one local assembly or another. They therefore removed from Article 24-3 any reference to representation of local councils according to population. To the government's relief senators also removed the recognition of regional languages and passed the first reading by 166 votes to 123. At that point the bill was some 70 votes short of what would be needed when Congress met.

Table 4.1 - **Constitutional Revision in the Senate June/July 2008**

	First Reading			Second Reading		
Group	**For**	**Against**	**Abst**	**For**	**Against**	**Abst**
CRC	0	23	0	0	23	0
Soc	0	95	0	0	95	0
RDSE	8	0	9	8	0	9
UDF	0	0	30	0	0	30
UMP	155	2	1+1*	153	2	3+1
NI	3	3	0	2	3	1
Total	166	123	40+1	163	125	43+1
*The speaker is usually accounted as not having voted.						

Before that could happen, the two chambers had to agree an identical text, and after the Senate vote they looked some way apart. In fact the real negotiations were only just beginning. Despite dark mutterings, senators had no intention of blocking the reforms: given certain guarantees, they were willing to follow the government in other areas.[12] Roger Karoutchi, now minister for parliamentary relations, shuttled between the chambers and a deal was struck. In exchange for the Senate's loss of its monopoly over expatriate representation, no attempt was made to reintroduce the population clause into Article 24-3. Deputies restored the reference to regional languages, but in Article

75. The bill passed its second reading in the National Assembly on 9 July, was adopted without amendment by the Senate on the 16th and Congress was summoned for the 21st. But it still was not clear that the bill would achieve the necessary majority.

The spread of votes in the two readings in the Senate admirably sum up the problem. The Communist, Republican and Citizen group (CRC) and the Socialists voted resolutely against the bill, though one or two voices were raised unofficially in favour of some of the changes. Views in the soft centre, the UC and the RDSE, as well as among the floating right-wing *non-inscrits* were equally unclear and gave the bill only 49 per cent of votes in the upper house.

Table 4.2 - **Vote of Congress - 21 July 2008**

Senate	Total	For	Ag	Abst
CRC	23	0	23	0
Soc	95	0	95	0
RDSE	17	11	4	2
UC-UDF	30	24	2	4
UMP	159	158	1	0
NI	6	2	2	1+1
National Assembly	**Total**	**For**	**Ag**	**Abst**
Soc/R/Citoyen	204	10	194	0
Gauche Dem	24	0	24	0
Nouveau Centre	24	23	0	1
UMP	317	310	6	1
NI	7	1	6	0
Congress	**906**	**539**	**357**	**9+1**

The bill looked to be in even greater jeopardy when *Le Monde* published an open letter from Lang to Sarkozy, expressing his frustration that a number of key aspects of the Commission's proposals had been ignored or rejected, including the clause regarding the demographic magnitude of *collectivités* in Article 24-3.[13] Sarkozy replied at length to Lang's reservations and to those of other sceptics the following day.[14] He made it clear that he saw the bill as only a first stage and promised, among other things, to ask the Senate to revisit the question of the electoral colleges, suggesting the tariff of one elector per 700 inhabitants in each commune as a starting point. This and other promises, allied to feverish lobbying, produced its reward. Lang and a handful of Socialist deputies voted for the reforms, but the margins were so tight that Bernard Accoyer, the UMP speaker of the

National Assembly and therefore chair of Congress, abandoned the practice of not having his vote counted just in case. The threshold was 538 votes. The bill passed by 539 to 357. The 24th revision of the constitution was promulgated on 23 July 2008.

Balladur II and the *millefeuille territorial*

If the Senate had been a difficult partner in drafting the 23 July law, there was a good reason. A month after inviting Balladur to think the unthinkable about the constitution, Sarkozy invited Jacques Attali to head the rather portentously titled Commission pour la Libération de la Croissance [growth] Française to do the same for the French economy. This was a much larger body than Balladur's: its 43 members included academics, businessmen and women, civil servants and journalists. But like the Vallon commission, it lacked local or national *élus*. The commission's conclusions, published in January 2008, took the form of *300 décisions pour changer la France* (316 in fact). The third section of the report tackled the question of reforming governance to foster growth. Decisions 258 to 267 focused on streamlining and clarifying decentralisation, a process the report described as 'a cause of confusion', a tangle (*enchevêtrement*) of responsibilities and cross financing leading to fragmentation, paralysis and waste of taxpayers' money. Decentralisation *Acte II* had failed to rationalise or to clarify the relationship between regions, departments and communes or make the system more efficient.[15] The report expressed a strong preference for restructuring local government around fewer regions, a new status to recognise the role of urban centres as the motors for growth and more thorough and widespread introduction of *intercommunes*. Decision 260 proposed nothing less than phasing out the departments.

Reaction in the Senate, so deeply sensitive about its prerogatives regarding local government and so intimately attached to the departments, was predictable and unequivocal. Puech, chair of the Observatoire de la Décentralisation, described the proposals as 'completely disconnected from reality'.[16] Poncelet echoed his sentiment at a meeting with the presidents of France's general councils: abolishing the departments, he insisted, 'demonstrated a profound misunderstanding of life at local level'.[17]

A shake up of local government was far from anyone's mind in the lead up to municipal and cantonal elections in March 2008, in which the government's supporters performed very poorly. The question was resurrected, however, by Sarkozy, first at Limoges in June 2008 and again at Toulon at the end of September. Speaking mainly about the response to the world economic crisis, he referred to the need to simplify France's complex local structures in order to deliver economies, reduce the fiscal burden on business and make the whole more transparent and comprehensible to citizens. Local government reform had become one of the 'major projects' for 2009 and Sarkozy once again asked Balladur to lead a committee of experts.[18] The Comité pour la Réforme des Collectivités Territoriales, or 'Balladur II', was formally established on 22 October 2008, to report by March 2009. Launching the committee, Sarkozy underlined the possibility of different solutions to different problems in different localities and, in more placatory terms than Attali, expressed his disappointment that so little progress had been made in promoting subsidiarity and using the right to experiment introduced into the constitution in 2003.[19] (Sarkozy had, after all, been interior minister when the reforms were introduced.)

The new committee comprised academics, civil servants and politicians, including two senior senators. The Socialist Pierre Mauroy was mayor of Lille from 1973-2001, prime minister at the time of the Defferre reforms and author in 2000 of a report into new directions for decentralisation for the Jospin government. He was joined by Gérard Longuet, a former minister, chair of the Association des Régions de France from 2002 to 2004, but principally chosen for the close support and advice he had lent to Sarkozy during his election campaign.

Despite their presence on the committee, Senate noses were, nevertheless, out of joint and there was a rapid response from the Luxembourg Palace, where the new speaker, Gérard Larcher, announced the creation of a 36-strong, cross-party *mission temporaire* to examine the organisation and development of local government, chaired by Claude Belot. A tart communiqué from the speaker's office reminded everyone of the upper chamber's constitutional vocation and primacy in the field.[20] Not to be outdone, his counterpart in the National Assembly, Bernard Accoyer, among whose constituents there were, after all, more local councillors than Larcher's, also set up a *mission*. Even before that, Jean-François Copé, chair of the UMP in the lower house, created a working group of majority deputies and senators.[21] Jean-Pierre Bel, chair of the Socialists in the Senate, responded by establishing a group for the opposition to co-ordinate their response. At the same time, the interior ministry promised consultations with various organisations representing local councillors; the Association des Maires de France (AMF), the Association des Maires de Grandes Villes de France (AMGVF), the Assemblée des Départements de France (ADF) and the Association des Régions de France (ARF). If the relationship between the various levels of French local government - the *millefeuille territorial* was the phrase of the day - was a tangle, this was more than adequately reflected by the muddle of *ad hoc* committees and working parties. Still, no-one could doubt the importance of local government to France's political elite.

The Balladur commission worked in three phases.[22] The first, during November 2008, finalised themes and methodology. The second, from early December to the end of January 2009, was occupied in hearing contributors, mostly, though not exclusively local and national *élus*, either individually or in groups. If senators had been excluded from the Attali commission's deliberations, they could hardly make that claim now. Many of the hearings took place at the Luxembourg Palace and there were more than a dozen senators among the 60 or so figures invited to present their views.

The chair of the legislation commission, Jean-Jacques Hyest, was the first senator to give evidence to the committee and was later followed by his counterpart on the finance commission Jean Arthuis. Arthuis appeared in tandem with the commission's *rapporteur général* Philippe Marini and they were asked to focus their comments on the fiscal burden on local authorities and rationalisation of the *taxe professionnelle* levied to fund them. That question was also a feature of the interview with Alain Lambert, Arthuis's immediate predecessor as chair of the commission and finance minister under Raffarin. In 2007 Lambert had been commissioned by the Fillon government to lead a working group examining relations between local authorities and state field agencies. Lambert reiterated the conclusions from his report - that there must be a clearer distinction of responsibilities between the different levels of local government, with the abolition of the *clause de compétence générale*, which allows a local authority at any level to interfere in any area of policy in the name of the public interest, and an end to the wastage caused by *financement croisé*, the tangled web of funding from different local authorities. His views were shared by a number of ministers and, according to various leaks, held favour within the committee too.[23]

Lambert's views were deeply at odds with Raffarin, who came down very firmly against abolition of *compétence générale* and cross-funding of infrastructure projects. Describing himself as an 'ultra-

Girondin', he pleaded instead for local authorities to be allowed to continue to experiment without constraints. On a more concrete note, he proposed to halve the number of regions and refocus the role of departments and regions, the former working closely with communes and the latter acting as the leader in relations between *collectivités* and the state. Nobody had ever called Jean-Pierre Chevènement a Girondin, but the senator for Belfort, invited to testify as the interior minister responsible for important legislation on intercommunal organisms in 1999, broadly agreed with Raffarin, even going so far as to argue against the whole principle of the reform. If anything needed to be made easier, it was the process of creating *intercommunes*. Chevènement also lent his support to the views of Philippe Dallier, the young UMP senator for Seine-Saint-Denis, whose 2007 report for the Observatoire de la Décentralisation laid the foundation of discussions for creating a Greater Paris authority (*le Grand Paris*).[24] Dallier made a very strong case for more active development of metropolitan centres and urban *agglomérations* as the economic and social motors of newly defined regions, a view supported by other contributors and by Mauroy.

Larcher spoke to the commission early in 2009, partly as the messenger for the Belot *mission* and also on his own behalf. The outcome of the *mission*'s preliminary work mostly told the committee what it already knew regarding the need for 'legible, coherent and effective' local government.[25] Larcher also gave his own views as speaker of the assembly that would have first sight of any bill emerging from the committee's deliberations, as a former minister and as a local *élu*. Rejecting the abolition of any one level of local government but also accepting that departmental and regional structures could not continue to ignore the impact of the 'le fait métropolitain', he nevertheless stressed the importance of the different levels in balancing the notions of proximity of representation with a strategic vision in economic and social planning. Most ordinary citizens, Larcher continued, were attached to their communes and their departments, but uncertainty remained regarding the regions. There was no reason, however, he argued for regions not to take a leading strategic role and he recalled his own role as *rapporteur* to a Senate enquiry that had put forward the idea of local authorities grouping themselves together an nominating one to act as the leader ('chef de fil'). As to *compétence générale*, Larcher opposed its abolition, preferring far clearer delimitation of different areas of responsibility between authorities.

Balladur was due to deliver his report in late February 2009 and, as with the revision of the constitution, the government hoped to have a bill before parliament in the spring and on the statue books by the summer recess. Press briefings by members of the committee towards the end of 2008 suggested the blanket abolition of any layer of local government had been jettisoned. Many of the contributors to the committee insisted on the importance of the departments in delivering vital 'services de proximité'. Several (including Larcher, Raffarin and Chevènement) picked up on the suggestion that members of the departmental assemblies might also becoming *ex officio* regional councillors, perhaps being re-christened *conseillers territoriaux* and functioning at both levels in different contexts, much as municipal councillors in Paris also function, on occasion, as *conseillers généraux* for the city-department. An advanced leak of the content of the final report, from committee-member Dominique Perben, suggested that Balladur would recommend a reduction of the number of regions from 22 to 15 and that eight of France's largest provincial cities should be accorded a new status.[26]

All these changes would have an impact on the Senate, but a far less profound or traumatic one than had been feared at the outset. Since Sarkozy had ruled out the abolition of communes at a conference of the AMF in November 2008, municipal delegates would continue to provide the critical mass in the Senate's electoral colleges. The question how still hung in the air.

By way of a coda, it became clear during the hearings and particularly in an exchange between Balladur and Hyest on 3 December 2008, that the former prime minister had not been impressed by the Senate's refusal to accept the amendment to Article 24-3, that the upper house should represent local authorities according to their population. He asked Hyest, bearing in mind Sarkozy's comments on the eve of the meeting of Congress in July 2008, whether he thought, privately, the Senate was now ready to accept a modification to the colleges. Hyest avoided the trap simply by answering that since the last *renouvellement* and with the likelihood that the left would take control of the Senate in 2011, the voices calling for change had fallen silent. Balladur did not pursue the argument.

Part II
Senators and the Senate

5

Departments, seats and colleges

There were 514,519 councillors elected at the 2001 municipal elections. In France the ratio of councillors to voters is better than one to 100.[1]

The 'Grand Council of the Communes of France' certainly exists, but it is ephemeral: it is the senatorial electoral college.[2]

The Senate has almost always been a mixed assembly. It comprised life and elected members between 1876 and 1916, elected and nominated members between 1946 and 1948, members representing the *collectivités* and expatriates from 1946 to the present and, over the same period, a varying number of senators elected by PR or by a majority system. The Senate of the Third Republic had 300 seats in 1876 and 314 from 1920 with the return of Alsace and Moselle. The constitution of 1946 fixed the Council of the Republic at between 250 and 320. In 1946 there were 315 senators (to 627 deputies) and in 1948 the number rose to 320. The 1958 constitution set no limit. The 'provisional' Senate numbered 282, the Senate proper 308. Algerian independence reduced the number to 274, which then rose again to 285 with the creation of new departments in the Ile-de-France and a seat for the islands of Wallis-et-Futuna. The new seats created in 1976 brought the number to 316 and then six more to represent French expatriates were added in 1982 to make 322. The 2003 *loi Poncelet* raised the total to 346. Two seats were added in 2006 for the new island *collectivités* of Saint-Martin and Saint-Barthélemy. The law of 23 July 2008 fixed the number of senators at 348. No department has lost a seat since the electoral law of 1958.

Debate over the Senate's representation breaks down into a series of separate questions: how many seats departments have or should have; what the ratio of inhabitants is to each senator; how senators are elected and how the way in which the departmental colleges are elected distort the 'real' political picture in each department. The Senate's defenders emphasise that it is a territorial assembly. It critics point out that it does not represent the *collectivités* equally, by which they often mean accurately.

The Senate in 1959

The first Senate of the Fifth Republic was nothing more than the old Council of the Republic, stripped of the African seats. The whole upper house was renewed in April 1959 on the basis of a revised distribution agreed in December 1958. In the *métropole*, 255 seats were distributed according to a *clé de répartition* - the scale of distribution – whereby each department was given one seat for the first 150,000 inhabitants (compared to 154,000 previously) with subsequent seats for every tranche of 250,000 inhabitants or part thereof. By coincidence, the only department to lose a seat at the changeover was the Lot, represented by speaker Monnerville, while ten new seats were created. The Seine (Paris and the districts of Sceaux and Saint-Denis) gained two, rising to 22 in total, while Calvados, the Oise, the Marne and the Var rose from two to three, the Loire and the Moselle from three to four, Seine-Maritime to five and Seine-et-Oise to eight. The four DOM retained their seven seats, while the number of senators for France's remaining dependencies (the *territoires d'outre-mer* or TOM) dropped to six. Representation of expatriates was also reduced, from nine senators to six. In Algeria, by contrast, the number rose to 34: 10 elected by the European population, the remainder by Muslim assemblies. Despite the increase, the national rate of representation, (the number of inhabitants per senator) was 1:174,000, compared to 1:165,000 in 1948, a reflection in the increase in the population to nearly 45 million.

Map 5.1 - **Metropolitan Seats in 1959**

The scale of distribution was not, however, applied rigorously, and some departments were entitled to feel aggrieved: there should have been an extra seat for the Gard, the Isère, the Gironde and a second for Seine-et-Oise. If it had been the intention to keep the metropolitan rate of representation as low as 1948, just 12 further seats would have done the trick, but distributing them would have necessitated a more thorough recalculation of the *clé de répartition* and more departments would have lost seats. The government wanted as little disruption as possible, though quite why the departments mentioned above were overlooked is unclear. In any case, as the redistribution stood in 1958, two-thirds of departments had a rate better than 1:174,000, while in 12 others it was below 1:200,000. Variation between top and bottom was another matter, however, with the senator for Lozère representing a population of 81,000 while each of his 22 colleagues for the Seine represented 250,000 inhabitants, with the Nord just behind.

Neither de Gaulle nor Debré liked PR, but they accepted that there was an argument for its use in larger districts and they retained the system adopted in 1948, a variation on d'Hondt's formula (V/(s+1), where V is the number of votes and s the number of seats already attributed), using a quotient in the first instance and a highest remaining average. The threshold was raised, however, from departments with four seats to those with five or more, or 60 seats in seven departments.

Map 5.2 - **Series A, B and C, 1962-2008**

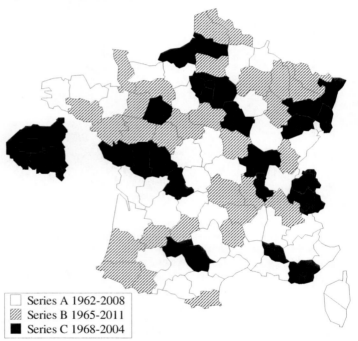

☐ Series A 1962-2008
▨ Series B 1965-2011
■ Series C 1968-2004

The electoral law restored the nine-year mandate, renewable by thirds every three years. In due course the seats were divided into roughly equal series, based on the alphabetical and numerical ordering of departments. Series A contained those listed from Ain (01) to Indre (36) plus Belfort (90), series B Indre-et-Loire (37) to Pyrénées-

Orientales (66), and series C Bas-Rhin (67) to Yonne (89). Seats for the DOM-TOM were distributed among the series and two expatriate senators would be elected in each too. The Algerian seats were abolished before the first *renouvellement* in September 1962.

Despite their arbitrary nature, each series had its own characteristics. Series A comprised departments that were principally rural and south of the Loire, though it also included three departments in the modern region of Brittany, three Norman departments and three in Champagne-Ardenne. The Bouches-du-Rhône was the only department in the series to use PR. Series B included a number of industrial, urban and commercial departments such as the Loire (Saint-Etienne), Loire-Atlantique (Nantes), the Isère (Grenoble) and Puy-de-Dôme (Clermont-Ferrand), as well as the Nord and Pas-de-Calais, though only the latter two fell under the PR rule in 1958. Series C was dominated by the Paris region, with the other departments clustered in Alsace and southern Lorraine, along the Vienne and Sèvre-Niortaise valleys, the two Tarn departments, two Provençal outposts in the Vaucluse and Var, Savoy, but also the Rhône, Saône-et-Loire and, away in the north, Seine-Maritime and the Somme. The order in which the series would proceed to be elected was decided by drawing lots, but as it happened, the letter A came out first and so the *renouvellements* ran in alphabetical order: series A in September 1962, B in September 1965, C in September 1968 and so on until 2008.

In 1964 the government announced the redrawing of the administrative map of the Paris region. Seine and Seine-et-Oise were replaced by seven new departments. Paris *intramuros* became a department in its own right (and kept the number 75), with its city council functioning at times as a municipal forum and at others as a *conseil général*. The *petite couronne* of suburbs just beyond the city limits became the Hauts-de-Seine (92), Seine-Saint-Denis (93), and Val-de-Marne (94). Seine-et-Oise disappeared altogether: a small northern slice became Val-d'Oise (95), the south-eastern corner the Essonne (91), and the remainder (including the towns of Mantes, Versailles and Rambouillet) became the Yvelines (which took the old number for Seine-et-Oise of 78).

The Seine's 22 seats were added to the eight for Seine-et-Oise and nine new ones were created to account for the region's demographic explosion and distributed in the manner outlined below in Table 5.1. PR was to be used in all the new departments, even those with only three and four seats. The distribution was also politically manipulated.

Paris should have had only 11 seats and the Val-de-Marne four, while Seine-Saint-Denis and Val-d'Oise, where the PCF was strong, should have had six and four respectively. The changes came into force for first time in September 1968.

Table 5.1 - **The Paris region in 1968**

Paris (75)	12	Seine-Saint-Denis (93)	5
Yvelines (78)	4	Val-de-Marne (94)	5
Essonne (91)	3	Val-d'Oise (95)	3
Hauts-de-Seine (92)	7	**Total**	**39**

1976 - a missed opportunity

In 1965 Gaston Monnerville had urged his colleagues to think about reform. Edouard Bonnefous came up with a new distribution of seats and Marcel Prélot devised a means of balancing distribution against demographic demands by creating intra-regional seats, but these ideas came to nought. The desire for change revived, however, with Giscard's narrow election victory in 1974, as the right, and especially the non-Gaullist right, sought to shore up its position. There were demographic pressures too. The population was creeping towards 53 million, which meant each senator now represented a shade more than 200,000 inhabitants. Giscard personally prompted Poher to encourage senators to revisit the question. The proposals they devised were imaginative and forward-thinking, but the outcome was disappointing, through no fault of their own.

A cross-party commission made two principal recommendations. Firstly, to raise the *clé de répartition* back to 154,000 for the first seat, then a seat per tranche of 250,000 thereafter, creating 33 new seats and taking one each from Paris and the Creuse. A campaign grew up rapidly around the Creuse, whose two senators (one Radical, the other Socialist) argued that the already small number of deputies for the department and its problems of rural depopulation and agricultural decline made the retention of both imperative. How the problems facing the Creuse differed from departments such as the Ariège or the Lozère, with only one senator, were glossed over, but the case met with sympathy in both houses.

The second proposal was rather more innovative. It involved the introduction of a system of rolling redistribution to take place every 18 years, linked to the most recent population census. Thus, the number of senators elected in series C in 1977 would be revised in

1995, those in series A elected in 1980 revised in 1998 and so on. The idea originally came from the Communists, but the commission thought it was an excellent one. The government was, however, determined to keep the *découpage* in its own hands and replied that while the census was an important aid to strategic planning, it should not be used as an automatic trigger for redistribution in either house. Deputies, for their part, objected on the more pragmatic grounds that such a mechanism might make senators look more representative and removed it when the bill came to them for its first reading. Senators reinstated it and were dismayed when deputies broke the unwritten rule that one chamber does not reinstate an amendment if the chamber affected by a change in electoral regime makes its views unequivocally clear by readopting the original text. In the end the opening threshold remained at 150,000, 33 new seats were created, none were abolished and automatic redistribution was abandoned.

Map 5.3 - **The 1976 distribution of seats**

The reform created the largest batch of new seats in the Senate's history: 32 were allocated to 28 metropolitan departments, with Bouches-du-Rhône, the Nord, the Rhône and Essonne each gaining two. Reunion also gained a seat, making a total of 316. The *clé de répartition* was generally respected: inconsistencies in the Ile-de-France were corrected, though the Hérault was denied a fourth senator for no very obvious reason, except that it was resolutely left-wing. The national rate of representation improved to one senator per 179,000, but the variation from one department to another widened. Bouches-du-Rhône was the worst off (1:233,000), just ahead of the Hérault (1:230,000). The Creuse had a senator for every 73,000 inhabitants, marginally better than the Lozère (pop.74,000) and the Lot, where a moderate rise in population gave it back the seat lost in 1958. All told, 56 departments were better off than the mean, but 20 had a ratio above 1:200,000.

The new seats were phased in over the subsequent *renouvellements* in 1977, 1980 and 1983. No attempt was made to rebalance the series: A now had 100 seats, B 101, C 115. From 1983 the numbers rose to 102, 103 and 117, when the Socialists doubled the number of expatriate seats to 12 bringing the total to 322. In practice, the real figure was 321: the seat for the Territoires des Afars-et-Issas (formerly Côte-des-Somalis) remained vacant from July 1980 until its formal abolition in 2003.

2003 – the *loi Poncelet*

Paradoxically, the origins of the 2003 *loi Poncelet* lay in Socialist plans to reform the upper house. The Socialists had had very little to say about the Senate in the 1960s and 1970s: its function as the refuge for the likes of Gaston Defferre and as the focus of parliamentary opposition to the regime established a state of grace that lasted well into the Giscard presidency.[3] The only contribution from the PS during the 1970s was a vague commitment to reducing the senatorial term to six years. The conversion to thoroughgoing reform came later, driven by the impact of bipolarisation and conflict in the Mitterrand years, coupled with the RPR's breathtaking success in its conquest of the notables, a success based in part upon the singular failure of the PS to fill the space created by the decline of the Radicals and the Communists as serious forces in municipal politics.

Although conflict between the Senate majority and the Socialist government reached its high-water mark with the dispute over the extension of the use of referenda in 1984, Mitterrand was not a constitutional reformer by instinct. Pierre Joxe aired the possibility of Senate reform after Mitterrand's re-election in 1988, but it was left to Guy Allouche, PS senator for the Nord, to set the ball rolling (albeit very slowly) with his private bill in 1989. Allouche was influenced by Jean Grangé's work and shared the view that creating and distributing more seats was not enough by itself. A more accurate and enduring solution, he argued, lay in producing electoral colleges that more accurately reflected each department's demographic and political balance. Allouche's main proposals, therefore, included ending the traditional link between the number of delegates and the size of the municipal council and linking it directly instead to the population of each commune. Once a 'true' picture of the political balance of the department had been achieved within each college, he argued, PR should then be used where there were three or more senators to elect: in those with only one or two seats, it would make little difference. Allouche's proposals would have been discussed in 1991, had they not been guillotined.

It was not until the election of the *gauche plurielle* in 1997, that serious rumours of reform resurfaced. In the autumn of 1997, François Hollande made it clear that the government would interpret good results in regional and cantonal elections the following spring as a mandate for political modernisation, so senators already knew the government would turn its attention to them sooner or later.[4] What really winded them after the Jospin's 'anomaly' interview in April 1998 was that when they turned to the Elysée for support, Chirac replied that a little reform might not be a bad idea. Like his predecessors Monnerville and Poher, Monory upheld the tradition of *autoréforme*, asked Jospin for time and delegated Daniel Hoeffel to lead an internal review. His fall in September and his successor's problems getting senators to accept parity and *décumul* prompted the government to publish its own plans in June 1999. These included changing the mechanism for electing municipal delegates to the colleges to a tariff of one per 500 inhabitants, creating new seats, redistribution on the basis of the 1999 census, reducing the threshold for PR from five seats to three and lowering the age of eligibility to 30. Curiously, Allouche now argued for going a step further, for *une assemblée proportionnelle* with PR for all except those departments with just one seat. Socialist electoral analysts calculated, however, that they had more to gain by sticking at three. The Senate legislation commission (chaired by Larché with Raincourt as *rapporteur*) had done its own sums, and offered four, which, it pointed out, would create a semi-proportional, semi-majoritarian assembly.

The government proposed 22 new seats in 21 departments (Seine-et-Marne would gain two), while the Creuse would lose one, Paris three and the redundant Afars-et-Issas seat would be abolished. As an organic law affecting the Senate, the bill had to get through both houses in identical form. The government knew it stood no chance, but it was worth embarrassing Chirac over modernisation. The legislation commission moved a *question préalable* motion and the government withdrew the bill. The other reforms (municipal delegates, PR) passed on the National Assembly's last word, though to the government's dismay, deputies lowered the ratio of municipal delegates from 1:500 to 1:300 (the Senate commission had suggested 1:700). Jospin might have forced 1:500 through by using Article 49-3, but on coming to power he had resolved never to use that mechanism and kept his word.

Right-wing senators petitioned the Constitutional Council on two counts: that the election of municipal delegates at the rate of 1 per 300 inhabitants introduced too many non-elected members into the colleges and that the threshold for PR should not be lowered without redistribution of seats (which they themselves had blocked). The first objection was upheld, the second rejected, with the result that the *renouvellement* of series B in 2001 saw PR used for the first and last time in departments with three or more seats. The Council did, however, suggest that the balance between population and representation in the Senate should be subject to regular review.

The Council's remarks were picked up by Patrice Gélard, eminent professor of constitutional law and RPR senator for Seine-Maritime. Gélard was prepared to break with the tradition of simply throwing more seats at the problem. He took the population figure in the 1999 census (a total of 60,186,184 inhabitants for France and the DOM) and divided it by the 304 existing seats. This produced a crude figure of one senator per 198,000 inhabitants, so he suggested raising the opening *clé de répartition* to 200,000. Every department with a population over the threshold would have a second seat, accounting for 186 altogether. Gélard then divided the population again by the remaining 118 seats, giving him a quotient of roughly 500,000, so he suggested distributing all remaining seats on this basis, using a highest remaining average system. He calculated that four departments (Bouches-du-Rhône, Nord, Yvelines and Seine-et-Marne) would gain two seats, while 13 others would have one extra. These would be paid for by 21 departments losing a seat each. Unlike earlier proposals which relied on creating a large number of one-seat departments, Gélard's had the virtue of taking seats principally from departments with three and four senators (the Loire and Meurthe-et-Moselle in the latter group).[6] Paris would drop to 11 seats. The Creuse would finally lose its second seat, as would the Gers, the Cantal, Haute-Marne, the Meuse and the Lot, doubling membership of the 'one-seat club' to twelve.[7]

Gélard's proposals were much too ambitious, not to say radical. Instead, the *loi Poncelet*, adopted in May 2003, created 25 new seats, while also reducing the senatorial term to six years, lowering the age of eligibility to 30, and raising the threshold for PR to four seats. The reform differed very little from the Jospin government's earlier proposals, except that Paris and the Creuse kept their seats. The Socialists appealed to the Constitutional Council against the 'Paris-Creuse' anomaly, but with moderation: they held both seats in the Creuse and the results of the 2001 municipal elections in Paris meant the left stood to win more when series C came round in 2004. The Council ruled that allowing the two to keep their seats did not create too great a disparity in the rate of representation in relation to other departments and was therefore acceptable. While retaining 12 senators put Paris in the middle of the representation league table (with 1:179,000), the Creuse was now the best off, with a ratio of 1:61,000, ahead of the Cantal (two seats) and Lozère (one), both with 1:74,000.

The reform went some way to redressing the representation gap, which had grown to 254,000, between the Creuse at one end and the Var and the Hérault, where each senator represented 315,000 inhabitants, and Seine-et-Marne (1:308,000). The gap between the Creuse and the Var (1:237,000 after the reform) closed to 176,000. But in fact interim population statistics for 2003 showed that the changes were already out of date. Paris, the Creuse and also the Cantal, whose population had dropped to 148,000, should have lost seats. Nine others should have been raised: Vienne and Pyrénées-Orientales to three seats, Calvados, Haute-Savoie and Morbihan to four, Var and Hérault to five and Loire-Atlantique and Essonne to six.

The *loi Poncelet* increased the number of seats to 346, the extra seats for two new Caribbean *collectivités* Saint-Martin and Saint-Barthélemy created in 2006 raised the total to 348 and that figure was incorporated into the constitution in July 2008. Of course, the number could be revised at a later date, but if that does not happen, then the moment is approaching when demographic growth and movement will make it necessary to reset the *clé de repartition* in the manner foreseen by Gélard or something like the Prélot proposal of intra-regional senators needs to be taken seriously. Whatever the second Balladur commission proposes may make that sort of solution much more attractive or may require wholesale changes.

Map 5.4 - **Distribution of seats from 2003**

The *loi Poncelet* also included the reduction of the senatorial term to six years, renewed by half every three. The transition was to be phased in over the next four *renouvellements*: in 2004, 2007, 2010 and 2013. Subsequent changes in the electoral calendar, however, caused by the glut of elections scheduled for 2007 (presidential, legislative, municipal and senatorial), led to municipal elections being delayed until the spring of 2008, with the next *renouvellement* also being put back a year, to September 2008. The departments of series C, re-elected in September 2004, were divided into two groups: the Ile-de-

France and the others. Lots were drawn to decide which group would
be elected for just six years: the Paris region drew the short straw. All
senators elected in 2008 (series A) would be elected for six years. In
2011 all series B and those senators elected for six years in 2004
become series 1. Three years later, senators elected for nine years in
2004 will come to the end of their mandate and form series 2 with
senators for series A elected in 2008.

Table 5.2 - **Departments in Series 1 and 2 from 2011**

Series 1 – to be elected 2011, 2017 etc Indre-et-Loire to Pyrénées-Orientales (formerly series B)	117
Paris, Seine-et-Marne, Yvelines, Essonne, Hauts-de-Seine, Seine-Saint-Denis, Val-de-Marne, Val-d'Oise (formely in series C)	53
Guadeloupe, Martinique, La Réunion	9
Nouvelle-Calédonie, Mayotte, Saint-Pierre-et-Miquelon	5
Assemblée des Français de l'Étranger	6
Series Total	**170**
by proportional representation	*108*
Series 2 – to be elected 2014, 2020 etc	
Ain to Indre (formerly series A)	102
Bas-Rhin to Haute-Savoie, Seine-Maritime, Deux-Sèvres to Yonne, Belfort (formely in series C)	63
Guyane	2
Polynésie française, Wallis-et-Futuna, Saint-Barthélemy, Saint-Martin	5
Assemblée des Français de l'Étranger	6
Series Total	**178**
by proportional representation	*68*
Total	**348**

As in 1976, the new seats were phased in, so that the Senate reaches
its full complement in 2011. Series 1 includes 40 metropolitan
departments, compared to 56 in series 2. The two are slightly
unbalanced. Series 1 includes 170 seats, series 2 178. In the former,
108 senators will be elected by PR, compared to just 68 in the latter,
unless the threshold is changed again. In total, 176 senators are elected
by PR, 172 by the majority system.

The electoral colleges

While the distribution of seats has been the main focus of the debate
over representation, Grangé and his disciples have persistently argued
that the problem can only be fully addressed if there is also thorough

reform of the electoral colleges. Their arguments found an echo in the Constitutional Council's comments in 2000 and were restated in the conclusions of the first Balladur committee report in early 2008.

Map 5.5 - **Series 1 and 2 from 2011**

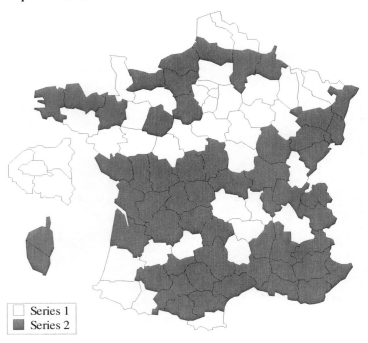

Except in 1946, the colleges have always comprised *ex officio* and elected delegates. Between 1875 and 1940 the *ex officio* element comprised deputies, all members of the general council and the *arrondissement* councils. In 1946 delegates were elected directly by universal suffrage at the level of the cantons, before the return, in 1948, to much the same arrangement as the Third Republic, though without district councillors, abolished under Vichy and never revived.

The ballast in the colleges has always been provided by delegates elected by the municipal councils. Until 1884, each commune elected just one each, irrespective of demographic magnitude. Then, a sliding scale was introduced linked to the size of the municipal councils, which are themselves based on a banded scale. Thus, the smallest communes, with just ten councillors, would send one delegate, those of 12 sent two and so on up to communes of over 60,000 inhabitants, whose 36 councillors elected 24 delegates. Paris city council elected 36 delegates. The system was broadly revived in 1948, with two important innovations: in communes of 9,000 or more inhabitants, all councillors became *ex officio* delegates and in those over 45,000, councils would elect supplementary delegates at the rate of 1 per 5,000 inhabitants.

Table 5.3 - Scale of municipal delegates 1983-present

Population	Council	Senate delegates
Fewer than 100	9	1
100 to 499	11	1
500 to 1,499	15	3
1,500 to 2,499	19	5
2,500 to 3,499	23	7
3,500 to 4,999	27	15
5,000 to 8,999	29	
9,000 to 9,999	29^8	All
10,000 to 19,999	33	
20,000 to 29,999	35	
30,000 to 39,999	39	All plus 1 supplementary delegate per 1,000 inhabitants over threshold
40,000 to 49,999	43	
50,000 to 59,999	45	
60,000 to 79,999	49	
80,000 to 99,999	53	
100,000 to 149,999	55	
150,000 to 199,999	59	
200,000 to 249,999	61	
250,000 to 299,999	65	
Over 300,000	69	
Lyon	73	
Marseille	101	
Paris	163	

The 1958 electoral law made very few outward changes. The threshold for supplementary delegates was lowered to communes of 30,000 at a rate of one per whole tranche of 1,000 inhabitants. In the Seine, all municipal councillors became *ex officio* delegates. The overall number of *grands électeurs* in metropolitan France was

108,465, more than half of whom came from communes of fewer than 1,500 inhabitants. A handful of small departments lost electors, most saw moderate increases, but in the Bouches-du-Rhône, Marseille's share rose from 184 delegates to 680 (of 1,500), shifting the balance within the department and significantly aiding Gaston Defferre in his campaign to be elected senator in 1959. The system was adjusted, as part of Defferre's own programme of local government reform, in 1982. Municipal councils in the middle and at the top of the scale were enlarged and the senatorial colleges expanded accordingly: while communes in the 2,500 to 3, 499 band rose from 21 to 23 councillors, those over 300,000 from 49 to 69.

Table 5.4 gives an account of the electoral colleges in each department, based on the 1998, 2001 and 2004 *renouvellements*. The table has been arranged by overall size of college, which is represented in Map 5.6. Column A shows the district magnitude at the elections. The following four columns show the number of deputies (B), regional councillors (C), general councillors (D) and municipal delegates (E). Column F gives the total college magnitude and G indicates the proportion of municipal delegates. Altogether, delegates account for 96 per cent (137,748 of 144,059) of seats in the colleges. This means that nearly one municipal councillor in four is a *grand électeur*. As the table shows, there is some variation from this norm. The two Corsican departments and Paris are anomalous. In the case of the former, the proportion of delegates is depressed by the presence of members of the Assemblée de Corse, whose number is out of all proportion to the number of regional councillors for mainland departments. In Paris, city councillors function as general councillors and elect 2000 supplementary delegates.

Variation of magnitude across the colleges is enormous, from just 341 in the Lozère to 5,700 in the Nord. The magnitude of the Nord college is not just a function of its demographic size, though it is the most populated department, at 2.5 million inhabitants. The size also reflects the large number of communes (654) , which is also the case in the neighbouring Pas-de-Calais (894), whose population is smaller than that of both the Rhône (293 communes) and Bouches-du-Rhône (119), though these are both relatively small departments: 3249km^2 and 5087km^2 respectively, compared to 6671km^2 for the Pas-de-Calais. What the table shows up less obviously is the ratio of electors to population. Here, Paris is the worst off, with each elector representing more than 1,000 inhabitants, while in the Meuse the figure is just 1:226. The national average is 1:400.

Table 5.4 - **Composition of Senate colleges (1998-2004)**

	A	B	C	D	E	F	G
Nord	11	24	72	79	5522	5697	96.93
Pas-de-Calais	7	14	41	77	3798	3930	96.64
Seine-Maritime	6	12	39	69	2912	3032	96.04
Rhône	7	14	41	54	2867	2976	96.34
Seine-et-Marne	4	9	25	43	2863	2940	97.38
Bouches-du-Rhône	7	16	49	53	2780	2898	95.93
Moselle	5	10	31	51	2720	2812	96.73
Gironde	5	11	36	63	2700	2810	96.09
Yvelines	5	12	28	39	2682	2761	97.14
Isère	4	9	29	57	2624	2719	96.51
Bas-Rhin	4	9	27	44	2476	2556	96.87
Loire-Atlantique	5	10	31	59	2290	2390	95.82
Essonne	5	10	24	41	2250	2325	96.77
Paris	12	21	41	163	2086	2311	90.26
Haute-Garonne	4	8	32	53	2181	2274	95.91
Oise	3	7	23	41	2151	2222	96.80
Val-d'Oise	4	9	21	39	2058	2127	96.76
Finistère	4	8	25	54	1980	2067	95.79
Hauts-de-Seine	7	13	28	45	1904	1990	95.68
Ille-et-Vilaine	4	7	24	53	1900	1984	95.77
Seine-Saint-Denis	6	13	20	40	1887	1960	96.28
Meurthe-et-Moselle	4	7	22	45	1881	1955	96.21
Val-de-Marne	6	12	22	49	1834	1917	95.67
Calvados	3	6	21	49	1816	1892	95.98
Hérault	3	7	24	48	1811	1890	95.82
Maine-et-Loire	3	7	21	41	1778	1847	96.26
Haut-Rhin	3	7	20	31	1768	1826	96.82
Var	3	7	25	43	1740	1815	95.87
Aisne	3	5	17	42	1693	1757	96.36
Alpes-Maritimes	4	9	28	52	1653	1742	94.89
Loire	4	7	22	40	1669	1738	96.03
Somme	3	6	19	46	1645	1716	95.86
Pyrénées-Atlantiques	3	6	17	52	1624	1699	95.59
Haute-Savoie	3	5	17	34	1626	1682	96.67
Puy-de-Dôme	3	6	20	61	1563	1650	94.73
Saône-et-Loire	3	6	20	57	1566	1649	94.97
Morbihan	3	6	18	42	1575	1641	95.98
Eure	3	5	17	43	1573	1638	96.03
Côtes-d'Armor	3	5	16	52	1528	1601	95.44

Table 5.4 continued	A	B	C	D	E	F	G
Manche	3	5	16	52	1484	1557	95.31
Marne	3	6	19	44	1466	1535	95.50
Gard	3	5	18	46	1456	1534	94.92
Loiret	3	5	18	41	1468	1532	95.82
Côte-d'Or	3	5	17	43	1463	1528	95.75
Charente-Maritime	3	5	18	51	1432	1506	95.09
Doubs	3	5	18	35	1436	1494	96.12
Vendée	3	5	17	31	1420	1473	96.40
Ain	2	4	14	43	1385	1446	95.78
Sarthe	3	5	15	40	1360	1420	95.77
Indre-et-Loire	3	5	17	37	1309	1368	95.69
Dordogne	2	4	12	50	1233	1299	94.92
Vosges	2	4	14	31	1176	1225	96.00
Eure-et-Loir	2	4	13	29	1134	1180	96.10
Vaucluse	2	4	14	24	1135	1177	96.43
Drôme	2	4	12	36	1123	1175	95.57
Charente	2	4	12	35	1032	1083	95.29
Savoie	2	3	10	37	1028	1078	95.36
Deux-Sèvres	2	4	11	33	1024	1072	95.52
Vienne	2	4	14	38	1008	1064	94.74
Yonne	2	3	10	42	1009	1064	94.83
Orne	2	3	10	40	976	1029	94.85
Pyrénées-Orientales	2	4	12	31	980	1027	95.42
Tarn	2	4	14	46	950	1014	93.69
Landes	2	3	10	30	969	1012	95.75
Allier	2	4	13	35	950	1002	94.81
Ardennes	2	3	11	37	937	988	94.84
Jura	2	3	10	34	926	973	95.17
Aude	2	3	10	35	921	969	95.05
Haute-Saône	2	3	10	32	907	952	95.27
Ardèche	2	3	9	33	900	945	95.24
Aube	2	3	11	33	894	941	95.01
Lot-et-Garonne	2	3	10	40	882	935	94.33
Loir-et-Cher	2	3	10	30	891	934	95.40
Haute-Vienne	2	4	21	45	833	903	92.25
Meuse	2	2	7	31	848	888	95.50
Cher	2	3	11	35	829	878	94.42
Mayenne	2	3	9	32	815	859	94.88
Haute-Marne	2	2	8	32	812	854	95.08
Hautes-Pyrénées	2	2	9	34	809	854	94.73
Aveyron	2	3	10	46	788	847	93.03

Map 5.6 - **Magnitude of electoral colleges 1998-2004**

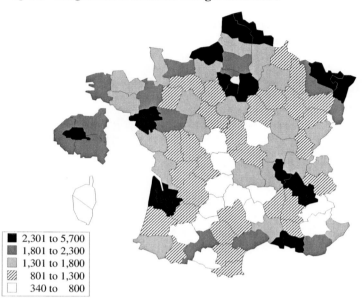

■ 2,301 to 5,700
▨ 1,801 to 2,300
▨ 1,301 to 1,800
▨ 801 to 1,300
□ 340 to 800

Table 5.4 continued	A	B	C	D	E	F	G
Nièvre	2	3	9	32	727	771	94.29
Gers	2	2	7	31	711	751	94.67
Corrèze	2	3	14	37	686	740	92.70
Haute-Loire	2	2	8	35	660	705	93.62
Indre	2	3	8	26	664	701	94.72
Lot	2	2	6	31	586	625	93.76
Tarn-et-Garonne	2	2	7	30	574	613	93.64
Ariège	1	2	6	22	579	609	95.07
Cantal	2	2	6	27	501	536	93.47
Haute-Corse	1	2	27	30	451	510	88.43
Creuse	2	2	8	27	469	506	92.69
Alpes-de-Hte-Prov	1	2	5	30	453	490	92.45
Hautes-Alpes	1	2	4	30	357	393	90.84
Corse-du-Sud	1	2	24	22	316	364	86.81
Belfort	1	2	6	15	331	354	93.50
Lozère	1	2	3	25	311	341	91.20

Source: Sénat, Service de la Séance

The total number of electors has more or less kept pace with national demographic growth since 1959: 32 per cent against population increase in metropolitan France of 34 per cent. Table 5.5 below, shows how the overall increase has affected different departments. The table has been organised by index of increase (1959=100 except in the Paris region, where the first figure is 1968). Six departments have lost electors. Paris, whose population has dropped by half-a-million since 1968, has lost 500 electors over the same period because the college, overwhelmingly composed of supplementary delegates, is highly sensitive to population shifts (and therefore offers something of a test case for advocates and opponents of electing all delegates in proportion to the population of communes). The Creuse has seen the next largest drop, as its population has fallen from 160,000 in 1962 to 124,000. The other losses are relatively minor. Three departments (Var, Seine-et-Marne and Essonne) have seen their colleges more than double, while nine others have increased by 170 points or more.

Table 5.5 - **Expansion of departmental colleges 1959-2004**

Department	1959	1998/ 2004	Increase	Index 1959=100
Var	807	1815	1008	225
Seine-et-Marne	1319	2940	1621	223
Essonne*	1103	2325	1222	211
Alpes-Maritimes	899	1742	843	194
Yvelines*	1431	2761	1330	193
Haute-Savoie	872	1682	810	193
Bouches-du-Rhône	1521	2898	1377	191
Vaucluse	629	1177	548	187
Rhône	1686	2976	1290	177
Haute-Garonne	1293	2274	981	176
Val-d'Oise*	1212	2127	915	175
Hérault	1115	1890	775	170
Isère	1686	2719	1033	161
Pyrénées-Orientales	645	1027	382	159
Oise	1404	2222	818	158
Loiret	986	1532	546	155
Loire-Atlantique	1584	2390	806	151
Val-de-Marne*	1299	1917	618	148
Gard	1051	1534	483	146
Bas-Rhin	1777	2556	779	144
Ain	1003	1446	443	144

Table 5.5 continued Department	1959	1998/ 2004	Increase	Index 1959=100
Eure-et-Loir	820	1180	360	144
Pyrénées-Atlantiques	1205	1699	494	141
Savoie	764	1078	314	141
Gironde	2008	2810	802	140
Maine-et-Loire	1320	1847	527	140
Seine-Saint-Denis*	1409	1960	551	139
Eure	1177	1638	461	139
Indre-et-Loire	987	1368	381	139
Haut-Rhin	1319	1826	507	138
Drôme	855	1175	320	137
Seine-Maritime	2223	3032	809	136
Ille-et-Vilaine	1460	1984	524	136
Doubs	1106	1494	388	135
Calvados	1427	1892	465	133
Marne	1165	1535	370	132
Belfort	268	354	86	132
Côte-d'Or	1176	1528	352	130
Nord	4487	5697	1210	127
Puy-de-Dôme	1300	1650	350	127
Loir-et-Cher	736	934	198	127
Moselle	2233	2812	579	126
Hautes-Alpes	313	393	80	126
Pas-de-Calais	3141	3930	789	125
Hauts-de-Seine*	1588	1990	402	125
Vendée	1177	1473	296	125
Sarthe	1159	1420	261	123
Landes	821	1012	191	123
Tarn-et-Garonne	499	613	114	123
Aube	769	941	172	122
Loire	1454	1738	284	120
Alpes-de-H-Provence	408	490	82	120
Lot-et-Garonne	786	935	149	119
Meurthe-et-Moselle	1655	1955	300	118
Charente-Maritime	1275	1506	231	118
Tarn	859	1014	155	118
Morbihan	1398	1641	243	117
Yonne	912	1064	152	117
Finistère	1776	2067	291	116
Ardèche	817	945	128	115

Table 5.5 Department	1959	1998/2004	Increase	Index 1959=100
Aude	848	969	121	114
Haute-Vienne	793	903	110	114
Mayenne	753	859	106	114
Somme	1521	1716	195	113
Côtes-d'Armor	1416	1601	185	113
Hautes-Pyrénées	754	854	100	113
Saône-et-Loire	1474	1649	175	112
Deux-Sèvres	955	1072	117	112
Lot	560	625	65	112
Aisne	1578	1757	179	111
Jura	875	973	98	111
Charente	987	1083	96	110
Haute-Marne	776	854	78	110
Vienne	980	1064	84	109
Orne	948	1029	81	109
Cher	802	878	76	109
Haute-Saône	877	952	75	109
Manche	1448	1557	109	108
Ariège	570	609	39	107
Dordogne	1228	1299	71	106
Meuse	850	888	38	104
Corrèze	709	740	31	104
Haute-Loire	677	705	28	104
Nièvre	744	771	27	104
Vosges	1188	1225	37	103
Ardennes	964	988	24	102
Gers	738	751	13	102
Lozère	342	341	-1	100
Allier	1022	1002	-20	98
Indre	725	701	-24	97
Aveyron	903	847	-56	94
Cantal	578	536	-42	93
Creuse	588	506	-82	86
Paris*	2853	2311	-542	81
Haute-Corse	820	510	/	/
Corse-du-Sud		364	/	/
* first figure 1968				

The system keeps track of demographic trends. In 66 departments, expansion is within +/-10 points of the index of demographic growth. There are, however, some quite dramatic departures at either end of the scale. As Table 5.5 shows, the indexed increase in the Var has been 225. The department's demographic growth has been impressive, from 470,000 to nearly 900,000, but only a 190-point increase. The distortion is repeated in those departments whose colleges have grown the most. The population index for Bouches-du-Rhône in 1999 over the 1962 census is 147 and for the Rhône 141. Seine-et-Marne, however, stands apart from this general rule. The indexed growth in the college (223) lags marginally behind its demographic expansion (227).

The principal problem with the colleges lies in the linkage of the number of delegates per commune to the size of the municipal council. In the first place, the banded scale used to determine the number of councillors in each commune is neither regular nor proportional (see Table 5.3). There are no outward reasons why the increments are staged as they are and why a commune with 5,000 inhabitants, for example, should have the same number of municipal councillors as one of 8,999, or why a commune of 27,000 inhabitants should have only six more councillors (35) than one of 9,000 (29). The impact of these initial distortions means that almost without exception, in every college, the populations of communes of fewer than 2,000 inhabitants are systematically over-represented. Thus, while the 'average' municipal delegate represents 426 inhabinatnts, delegates for Lyon and Marseille represent 932, while each delegate for a commune of fewer than 3,500 represent 292.[9] The only colleges that escape this general rule are Paris, the Hauts-de-Seine, which has no small communes and, perhaps unexpectedly, the Vendée, whose 212 communes of fewer than 2,000 inhabitants are counterbalanced by 64 in the 2,000 to 9,999 category.

The Raincourt proposal

Intuitively, one would tackle this problem by simply uncoupling the number of delegates from the size of the municipal councils and linking it directly to the population, while retaining their election within the councils. This was the basis of the Jospin government's proposals: a flat rate of one delegate per 500 inhabitants. Allouche anticipated the Constitutional Council's reservations and came up with a mixed proposal. First, he proposed making all municipal councillors in communes of 3,500 inhabitants (i.e. with 27 councillors) *ex officio* delegates. Secondly, he lowered the point on the scale where supplementary delegates would be elected from communes of 30,000 to those with 20,000 and at the rate of 1 per 500 inhabitants rather than 1 per 1000. Henri de Raincourt, *rapporteur* to the Senate legislation commission, suggested lowering the threshold for supplementary delegates to all communes of 9,000 or more at the rate of 1 per 700.

Of the three proposals the government's looked the most moderate on paper. By reducing representation at the lower end and increasing it at the upper, it created fewer than 400 new electors across the country, though the proportion of co-opted delegates would rise from 8 per cent to 21 of the total. Raincourt's proposal froze the number of electors in communes below 9,000 and created nearly 20,000 new ones at the top end, though it kept the proportion of supplementary delegates down to 18 per cent. Of the three proposals, Allouche's performed best in this regard, restricting supplementary delegates to just 16 per cent, though at a cost of increasing the national college by 40,000.[10] As has already been seen, the National Assembly lowered the rate to 1 delegate per 300 before passing the bill on the last word in June 2000. The Constitutional Council ruled that this created far too many 'élus du troisième degré' and the reform was struck down.

The *loi Poncelet* completely ignored the colleges, but the first Balladur Committee, with its remit to modernise and 'rebalance' the institutions of the Republic, could hardly avoid the question. Balladur returned to the debates of June 2000 and Constitutional Council's insistence that the Senate must remain 'elected by an electorate that itself emanates from the collectivités'. He was equally firm that change was necessary.

> Whatever the mission assigned to the Senate by the
> Constitution to represent the *collectivités territoriales*, sparsely
> populated areas cannot be represented in a way that acts to the
> detriment of more heavily populated ones.[11]

The committee proposed to get around the Constitutional Council's concerns by extending the second sentence of Article 24-3 to read 'The Senate ensures the representation of the *collectivités territoriales* of the Republic *according to their population*' [author's italics], thereby applying gentle pressure on both the Senate and the government to seek a better balance within the colleges between rural and urban communes. In the preamble to the bill based on the committee's report, the government reinforced the point by insisting that strengthening the role of parliament must be matched by better representation. Article 9 of the reform bill proposed, therefore, that the Senate should ensure the representation of the *collectivités*, 'taking account of their population'. The government also added a modification to Article 25 of the constitution, making all electoral boundaries and the distribution of seats in both assemblies subject to review by an independent body.

The biggest obstacle to the government's proposals came not from the left (Socialist senators had made similar proposals in July 2007 in direct response to the Épinal speech),[12] but among its own supporters, whose institutional memory was marked by a profound dislike of change imposed from outside. The legislation commission insisted on the importance of the Senate's difference and deleted the reference to demographic magnitude at the first reading. It also amended the change to Article 25, so that the independent body would only examine the boundaries question for deputies, though it would still examine distribution of seats for both houses.

That, however, was not the final word on reforming the colleges. In his open letter to President Sarkozy, Jack Lang expressed dismay that the text would not include the population clause. With the final vote in Congress looking very tight, Sarkozy promised to ask the Senate to consider the question of reform of the colleges, with the *proposition Raincourt* as the preferred starting option.[13] And in his inaugural address to the Senate, Gérard Larcher, made a fleeting reference to *autoréforme*, though it is not clear whether he meant by this a commitment to reviewing the colleges.[14] At the time of writing no progress has been made on this direction.

Mayfly electors

Supplementary delegates remain, then, a sticking point for reform. To be eligible, they must be enrolled on the electoral register in the commune. In most departments they represent a small minority of electors, but in the city-department of Paris in 2004 they numbered 2086 of a college of 2311. In Bouches-du-Rhône, Alpes-Maritimes and the Rhône, they constitute 32, 25 and 18 per cent respectively of the total college, though because of the communal distribution, they are only 7 per cent of the college in the Nord and 2 per cent in the Pas-de-Calais. Their existence raises a number of problems, the principal being the question of the *mandat impératif*. Article 27 of the constitution enshrines the principle that 'tout mandat impératif est nul', that is to say that all instruction to vote one way or another is null and void, but the co-option of supplementary delegates onto the colleges comes very close to crossing the line.

The delegates are elected by municipal councillors, using PR and with the intention to reproduce the political balance within the council. It is reasonable to expect, therefore, that they might vote according to instruction. The ability to control these supplementary electors, particularly in colleges where they are numerous and margins are tight and to deliver them as a block can become a powerful lever. Charles Pasqua and Jean-Pierre Fourcade, who both stood on dissident lists in 2004 in the Hauts-de-Seine, were certainly helped by their ability to call in favours from their friends and clients. As many as half the 211 (of a college of 1900) votes that saw Pasqua return to the Senate, were provided by his former protégés, Patrick Balkany and Patrick Devedjian, the mayors of Levallois-Perret and Antony respectively, probably acting on orders from Sarkozy, who was UMP president at the time and had secured Pasqua's resignation as chair of the departmental assembly in his favour in exchange. Similarly, Fourcade could count on a reasonable level of support among electors from Boulogne-Billancourt (whose 103,000 inhabitants make it the second most populous commune in the region), where he was mayor, and Saint-Cloud, where he had been from 1971 to 1992.

How these delegates are chosen in the first place remains one of the more opaque aspects of the colleges. Like all elections, they are managed by the ministry of the interior which keeps a jealous guard on the results: even the Senate's own Service de la Séance cannot easily get hold of a breakdown of who the delegates are. Sometimes, however, details slip out. In 1998, *Le Monde* reported the results of an enquiry by one inquisitive citizen in the Hérault, who took the trouble to scrutinise the list of 238 electors (61 councillors and 177 supplementary delegates) for Montpellier city council.[15] He discovered that 54 delegates had close family ties (wives, husbands, sons and daughters) either to one another, to members of the council or even to one senator-candidate. In their defence, the local PS, the principal subject of the article, led by the notorious Georges Frêche, argued that it was not always easy to find delegates willing to give up a Sunday at the beginning of the hunting season, while the party's decision to set an example and voluntarily present lists alternating men and women candidates had imposed certain constraints.

Whatever the explanation or the excuses, there is no reason to believe that the PS in the Hérault operates differently from federations or parties in other departments when it comes to drumming up a group of reliable 'électeurs d'un jour'.

Representing expatriates

Until 2008, the Senate enjoyed the specific constitutional task to ensure the representation of French nationals living abroad. Pressure groups lobbying for better protection of and provision for expatriate interests existed before the Second World War, and there was a distant Revolutionary tradition of representing citizens whether at home or abroad. The real impetus to represent expatriates, however, lay in the determination at the Liberation to reunite the whole national community, including those living in the protectorates, beyond the French Union, over whose support Vichy and the Resistance had fought a ferocious battle. Both Constituent Assemblies included expatriate representation, but the National Assembly of 1946 did not. The oversight was redressed in December 1946, when deputies set aside eight of their 50 nominated seats for expatriate representation. Three were allocated specifically to Morocco, two to Tunisia and one each to Africa/Europe, Asia/Oceania and America. In 1948 an extra seat was added for Indochina and nomination passed to the Conseil Supérieur des Français de l'Étranger (CSFE), a body chaired by the minister of foreign affairs that brought together government-appointed experts, alongside delegates elected by overseas chambers of commerce, teachers' organisations, veterans' associations and the Union des Français de l'Étranger (founded in 1927). In 1950, election of delegates was extended to all expatriates registered (*immatriculés*) with their local consulate and affiliated to one of the accredited organisations, which were in turn allotted seats on the CSFE according to their size. Delegates voted in regional electoral colleges, which used a two-round majority system. To get around the constitutional requirement that all members of parliament must be elected by direct or indirect universal suffrage, the CSFE only nominated candidates, who were then formally elected by senators. The number of expatriate senators was reduced to six in 1958, but the new constitution formalised the Senate's special role in this domain.

The Socialists introduced a number of changes in the 1980s. The number of seats was doubled to 12 and the regional constituencies were re-organised. The electoral system was reformed to allow all registered expatriates to elect delegates directly and PR was introduced across the board. Superficially, the reforms looked like a right-minded attempt to reduce the democratic deficit, but the real goal was to build on the efforts of Socialists Guy Penne and Jean-Pierre Bayle, who after Mitterrand's narrow defeat in the 1974 presidential election had set about reorganising PS federations among expatriates. In 1980 they created the Association Démocratique des Français de l'Étranger and by 1989 the left had three expatriate senators (Bayle, Penne and Pierre Biarnès).

The change in the electoral system did nothing, however, to reverse chronically poor participation. Despite the explosion of emigration from the 1990s - the number of French nationals living in Great Britain and registered with their consulate alone doubled in the period 1995-2005 to over 100,000 - only 24 per cent cast their vote in the 1997 delegate elections and the figure was just 19 per cent in 2000. The CSFE responded by setting up a commission to propose a series of internal reforms, which led, in August 2004, to its transformation into the Assemblée des Français de l'Étranger (AFE), a semantic shift intended to reflect the body's formal status as a *collectivité publique*. Other changes included a reorganisation and increase in the number of constituencies from 48 to 52 and of delegates from 150 to 155. The reform reduced the number of government-appointed advisors from 20 to 12 and downgraded their role to a consultative rather than a deliberative one. The legislation also allowed the AFE to tackle voter indifference with experiments in electronic voting - a particular passion of expatriate senator Robert Del Picchia. The impact of these changes appears to have been minimal: in 2006, the rate of participation in the delegate elections for the Great Britain constituency was below 10 per cent.

The constitutional revision of July 2008 brought the upper chamber's monopoly of expatriate representation to an end. From 2012 *les Français établis hors de la France* will also be represented in the National Assembly, though it is not clear how many expatriate deputies there will be. The government's proposals suggested between seven and nine, but the Constitutional Council's ruling on the *redécoupage électoral* suggest the number may have to be as high as 11.[16] It remains to be seen whether expatriates will be more enthusiastic about the prospect of electing deputies than senators.

6

Les élus des élus

There are five hundred thousand municipal councillors in France, each and every one of whom dreams of one day becoming a senator.[1]

The electoral code says two things about the Senate colleges. Firstly, they must meet no more than 60 days before the senators being elected are due to take their seats, at the beginning of the autumn sitting. Secondly, that the election must take place on the seventh Sunday after the convocation of the colleges is published. In practical terms this normally means the last Sunday in September and, as they have done since 1876, the entire college assembles in the *chef-lieu* of each department (the specific venue varies according to the size of the college and availability) to cast their votes. In departments using PR the ballot is open from 9.00 a.m. until 3.00 p.m. In those using the majority system the first ballot is between 8.30 and 11.00 in the morning and the second, where necessary, opens at 3.30 in the afternoon and closes two hours later or as soon as all electors present have voted. In 1959, 29 departments did not need a second ballot but few now elect all their senators in the first round. In 1998, only nine of 38 'majority' metropolitan departments went to lunch with the day's business completed. In 2001 the number was three of 14, four of 16 in 2004 and 10 of 31 in 2008.[2] Some departments have more impressive records than others in this regard. Electors in the Vienne have only once been troubled by a second round, in 1968, when René Monory ended a tradition of Radical representation for the department stretching back to the 1890s. Since then, four elections (1977, 1986, 1995 and 2004) have come and gone with the victors enjoying a relaxed lunch.

Until 2001, the election of municipal delegates took place a minimum of three weeks before the *renouvellement*: the period was lengthened from 2004 to six to allow officials to verify the credentials of all members of the college, a complicated process when dealing with the various *suppléants* and replacement delegates. In spite of the precautions, the Constitutional Council was obliged to order a re-run of the 2004 election in Bas-Rhin after it upheld a challenge to the eligibility of some of the delegates.

The timetable also allows candidates and party officials to size up the results of delegate elections, estimate where votes will fall and target the *grands électeurs* whose influence might make a difference. With so few electors and such tight margins 'pas une voix ne doit s'échapper' – not a single vote must go astray and candidates work the stump to ensure maximum visibility. Even then, with so many non-aligned delegates, predicting the outcome is a dark art. Senators leave as little to chance as possible and do not like surprises, but the colleges can be volatile and headstrong.

Campaigning for Senate elections is all about *proximité* and even the safest candidate makes sure that he or she is seen around the department long before official campaigning gets underway, either just before or just after the public holiday on 15 August (Assumption Day): in 2008 campaigning opened formally on the 10th. This date has the advantage of coinciding with the opening of the summer sessions of the *conseils généraux*, at which many key players are assembled. Candidates have little time to draw breath. For example, in 2008, the web log of Raymond Couderc, UMP *candidat-sortant* in the Hérault, published a list of more than forty meetings with electors spread over 20 days between 19 August and the 19 September.

In departments using the majority system, candidates can stand alone or present themselves as a list, but in either case votes are counted individually. As with other majority elections in France, voters take slips with candidates' names (and those of their *suppléant*) on into the polling booth and place these in an envelope which is then dropped into the ballot box. Electors are not obliged to cast all their votes. Where PR is used, each list must present as many candidates as there are seats being contested plus two to cover the need for *suppléants*. The list system is blocked, so there are no transferable votes. In both cases, candidates must formally register ten days before the election: in 2008, for example, registration closed on Friday 12 September for the election on the 21st.

Sometimes lists of candidates are settled well in advance, but just as often the final decision is only taken days or even hours before registration closes. In the 2004 election in Paris, for example, an argument over who would be placed where on the UMP list was resolved at the very last minute, after an impressive piece of brinkmanship. The UMP had calculated that it could be sure of three seats and put up a list headed by Chirac loyalist Roger Romani, with Marie-Thérèse Hermange in second. The third place was assigned to Philippe Goujon, Balladurien chair of the UMP federation in Paris. Pressure from the Elysée saw him replaced by someone more congenial to the President. Goujon responded by setting up his own list and campaigned with such success that party analysts predicted he would finish ahead of Romani. The Chiraquiens came under even more pressure three days before the deadline when Goujon registered his list. A photograph of Goujon, his *colistiers* and Sarkozy and Fillon (running in the Sarthe) then appeared in local and national papers.[3] All Goujon had to do was wait. Just hours before the 6.00 p.m. deadline, Romani accepted third place on a new list, behind Goujon and Hermange.

Senate elections are hard-wired to the complex network of municipal, departmental, regional and national elections and inter- and intra-party relations. The deals cut can have a local dimension, perhaps ensuring that the seats are equally distributed between the geographical, economic or psychological subdivisions of a department, or they may be used to relieve pressure elsewhere. The case of Charles Pasqua in the Hauts-de-Seine in 2004 has already been outlined in the previous chapter. Another case concerned the 2008 municipal elections in Lyon and underlines the long-term view French politicians take regarding the division of the spoils. In 2003, Dominique Perben, minister of justice in the Raffarin government, announced his intention to lead the UMP's bid to take the city from the Socialists. As well as having to overcome opposition within the local UMP and take on the PS senator-mayor Gérard Collomb (in alliance with Michel Mercier), Perben would have to deal with Charles Millon, the maverick former defence minister who had courted controversy in 1998 by accepting the support of the FN to secure the chair of the Rhône-Alpes regional assembly.

In 2001, Millon had split the right-wing vote in Lyon, allowing Collomb to take city hall. In a bid to clear the path for Perben, Sarkozy suggested that Millon might think of running for the Senate, in the neighbouring Ain come September 2008. The *loi Poncelet* gave the department an extra seat, so there would be no *sortant* to upset. In any case, Millon is native of the department, born in Belley, where he was mayor from 1977-2001, and a former deputy, but with 17 candidates on the right, the UMP and its allies held a primary to establish their three preferred candidates. Eleven hundred of the department's 1600 electors were invited to participate, 700 attended and Millon emerged as one of the three nominees, along with Sylvie Goy-Chavent and Henri Guillermin (both UMP). The results of the primary came unstuck, however, on the unpredictability of the voters.

Table 6.1 - **Election in the Ain, September 2008**

		1st round	2nd round
	Registered electors	1615	1615
	Electors present	1587	1591
	Valid votes cast	1549	1556
	Absolute majority	775	N/A
Rachel Mazuir	PS	588	771
Jacques Berthou	Divers Gauche	509	723
Sylvie Goy-Chavent	UMP	634	720
Henri Guillermin	UMP	553	675
Charles Millon	UMP	580	634
Jean Chabry	Divers droite	209	516

The left had made good ground in the municipal and cantonal elections in March, taking the departmental capital Bourg-en-Bresse and the *conseil général*, both hitherto impregnable right-wing bastions.[4] Still, the balance across the department suggested a close contest and none of the candidates achieved the 775 votes required in the first round. By way of comparison, in 1998 the UDF *sortants* had been re-elected in the first round, with more than 900 of 1400 votes cast. Goy-Chavent led the way, ahead of the new PS chairman of the departmental assembly, Rachel Mazuir, with Millon in third. On paper, the distribution of votes suggested the right would take two of the three seats in the run-off. Left and centre electors duly coalesced behind to Mazuir and Jacques Berthou, mayor of Miribel, in the far south of the department. The real surprise, however, was the enormous right-wing protest vote that rallied against Millon behind Jean Chabry, general councillor and mayor of the small town of Jujurieux, whose share of the vote leapt by more than 300, while Guillermin picked up more than 200, overhauling Millon, who gained a paltry 54 votes and finished a lame fifth.

The election in the Ain attracted no fewer than 19 candidates in the first round. The total number of candidates varies from one election to the next and because no two series are alike, comparisons are not always easy, but the 2004 and 2008 campaigns are instructive. In 2004 (series C), there were 201 candidates in the 16 metropolitan departments using the majority system, or 12/13 per department for 37 seats, giving an average of between five and six candidates per seat. In the 13 departments using PR there were a total of 1006 candidates on 124 lists, giving an average of 77 candidates and 10 lists, though the range went from six lists in the Yvelines to 14 chasing the seven seats in the Hauts-de-Seine. *Outremer* there were 50 candidates for eight seats (all *scrutin majoritaire*), while the four expatriate seats were contested by seven lists.

Four years later, there were 328 candidates chasing the 67 seats to be elected by majority in 31 departments, or a shade under five candidates per seat. Among this category of department, the number of candidates ranged from just three in the Corsican departments (for one seat each) to 21 in Calvados (three seats), with the Ain on 19 and Côtes-d'Armor and Côte-d'Or (both three seats) just behind with 18. The situation among the PR departments was rather calmer too. Haute-Garonne saw nine lists chasing five seats and there were eight lists in the Gironde (six seats), Alpes-Maritimes (five) and Hérault (four), but there was no repeat of the profusion of dissident lists that had marked the 2004 election. In four of the departments the seats were shared between three lists and in the remaining three between just two.

The *renouvellement* marks the culmination of an intense period of networking and lobbying. And because all members of the college meet in one place to cast their votes, election day itself can become the focus of intense last-minute negotiations. Attendance is compulsory, on pain of a modest fine, and absences must be justified, but few electors fail in their duty. Membership is an honour, a moment when *les élus* gather to assert their collective identity as active citizens.

Though the election is in deadly earnest, there are moments of conviviality. Electors who arrive early enough may well breakfast with one or other candidate or group of candidates, but the real test of where allegiances lie comes over lunch. This is particularly the case in departments using the majority system, where luncheon can become either celebration of victory or the focus of horse-trading and shuttling from one group of electors to another. In departments using PR, the break allows candidates to estimate how many votes they and their rivals already have and to try to sway those who are playing hard to get. Either way, restaurants in the *chef-lieux* will be full of greater and lesser notables spending their subsistence allowances.

Once the polls have closed and the votes are counted, the day is rounded off with a *vin d'honneur*. Disappointed candidates return home, while the successful ones make every effort to get to the Luxembourg Palace. There, the *salle des conférences*, the old throne room, which normally functions as the parliamentary lobby, is set up with boards detailing the results as they come through, to be scrutinised by senators and various party figures, electoral analysts and reporters. The arrival of each new or returning senator allows colleagues a more or less staged moment of collective congratulation or sly comment. In 2004, for example, the absence of ecologist Dominique Voynet, elected in Seine-Saint-Denis, prompted one wag to suggest that she was still trying to find the department into which she had been parachuted. The ostentatious embrace given by UMP group president Josselin de Rohan for the returning Pasqua struck more than one observer as both forced and misplaced, while the warm handshake reserved by Sarkozy for Alain Lambert signalled the UMP president's support for the latter's decision to contest Poncelet's bid for a third presidential term.

Continuity and change

As luck would have it, when Gaston Monnerville put his hand into the green marble urn to decide in which order the renewal of the series would proceed, he pulled out the letter A. Thus, the *renouvellements* continued in a regular pattern, from 1962 to 2008. One might be tempted to think of Senate elections as a series of nine-year cycles, each ending with the *renouvellement* of series C in 1968, 1977, 1986, 1995 and 2004. This is not, however, how they are perceived by senators, electors or commentators, principally because the cycle of *renouvellements* has been punctuated at different points by the six-year cycle of municipal elections and these have a determining impact: the left-wing surge in the 2008 Senate elections can be entirely attributed to their impressive performance (and the right's catastrophic one) the previous March.

Its indissolubility and its nine-year term have consolidated the Senate's reputation for stability in the minds of the public and the media. This reputation is reinforced by external factors such as the periodic 'rejuvenation' of the National Assembly, in 1962, 1981 or 1993 for example, coupled with the institutionalisation of *alternance* between 1981 and 2002, while senators themselves place a rhetorical premium on the stability and balance that they bring to politics. The rates of institutional and departmental stability can be prone to overstatement and require some exploration.

Table 6.2 - **The rate of change at *renouvellement* 1959-2008**

		Seats	**Sortants**			**New**	**Change (%)**
			r	b	dns		
1959	All	274	176	*l*	*l*	85	*l*
1962	A	89+*1*[5]	81	8	1	8+*1*	8.9
1965*	B	90	57	12	15	27	30.0
1968	C	94+9	56	15	22	35+9	37.2
1971*	A	90	50	20	20	40	44.4
1974	B	90	46	15	28	44	48.8
1977*	C	103+*12*	42	12	49	49+*12*	50.2
1980	A	90+*10*	49	11	28	39+*10*	43.3
1983*	B	89+*11*+2	52	5	32	37+*13*	41.5
1986	C	115+2	68	18	29	47+2	40.9
1989*	A	100+2	60	14	26	40+2	40.0
1992	B	102	60	16	26	42	41.2
1995*	C	117	49	19	49	68	58.1
1998	A	102	51	14	35	51	50.0
2001*	B	102	43	40	19	60	58.8
2004	C	117+*10*	57	15	45	60+*10*	51.2
2008**	A	102+*12*	49	10	42	53+*12*	52.0
* indicates municipal elections ** one seat vacant							

Table 6.2 above offers an assessment of the degree of continuity and change of each *renouvellement* since 1959. Figures in italics indicate the introduction of new seats. The three categories under the heading *sortants* refer to the fate of outgoing senators who were either re-elected (r), beaten (b) or did not stand (dns). In the column headed 'new', figures in italics represent new seats. Finally, the figure in the

far right-hand column represents the rate of change for each *renouvellement* calculated as a percentage of new senators, i.e. those who have defeated an outgoing senator or replaced one who has retired. Including new seats in this calculation would give a false impression and by-elections have not been included.

It is not surprising that only eight seats changed occupant in September 1962. The municipal councils had not changed since the spring of 1959 and the worsening tension between the government and *la classe politique* incited local notables to return the same men and women that they had elected three years previously. A new round of municipal elections in the spring of 1965 and the more widespread use of PR in series C help to explain the rise in the rate of change in 1965 and especially 1968, which then gathered pace in the 1970s, with the passing of the Liberation generation, culminating in 1977 with a *renouvellement* described by Jean-Luc Parodi as 'quite unlike any other', when 49 senators, still a record, did not seek re-election, pushing the rate of change above half and close to 60 per cent with the new seats created the year before added in.[6] Among the *sortants* who did not to run, half had Senate careers pre-dating the Fifth Republic.

In 1980 the rate of change dropped back to 43 per cent, and then hovered around 41 per cent until 1992. It rose spectacularly again, however, in 1995, when there were 68 new senators (58 per cent), as the RPR, which had exploited an older generation of Gaullists to win seats in the 1980s (a process nicknamed *Neuwirthisation* after Lucien Neuwirth and including such unlikely senators as Couve de Murville and Philippe de Gaulle) now obliged many of these elder statesmen and women to stand down. The rate of change dropped to half in 1998, before a surge to 58 per cent in September 2001, which can largely be attributed to the reduction of the threshold for PR from five to three seats and to parity legislation. What really sets 2001 apart is the unprecedented number of *sortants-candidats* (40) who were beaten. Its nearest rival is 1971, with 20 *sortants battus*. Even 2008, with its swing to the PS, saw only 10 *sortants-candidats* fail.

In 2004 (series C) the PR threshold was raised again, to departments with four seats, affecting more than half the series. The rate of change dropped to 51 per cent and only 15 *sortants-candidats* lost their seats. The availability of 10 new seats certainly helped to reduce demand, while among the senators counted as 'new' were returnees such as Pasqua and Jean-Luc Mélenchon, as well as prime minister Jean-Pierre Raffarin and three cabinet colleagues who had resigned their seats on appointment to the government in 2002. What really marked the 2004 election was the number of dissident lists that sprung up in response to parity legislation, usually where outgoing male UMP senators objected to standing third or fourth on a list.

Four years later, the UMP could not afford the luxury of disunity. The poor performance in the municipal elections had a salutary effect and Alain Marleix, the UMP's election strategist and minister for state reform, managed to limit the damage, with some notable exceptions, including the defeat of Jean Puech, chair of the Observatoire de la Décentralisation. Not all was sweetness and harmony on the left either, but careful department-by-department negotiations still brought the opposition considerable reward. Officially PS analysts predicted a dozen extra seats at best, but this was a bluff. It was no real surprise that the final figure was more than 20. The swing to the left and the local federations' general determination to introduce new (if not always young) blood is reflected in the 52 per cent rate of change.

It is difficult, with any assembly that has a system of rolling renewal, to establish firm criteria by which to judge turnover or to give that some value. But it is worth noting that, after the 2008 *renouvellement*, 56 per cent of senators were serving their first term of office, which does not seem like an unreasonable rate of change, if that suggests the democratic deficit is closing.

Departmental turnover

It is equally unreliable trying to calculate and compare rates of stability and change within and between departments. Whatever the census point, some will have only recently re-elected their senators, making a firm calculation of average length of term in office elusive. The use of *suppléants* to replace senators who become ministers and who then stand down when a minister loses his or her portfolio skew the figures, while district magnitudes have also changed since 1959, so simply dividing the number of senators by the number of seats cannot be easily done across the board. Different electoral systems also make direct comparisons difficult.

Nevertheless, and taking the foregoing caveats into consideration, an attempt has been made, in Table 6.3 below, to provide an idea of the degree of continuity in France's metropolitan departments. The table shows departments by series and in the first three columns lists the number of seats allotted to the department in real years: new seats created in 1976 and 2003 are indicated under the year they became available. The table lists the total number of different senators who have represented a department between 1959 and the 2008 *renouvellement*. Stress is laid on the word 'different', because some departments have been significantly distorted by ministerial appointments. This is not an altogether satisfactory decision, because a few former senators have returned to the upper chamber after many years away: for example, Edgard Pisani (Haute-Marne) was out of the Senate between 1961 and 1974, while André Lejeune represented the Creuse briefly from September 1980 before becoming a deputy in June 1981. He then returned to the Senate in 1998 and was re-elected in 2008. Pisani, Lejeune and the handful of others like them have, however, been counted as one senator.

The census point is the 2008 *renouvellement* and has been adjusted to include sitting senators by adding the years that they are still due to serve until to the end of their term: so senators in departments from the old series B plus senators for the Paris region still have three years ahead of them, while those in series A and the 'provincial' half of the old series C have six. Of course, there will be changes before 2011 and 2014, but the Senate is generally stable. The rate of longevity of each senator in each department has been calculated by creating a total tariff for each department and dividing that by the number of senators. The tariff is arrived at by multiplying the constant number of seats since the beginning of the Republic by 53 or 56 years, then adding 37 years for seats that became available in 1977, 34 for 1980 and so on. The figures for Corsica and for the Paris region have been adapted to reflect the boundary changes made there too.

While the Senate went through five electoral cycles between 1959 and 2004, the average rate of change, i.e. the number of senators per seat per department, is a little over 4 senators per seat, with a variation of between 2.6 (Calvados) and 6 (Nièvre). Intuitively, it follows that stability of personnel results from political stability. Before the advent of the UMP, Calvados had a long Independent tradition and has only elected eight different senators since 1959 (despite the fact that there were 21 candidates in 2008). The Creuse, where the Socialists have held a comparable stranglehold, has had only six different senators and the same was true of the Hérault until 2007, when Raymond Couderc won a seat for the right for the first time since anyone could remember. In the Ariège, which has only had three different senators since 1959, Socialist domination of the department is so strong that in 2008 the UMP had difficulty finding a candidate willing to stand against Jean-Pierre Bel, who won with 455 of 597 votes cast.

Table 6.3 - **Rate of departmental change 1959-2014**

Series A	1959	1980	2008	No.	Long
Ain	2	2	3	9	13.1
Aisne	3	3	3	13	12.9
Allier	2	2	2	11	10.2
Alpes/Hte-Provence	1	1	1	4	14
Hautes-Alpes	1	1	1	4	14
Alpes-Maritimes	3	4	5	17	12.2
Ardèche	2	2	2	7	16.0
Ardennes	2	2	2	6	18.7
Ariège	1	1	1	3	18.7
Aube	2	2	2	10	11.2
Aude	2	2	2	8	14.0
Aveyron	2	2	2	10	11.2
Bouches-du-Rhône	5	7	8	33	10.7
Calvados	3	3	3	8	21.0
Cantal	2	2	2	10	11.2
Charente	2	2	2	9	12.4
Charente-Maritime	3	3	3	10	16.8
Cher	2	2	2	9	12.4
Corrèze	2	2	2	9	12.4
Corse	2	/	/	4	10.5
Corse-du-Sud	/	1	1	3	8.6
Haute-Corse	/	1	1	4	6.5
Côte-d'Or	2	3	3	12	12.2
Côtes-d'Armor	3	3	3	14	12.0
Creuse	2	2	2	6	18.7
Dordogne	2	2	2	12	9.3
Doubs	2	3	3	10	14.6
Drôme	2	2	3	8	14.8
Eure	2	3	3	11	13
Eure-et-Loir	2	2	3	10	11.8
Finistère	4	4	4	19	11.8
Gard	2	3	3	11	13.3
Haute-Garonne	3	4	5	17	12.2
Gers	2	2	2	9	12.4
Gironde	4	5	6	17	15.5
Hérault	3	4	5	13	16.0
Ille-et-Vilaine	3	4	4	18	11.2
Indre	2	2	2	8	14.0
Belfort	1	1	1	6	9.3

Table 6.3 continued					
Series B	**1959**	**1983**	**2011**	**No.**	**Long**
Indre-et-Loire	3	3	3	11	14.5
Isère	3	4	5	13	14.6
Jura	2	2	2	9	11.8
Landes	2	2	2	6	17.7
Loir-et-Cher	2	2	2	8	12.5
Loire	4	4	4	17	11.2
Haute-Loire	2	2	2	9	11.8
Loire-Atlantique	4	4	5	19	11.2
Loiret	2	3	3	10	13.7
Lot	1	2	2	6	14.0
Lot-et-Garonne	2	2	2	7	15.1
Lozère	1	1	1	5	10.6
Maine-et Loire	3	3	4	13	12.2
Manche	3	3	3	10	15.9
Marne	3	3	3	12	13.3
Haute-Marne	2	2	2	8	13.3
Mayenne	2	2	2	8	13.3
Meurthe-et-Moselle	3	4	4	14	13.6
Meuse	2	2	2	6	17.7
Morbihan	3	3	3	10	15.9
Moselle	4	5	5	20	12.2
Nièvre	2	2	2	12	8.8
Nord	9	11	11	43	12.5
Oise	3	3	4	8	19.9
Orne	2	2	2	7	15.1
Pas-de-Calais	6	7	7	30	11.6
Puy-de-Dôme	3	3	3	11	14.5
Pyrénées-Atlantiques	3	3	3	14	11.4
Hautes-Pyrénées	2	2	2	10	10.6
Pyrénées-Orientales	2	2	2	10	10.6

Between 1959 and 2003, the average senator could expect to be re-elected for a second term. At the other end of the scale, nearly 40 senators, not including those called to ministerial office, have left the Senate after less than a year in office. For example, Jean Bailly, former deputy for Belfort, was elected senator for the territory in September 1971, but resigned his seat at the beginning of November. Belfort provided an interesting, if unfortunate, instance again in 2008. Among the candidates for election there were Jean-Pierre Chevènement and the official PS candidate Yves Ackermann, who in

Table 6.3 continued					
Series C	**1959**	**1977**	**2004**	**No.**	**Long**
Bas-Rhin	4	4	5	17	13.8
Haut-Rhin	3	3	4	14	12.8
Rhône	5	7	7	24	14.7
Haute-Saône	2	2	2	8	14.0
Saône-et-Loire	3	3	3	12	14.0
Sarthe	3	3	3	13	12.9
Savoie	2	2	2	11	10.2
Haute-Savoie	2	3	3	10	14.8
Seine-Maritime	5	6	6	24	13.2
Seine-et-Marne	3	4	6	19	11.8
Deux-Sèvres	2	2	2	6	18.7
Somme	3	3	3	14	12.0
Tarn	2	2	2	11	10.2
Tarn-et-Garonne	2	2	2	8	14.0
Var	3	3	4	16	11.1
Vaucluse	2	2	3	9	13.6
Vendée	2	3	3	12	12.3
Vienne	2	2	2	8	14.0
Haute-Vienne	2	2	2	6	18.7
Vosges	2	2	2	6	12.4
Yonne	2	2	2	9	10.4
Paris region					
Series C	**1968**	**1976**	**2004**	**No.**	**Long**
Paris	12	12	12	43	14.8
Yvelines	4	5	6	23	11.0
Essonne	3	5	5	20	11.4
Hauts-de-Seine	7	7	7	26	14.3
Seine-Saint-Denis	5	6	6	21	14.2
Val-de-Marne	5	6	6	21	14.2
Val-d'Oise	3	4	5	16	12.5

1998 had been the *suppléant* to the outgoing senator, Michel Dreyfus-Schmidt. De-selected by the Socialists, Dreyfus-Schmidt nevertheless decided to stand again, as a dissident and mainly to steal votes from Chevènement, but on 5 September 2008 he unexpectedly died. Ackermann thus became senator, but his tenure was fleeting, as Chevènement won the election. Ackermann uncharitably commented that delegates had confused the meeting of the college with national heritage day (taking place on the same day) and voted for a historic monument.[7]

Senators, ministers and suppléants

Senators are subject to the same *incompatibilité* or prohibition concerning ministerial office as deputies, but because senators are elected in different ways, the matter of *suppléance* is handled differently. In departments using the majority vote, each candidate has to name a *suppléant(e)* when they register. It is not permitted for one candidate to also act as the *suppléant* to another and candidates cannot change *suppléant* between rounds. The *suppléant* takes the seat only if the senator becomes a minister, is nominated to the Constitutional Council, is appointed to a government mission for more than six months or dies in office. A senator cannot simply resign in favour of his or her *suppléant*.

In departments using PR, the next unelected candidate on a list acts as *suppléant*. Until 2000, each list was obliged to put up only as many candidates as there were seats available, but with the lowering of the threshold for PR to three seats and the possibility that a single list might take all three, the Jospin government introduced the stipulation that each list must contain two more candidates than there are seats. Although the threshold was raised in 2003, the *s+2* condition remained in place. Where PR is used it is permitted for a *suppléant* to replace a senator who resigns, thereby adding a further dimension to such elections. Most ministers or *ministrables* feel that they ought to head their list, but in some instances they put themselves in what they anticipate will be the 'first reserve' position, becoming the *suppléant* and providing insurance against losing ministerial office. Thus, in 2004, while his cabinet colleague Nelly Olin was leading her troops in Val-d'Oise, Gérard Larcher, minister for labour relations, stood fifth on the UMP list which took four seats in the Yvelines, making him *suppléant*. Though he was retained by Dominique de Villepin, Larcher did not figure (or asked not to figure) in the Fillon government appointed in May 2007. Many pundits, alerted to his ambitions for the presidency of the Senate, expected an immediate return to the upper house. *L'Express* asserted that it was no secret that Adeline Gousseau, fourth on the UMP list in 2004, would resign her seat as soon as Larcher left office.[8] In fact, Gousseau saw out the parliamentary session and did not resign until 1 October 2007, though the effect was the same.

Most *suppléants* are only senators for short periods, though Maryse Roger-Coupin set some kind of record in January 2007 when she resigned within one day of replacing Yves Coquelle (CRC, Pas-de-Calais), preferring to concentrate on her role as mayor of Angres and was replaced in turn by Jean-Claude Danglot. Others have had extended stays. Guy Robert enjoyed a sixteen year career as senator for the Vienne between May 1977 and June 1997, as *suppléant* first to Monory and then to Raffarin and standing in his own right on one occasion. Other senators who started out as *suppléants* have gone on to establish considerable reputations in the upper chamber. Michel Charasse (Puy-de-Dôme) first entered in 1981 as *suppléant* to Roger Quilliot. Charasse stood in his own right alongside Quilliot in 1983, before becoming a minister in 1988. Like Pierre Mauroy, in September 1992 Charasse foresaw the train wreck that the 1993 general election would be for the left and returned to the upper house. Often an errand runner when Mitterrand was at the Elysée, Charasse became one of the Senate's more colourful personalities, usually puffing on a cigar and happier in the company of Poncelet than his fellow Socialists, which goes some way to explain why the PS withdrew its support for him to continue as *questeur* in 2004.[9] In June 2008 he left the Socialist group for the RDSE.

While it is forbidden for members of the government to hold a seat in parliament, it is regarded as perfectly normal for ministers who have come from the upper house to seek re-election when their series comes. Although questions were asked about prime minister Raffarin's reasons for standing in the 2004 *renouvellement*, he was doing nothing more or less extraordinary than the other former senator-ministers in his cabinet. And like them, he had a thirty-day period in which to declare whether he intended to take up his seat or not. Raffarin, of course, did not, and three other members of his cabinet - Larcher, Fillon and Olin - also resumed their government responsibilities. Plenty of others - Charasse in 1992, Hubert Falco in 2004 - preferred to take up their seats, though Falco became a minister again in April 2008. The case of Fillon in 2004 was slightly unusual in that here was a politician who had not been a senator seeking election to a seat he was unlikely to take up. His profile in local politics in the Sarthe made him excellent senatorial material. When Villepin dropped Fillon from the government, his *suppléant* resigned and Fillon entered the Senate through a by-election in September 2005. Three years later, as part of the raft of legislation designed to bring the constitutional revision of July 2008 to life, Fillon's government introduced an organic law allowing former deputies and senators who become ministers to resume their seats 30 days after leaving office. If they chose not to return to parliament, the law continued, their *suppléants* would stay on. On 8 January 2009, however, the Constitutional

Council ruled the new conditions did not conform to the constitution, meaning that if a minister opted not to return to their seat, a by-election would have to be held.[10]

Deputies and senators

Half of all senators under the Third Republic had previously served as deputies, while just a handful went the other way.[11] The 'rate of progression' from lower to upper house since 1945 has been far lower. The first Council of the Republic included only a handful of former deputies and constituents and in 1949 only 39 senators (16 per cent of the total) had been deputies, 23 of them under the Third Republic and 29 in either Constituent Assembly or the National Assembly. A decade later, after the complete renewal in April 1959, the proportion had risen to 22 per cent. Thereafter it dropped again below one-fifth: in 1980 there were 54 former deputies among the 305 senators for France and the DOM-TOM (17.7 per cent), and although this had increased by 1995 to 76 of 309 (24.6 per cent), the figure was much the same a decade later.[12] Of 304 metropolitan senators in October 2006, 74 (24.3 per cent) were former deputies.

The legislative role and the prestige of the 'old' Senate go some way to explaining the difference. Other constraining factors enter into the equation too. French political parties may still be relatively weak, but local federations have had more success in preventing deputies who want to move to the Senate from doing so, while *suppléance* and the low rate of mortality among senators have reduced the number of by-elections to allow a deputy to step up. In 1995, Christian Demuynck, RPR deputy-mayor for Neuilly-Plaisance (Seine-Saint-Denis), was expelled from the party when he defied orders and stood for the upper chamber. He was one of just eight deputies who moved to the upper house in the 1995, among 68 new senators. Three years later, 26 deputies who had lost their seats at the 1997 dissolution made a bid to return to parliament, but only ten were successful.[13] Thus, while in some political cultures, membership of the 'first' chamber is recommended or even a pre-requisite for entry into the second, in France senators and deputies are, for the most part, distinct.

In the popular imagination, a deputy who moves to the Luxembourg Palace is, typically, a figure who has passed a certain stage in their career, for whom the Senate represents a comfortable pre-retirement. The career of Jean-Claude Gaudin, senator-mayor for Marseille, offers just one emphatic counter-example of a well-established politician whose best has been reserved for his time in the upper house. First elected to the city council in 1965 as an Independent, as part of Defferre's broad anti-Communist list and at the age of 26, in 1978 he became a deputy and held his seat in 1981 against the *vague rose*. Two years later, in the municipal elections, Gaudin's UDF-RPR list won more votes overall than Defferre's, but failed to take the *mairie* because of the electoral *découpage*. Instead, in 1986, Gaudin became the first elected president of the Provence-Alpes-Côte-d'Azur regional council. Chair of the UDF group in the National Assembly, he was unable to prevent Centrist deputies forming their own group after the 1988 general election. The following year the disappointment of a second failed bid for mayor - Gaudin was beaten by the *mitterrandiste* Robert Vigouroux - was offset by election to the Senate.[14] Gaudin finally became mayor in 1995 and retained the post in 2001 and 2008. Victory in Marseille was enough for Juppé to make Gaudin regions minister in the 1995 autumn reshuffle. Out of office after the dissolution, Gaudin only had to wait until September 1998 to stage his return, leading the right to three seats in the Bouches-du-Rhône for the first time ever. He returned to the Luxembourg Palace just as the old UDF groups - the Union Centriste and the Union des Républicains et Indépendants - failed to prevent the RPR taking the speakership. A man of Gaudin's stature could not, however, be ignored and he was immediately elected vice-president, a position he retained in both 2001 and 2004, when he became *premier vice-président*. One of the grey eminences behind the UMP in 2002, he took over as interim chairman of the party when the courts stripped Juppé of his political eligibility in 2003. After Sarkozy's election to the party chair, Gaudin resumed his role as *président-délégué* and quietly shifted his support to the young pretender. With Sarkozy's election to the Elysée, Gaudin became one of a triumvirate who took temporary charge of the party. Gaudin began to look a possible successor to Poncelet and his victory in the 2008 municipal election, one of the majority's few successes, appeared to reinforce his position. Within weeks, however, his chances took a serious blow, when the UMP failed to secure the chair of the *intercommunal* council for greater Marseille. Although Gaudin maintained well into September that he was a candidate, other men were better placed and he gracefully withdrew.

As a deputy, Gaudin had been sufficiently well entrenched in his constituency to weather two poor elections for the right, in 1981 and 1988, but successive *alternances* in general elections between 1981 and 2002 made other politicians less secure and may account for the gentle rise in the rate of progression since the 1980s. A seat in the Senate can offer insurance against bad times ahead or an opportunity for a return to the parliamentary fray. The former was certainly true for Mauroy and Charasse and it worked out neatly for both that their departments were up for re-election in 1992. Michel Rocard did not have that luxury and had to wait until 1995. After the colossal failure of his 'Big Bang' in 1993, Rocard was ready to return to parliament as senator for the Yvelines in 1995. He never really settled, however, and when, in 1997, Jospin asked senior PS figures to set a voluntary example over *décumul*, Rocard chose to remain an MEP. Similarly, the 2004 *renouvellement* offered seven *gauche plurielle* casualties of the 2002 general election, including Voynet and the PCF's Robert Hue, an unlikely way back into parliament.

Sometimes senators have gone the other way. In 2007, four senators, one on the right, three on the left, moved to the lower house in the legislative elections.[15] Three of them were senators of relatively recent vintage. Roland Muzeau became Communist senator for the Hauts-de-Seine in 2000, when Michel Duffour joined the Jospin government. The *fabiusienne* Sandrine Hurel became a senator in 2004, in succession to Henri Weber, for whom she had worked as parliamentary assistant. Her decision to stand in Dieppe (where she was already municipal and departmental councillor) was a deliberate strategy to build on Ségolène Royal's remarkable performance there in the presidential election and help prepare the left for a triumphant municipal election in 2008.[16] Philippe Goujon, whose remarkable act of brinkmanship is related above, was elected to succeed his political mentor, Edouard Balladur, as deputy for the 15th *arrondissement*, though his election was not formally ratified by the Constitutional Council until 29 November 2007 and so his *suppléante* could not replace him in the Senate until that date.

The decisions of Hurel, Goujon *et al.* point to a small-scale practice of 'chamber hopping', a phenomenon almost completely unknown under the Third Republic. Perhaps the best example of this practice was Edgar Faure, who became senator for the Jura in April 1959 after losing his seat in the National Assembly. A Radical, but close to the Elysée, Faure became minister of agriculture in January 1966 in the reshuffle that followed de Gaulle's re-election. Like the other members of Pompidou's cabinets, he stood for the National Assembly in the 1967 and 1968 general elections, though this time for the Doubs, resigning on each occasion to resume his ministerial duties. Elected deputy for the Doubs in 1973 he ascended directly to the *perchoir*, but five years later lost a bitter contest to Chaban-Delmas. In 1980 he opted to return to the upper house for the Doubs, and became the only senator in the history of the Fifth Republic so far to have represented two different departments (not counting the reorganisation of the Paris region). Other chamber hoppers have included Maurice Pic, who was senator for the Drôme from 1948 to 1959, then deputy for 12 years, before returning to the upper chamber from 1971 until 1989, and Bernard Chochoy, senator for the Pas-de-Calais from 1946 to 1967, then a deputy, and then senator again from 1974 until his death in 1981. Jean Lecanuet's career as senator for Seine-Maritime from 1959 until his death in 1993 was punctuated by two spells in the Bourbon Palace: the first lasted just a year, from March 1973 to April 1974, before he became a minister under Chirac and then Barre. He returned to the Senate in 1977. Then, in April 1986, he stood for the National Assembly again, only to resign when he was re-elected to the Senate five months later. Strangely, he was not alone. Roger Quilliot, who had returned to the Senate in 1983, secured the seat of deputy for Clermont-Ferrand for the PS before standing in a Senate by-election to fill the vacancy he had himself created. Of course, both men stood in the general election to secure a seat they knew they would abandon to their *suppléant*. It may be that, in the future and with the reduction of the senatorial mandate to six years, movement between the two chambers will increase.

Sometimes deputies move to the Senate, find it is not for them and return to the National Assembly. Raymond Marcellin represented Morbihan as an Independent in the lower house from 1946, until Pompidou appointed him to his government in May 1962. He remained a ministerial *incontournable* until Chirac dispensed with his services in May 1974. Marcellin returned to parliament via the Senate in that year's *renouvellement*. It was, in many ways, a curious choice, given that during his time as interior minister, Marcellin had had regular run-ins with the Senate and had, moreover been one of the few Independents who openly campaigned for a 'yes' vote in 1969. On the other hand, he was president of the *conseil général*, mayor of Vannes and controlled most political patronage in the department. And it would hardly be the first time that a politician who had spent part of their career at loggerheads with the Senate, later became one of its stalwarts. This was not to be the case, however, for Marcellin. In 1981 he became a deputy once more and fought three more general elections before standing down in 1997.

The flow of parliamentarians from one house to the other is necessarily subject to the availability of seats and the timing of the electoral cycle. The 1997 general election created a large potential pool of right-wing former deputies, but only those whose departments were due to come up for re-election in September 1998 could hope to take advantage and only then if there were vacancies. Only twelve deputies who lost their seats in 1997 moved to the Senate in the intervening decade, mostly in 1998 and 2001. The 2002 general election allowed many *orphelins de la dissolution* to return to the Bourbon Palace and the 2007 election allowed them to stay there. Some deputies, of course, prefer to fall back on their local offices and prepare for the next general election.

The *cumul des mandats*

Local politics provides a training ground for would-be parliamentarians in many countries, but in few is the vertical link between local and national representation in one person retained. In most advanced democracies, where not expressly forbidden, culture and practice preclude accumulation of elected offices. In France, this is not the case, though recent administrations have sought to limit the practice of *cumul des mandats*, either by compulsion or persuasion: the Socialists passed legislation in the 1980s and again under Jospin, while on the right the process has been more a question of unofficial pressure. As President, Chirac tried to insist that ministers should not also be mayors, though he was not always successful. The first Balladur commission proposed prohibition, but the government dropped that.

Paradoxically, the limitations upon *cumul* have seen a parallel increase in the practice among deputies, encouraged by the risks of *alternance* in general elections and the enhanced responsibilities of local office brought about by decentralisation, to prepare themselves a safety net. If the Senate, where the cultivation of clienteles and the interaction between national and local representation was once the *chambre des cumulards*, the numbers no longer back up the case. Table 6.4 shows the number and proportion of members of each assembly who hold elected office at the level of the communes, departments and regions. For each category, the number of mayors and presidents of general and regional councillors has also been added and the proportion of executive officers (e.g. mayors among the total number of municipal councillors) calculated.

Table 6.4 - The *cumul des mandats* December 2008

	Senate - 343 seats		National Assembly - 577 seats	
Commune	189	63%	378	66%
Mayors	115	61%	267	71%
Department	111	35%	127	22%
Chairs	31	29%	21	17%
Region	31	7%	60	10%
Chairs	4		6	
None	88	28%	75	13%

The figures underline a growing, if gentle, trend away from *cumul* in the Senate: on the eve of the 2008 *renouvellement*, the number of *non-cumulards* was 68, or 21 per cent of the total. The discourses of modernisation and *non-cumul* on all sides of the political argument since the election of Sarkozy, reiterated most clearly in the conclusions of the first Balladur committee, had an impact on Senate elections in 2008 that they could not have on the general election in June 2007. At 13 per cent, the rate of *non-cumul* among deputies in the 2007-2012 legislature is the same as its predecessor. The gap between the two chambers is growing and it is the upper house that has taken the greatest strides forward in this area. The Senate's case in this regard is boosted by the twelve members for expatriate nationals, who are almost by definition unable to hold local office. And the list of current senators who today hold no local office requires close examination. It includes, after all, the likes of Pasqua, for so long the boss of the Hauts-de-Seine, or Raffarin, or even the ecologist Marie-Christine Blandin, whose place in history was assured when she became the first woman president of a regional assembly in 1992. Few senators have never held local office of any sort. Others, however, owe their seats purely to national celebrity: Robert Badinter, for example, who became a senator in 1995, has never won an election by universal suffrage, though he has lost a couple.

When comparing and distinguishing *cumul* in the assemblies, it is generally said that senator-mayors come from smaller communes, deputy-mayors from larger ones. In 1965, Monnerville was delighted to welcome among the new cohort the mayors of Nantes, Saint-Etienne and Valenciennes to the 'sleepy, rural Senate', but it was, nevertheless the case that most senator-mayors held office in towns of fewer than 12,000 inhabitants and even well into the 1980s the mayors of France's larger cities tended to head for the National Assembly. One who did not, however, was Quilliot, who became mayor of Clermont-Ferrand in 1973 and entered the Senate the following year.

Chairman of the Association des Maires de Grandes Villes de France from 1977 to 1983, he made the Senate his parliamentary base and by the 1990s the mayors of other major cities did likewise. The Senate has not become the *chambre des grandes villes de France* but on the eve of the 2008 municipal elections it included the mayors of four of the most heavily populated cities – Marseille, Lyon, Nice and Strasbourg – as well as Toulon (15th) Mulhouse (33rd) and Perpignan (36th). It would have been very interesting if Jean-Claude Gaudin, mayor of Marseille, had made a serious bid for speaker in 2008. It is also arguable that his responsibilities in the *cité phocéenne* excluded his candidature.

The main distinction between the chambers is at the departmental level. There are more general councillors in the National Assembly than the Senate, but as a proportion, their share of the upper house is more significant, and the number of chairs of the departmental assemblies is higher too. Given that the departments serve as the Senate's electoral districts, this is not surprising and is confirmed when figures for the rate of double *cumul* are taken into consideration. Of the 255 *sénateurs-cumulards*, nearly one quarter (62) hold offices at municipal and departmental level. In the Assembly, 54 deputies (11 per cent) hold municipal and departmental office.

Parity and *sénatrices*

While the Senate has inherited certain constitutional and institutional characteristics from its predecessors, ancestral reputations have also clung on and this is nowhere more evident than over representation of women. Senators were the principal obstacle to women winning the vote before the Second World War, despite repeated expressions of support in the lower house. Despite the relatively high proportion of women involved in local politics (14 per cent of municipal councillors in 1983, 22 per cent in 1995 and 32 per cent by 2001), the glass ceiling has prevented that performance from being reflected in parliament. Until recent times the Senate lagged behind the National Assembly, though the record in the lower house is scarcely better. In 1993, when the parity campaign began to work up a head of steam, there were 35 *députées* (6 per cent) compared to 14 *sénatrices* (5 per cent). Still, it was not too difficult for parity's advocates to draw a parallel between the modern Senate's reticence regarding parity legislation and its ancestor's objections to votes for women.

Setting aside their philosophical and political objections, one of the practical concerns senators raised to parity legislation was that it would not be applied in the same way to all elections and the Senate provides a peculiar case in point. Parity only applies to departments using PR, where lists are obliged to alternate candidates by sex. The legislation has had two effects since 2001. The first, predictably, was to create a lot of grumpy male senators who found themselves pushed down the order and less likely to be elected. The second was that, in response, male *sortants* took to getting around parity by setting up their own lists. This was particularly evident in the 2004 election. In the Hauts-de-Seine, for example, neither Jean-Pierre Fourcade nor Jean-Pierre Schosteck were prepared to appear at third or, worse, fifth on the official UMP list and duly set up their own separate lists. Fourcade managed to find 191 friends to vote for him and was re-elected in seventh and last place. In the same department, the PS and PCF won a seat each. Had they run a joint list, they would have won a third seat, which would have gone to a woman candidate. Given, however, that the Socialist candidate was Robert Badinter, husband of one of parity's most forthright critics, philosopher Elisabeth Badinter, perhaps that was asking too much. In Val-d'Oise the official UMP list was led by social exclusion minister Nelly Olin, one of the few women to head a list. In second place was Hugues Portelli, professor of constitutional law and political science at the Université de Paris II-Assas. Portelli's nomination infuriated François Scellier, chair of the departmental assembly, who believed that fourth spot was beneath his dignity and ran his own list. His fit of pique was utterly counterproductive: his 268 votes deprived Olin's list of a third seat for Lucienne Malovry, but since Olin remained a minister, Malovry became a senator anyway. Had Scellier swallowed his pride, Malovry would have been elected by right and he would have taken his seat as Olin's *suppléant*.

The same department witnessed a rather less savoury but certainly inventive approach to the problem. Alain Richard, a Rocardian middle-weight in the PS, senator from 1995 to 1997 and defence minister under Jospin, found himself pushed down to third place on the party list, when the local federation voted to put the *sortant* Bernard Angels, Richard's *suppléant* in 1995, at the top. Richard used all his charm to try to persuade Raymonde Le Texier to resign immediately after the election and thereby allow him to resume his seat. Le Texier politely but firmly refused.[17]

The pattern of misbehaviour was repeated in many of the departments using PR, but it is difficult to say how many *sénatrices* would have been elected if all male candidates and the parties had played to the rules, because there were also cases where dissident lists split the vote and presented the other side with unexpected gains, as happened in the Haut-Rhin, where Patricia Schillinger won a seat PS analysts had not been expecting. Women headed only three lists with a chance of winning seats: Olin in Val-d'Oise, Catherine Tasca (PS) in the Yvelines and Hélène Luc (PCF) in Val-de-Marne. The legislation was by no means ineffective however. There were 34 women in the Senate before the election, 57 after it, comprising 17 per cent of the total compared to 12 per cent in the lower house. On the eve of the 2008 *renouvellement* the number of *sénatrices* had risen to 60 (18.2 per cent of the total), compared to 107 *députées* (18.5 per cent) in the new legislature. The 2008 *renouvellement* saw a generally better pattern of behaviour: the UMP had done so badly in most departments that there was no room for dissent, though it was not completely unknown (e.g. in the Alpes-Maritimes). The number of *sénatrices* rose to 75 or 22 per cent.

Table 6.5 - **Women in the Senate 1946-2008**

Year	No.	%	Year	No.	%
1946/7	22	7	1995	18	5.6
1948	12	3.8	1998	18	5.6
1959	5	1.9	2001	35	10.6
1968	5	1.8	2004	56	16.9
1977	5	1.7	2008	75	21.9
1986	9	2.8			

François Chevalier underlined that, between 1947 and 1989, of the 47 women who had sat in the upper chamber, 23 had been Communists, seven Socialists and the remainder shared out evenly between the other parties. Chevalier also noted that women senators tended to be elected in departments using PR, where parties had greater leverage.[18] A report into the 2004 *renouvellement* by UMP deputy Marie-Jo Zimmermann, commissioned by the Observatoire de la Parité, demonstrated that the left-wing bias had been corrected in the manner outlined in Table 6.6 below, but the importance of PR, reinforced by parity legislation, had not diminished. Zimmermann reckoned that raising the PR threshold from three to four seats had meant women won five fewer seats in 2004 than they would have in 2001. Still, the relative influx of women into the upper chamber, allied to changing attitudes towards feminisation of the language has resulted in one important innovation. A decade ago few people used the term *sénatrice*. It is, moreover, important to note the impact that parity legislation has had even in elections where it does not apply. In some departments using the majority system some parties, (e.g. the PS in the Corrèze in 2008), made a conscious effort to put up candidates of both sexes. The results for 2008 (below) suggest that the gap between the two systems is closing, though the differences between the series make like-for-like comparison impossible.

Table 6.6 - Sénatrices **by party and electoral method 2001-8**

	2001			2004			2008		
	M	PR	All	M	PR	All	M	PR	All
Ecologist	0	1	1	0	2	2	0	0	0
PCF	0	5	5	0	3	3	1	1	2
PS	1	5	6	1	9	10	4	4	8
Other Left	0	2	2	0	0	0	1	1	2
UDF	1	4	5	0	3	3	0	0	0
UMP	0	4	4	1	10	11	1	3	4
PRG	0	0	0	0	0	0	0	1	1
Other Right	0	0	0	0	2	2	0	1	1
All	**2**	**20**	**22**	**2**	**29**	**31**	**7**	**11**	**18**

Mortality, age and longevity

Edouard Herriot, the Radical speaker of the lower house under both the Third and Fourth Republics, began his distinguished parliamentary career as a senator for the Rhône between 1912 and 1919. It was not an experience he enjoyed. The Senate, he once wrote, is 'an assembly of old men, tempered by a high death rate'. Under the Third Republic the observation was fair: one senator in three died in office. In the 1930s, 104 of 184 new senators owed their seat, in the first instance, to the death of the incumbent.[19] The postwar upper chambers have witnessed nothing like that rate of mortality. To December 2008, only 183 of more than 1200 senators (less than 15 per cent) had died in office, which says as much about social attitudes to retirement as the robust good health of France's political elite. The highest number of deaths in any one year has been eight (in both 1981 and 1983).

The popular idea of the Senate as an assembly of old men is reinforced by a tendency within the political media to focus on the relative *rajeunissement* of personnel at each election, a phenomenon which is, of course, perfectly natural in the normal scheme of things. The Fourth Republic reduced the age of eligibility to the upper house from 40 to 35 and there it remained until 2003, when it was lowered to 30. By definition, then, senators start their careers later than deputies (though deputies themselves are seldom under 30). The Senate is a chamber of elders. The nature of senatorship, with its emphasis on connections, political networks and the *cursus honorum* of local office, means that senators under 40 are few and far between. In the 1998, 2001 and 2004 *renouvellements* the average ages of the incoming cohort were 59, 58 and 58 years, but in 2008 this rose to 60, although it was 57 amongst the new senators.

Table 6.7 - **Average age of all senators 1983-2008**

1983	61	1992	62	2001	61
1986	61	1995	61	2004	61
1989	62	1998	59	2008	62

In 1973 the age gap between senators and deputies was six years (59 to 53). It rose in 1978 to nine (60 to 51) and remained steady until 1995, when the average age of senators was 61 compared to 54 in the National Assembly.[20] Since then the gap has remained at around five or six years, although the more frequent renewal of the Senate allows for periodic reductions. There were, for example, two Senate *renouvellements* during the life of the 1997-2002 legislature. On the eve of the general election in June 2007, the average age of deputies was 58 years and six months, while among senators it was 63. Although only 132 new deputies entered the National Assembly at the general election, the average age dropped to 55, with the youngest aged a little over 28, giving some 50 years to the *doyen d'âge*. In the Senate in September 2008, there was a similar gap between the new *benjamin* Richard Tuheiava (Polynésie Française), at 34 and the 83 year-old Serge Dassault.

The image of the ageing senator is not altogether without justification. The re-election of Poher to the presidency in 1989 at the age of 80 may have been politically expedient, but it marked the apogee of a decade during which a number of prominent, veteran Gaullists had moved to the Senate through *Neuwirthisation*, whereby the RPR exploited the names and reputations of such figures to boost their performance at the polls. No fewer than 13 of the senators elected in 1986 were over 71, and in 1989 24 were 66 or over. Although the trend through the 1990s and 2000s has been downwards, in 2008 nearly 14 per cent of the Senate was aged 71 or over. It should also be said, in fairness, that the right has not been alone in putting forward candidates of more advanced years. In 2008 André Lejeune was re-elected at the age of 73, while in the Corrèze one of the new team was René Teulade, the 77 year-old president of the departmental assembly: a new face perhaps, but not a young one.[21]

While political culture places a premium on local office and networks as a prerequisite for senatorship, family connections have seen some seats pass from parent to child. Antoine Courrière was a Resistance hero, elected to the upper house for the Aude in 1946, a seat he occupied until his death in 1974. During the 1960s, he chaired the Socialist group and was one of Monnerville's staunchest allies, a forthright critic of colleagues who believed replacing their speaker might save the Senate from de Gaulle. On his death, his seat was filled by his son Raymond, who served the department from 1974 until 2006, except between 1981 and 1986, when he was a minister. Courrière *fils* was struck down by a heart attack in August 2006, while out for a walk in his native village of Cuxac-Cabardès, where he had been mayor since 1974, again in succession to his father. In his tribute, Poncelet made a virtue of the sixty years of service rendered to their *administrés*, to the upper chamber and to the Republic by Courrière *père et fils*.[22] A similar case arose in the Sarthe in 1977, when Roland du Luart succeeded to the seat vacated by his father, the Marquis Ladislas du Luart, elected senator nine years earlier. Luart *fils* entered the Senate at the age of just 37 and has been a fixture ever since, simultaneously holding the office of mayor of the commune that bears the family name and chair of the departmental assembly.[23]

A more complex dynastic link exists in the Pyrénées-Orientales, where the Alduy family have made their mark on politics. Paul Alduy became mayor for Amélie-les-Bains in 1952 and was re-elected in 1959, but also stood in the same year in Perpignan, where he won and took over the town hall. Back in Amélie, wife Jacqueline became mayor and it was she who first entered the Senate in 1982, as *suppléante* upon the death of Léon-Jean Grégory. She did not stand for re-election to the Senate in 1983, but her husband, who had lost his seat as deputy in the 1981 *vague rose*, did. Investigations into his handling of the city's finances led him not to stand in 1992. In 1993 the city budget was frozen and the municipal council dissolved. After fresh elections, his son, Jean-Paul Alduy became mayor and in 2001 he upheld the family tradition by entering the Senate.

The 2004 *renouvellement* saw two similar attempts to carry on a family senatorial tradition. In Paris, Philippe Dominati was successful in his campaign to replace father Jacques, despite failing to win the UMP nomination and having to lead his own dissident list (he was elected with 180 votes or 7.8 per cent).[24] Joëlle Ceccaldi-Reynaud, who was hoping to pull off a similar feat in neighbouring Hauts-de-Seine, failed to succeed father Charles. But in the same department another political dynasty returned to the Senate, as Isabelle Debré, daughter-in-law of the late Michel Debré was elected in second place on the official RPR list headed by Roger Karoutchi.

When this work was first in draft form, in 2007, the longest serving senator was Jacques Pelletier, first elected to represent the Aisne in 1966, though his time had been interrupted with periods as a minister (under Barre in the 1970s and Rocard in the 1980s) as well as a nine-year term as *médiateur de la République* (ombudsman). Pelletier died, however, on 3 September 2007, at the age of 78 and on the eve of what would have been the next *renouvellement* of his series. Just two months earlier another veteran Maurice Blin, who entered the Senate for the Ardennes in 1971 stood down. After the 2008 *renouvellement* outgoing speaker Christian Poncelet was one of only three senators, along with du Luart and Fourcade, who had been ever-present in the Senate since 1977. Another of the class of 1977, the former Communist group chair, Hélène Luc, resigned 18 September 2007, a tenure made all the more remarkable given the PCF's dislike for its members to establish themselves in office. Blin and Luc's decisions to retire were almost certainly due to the postponement of the *renouvellement* of series A to 2008. As it was, Blin's service to the Senate put him level with Louis Jung (Bas-Rhin 1959-95) and Etienne Dailly (Seine-et-Marne 1959-95) as the longest serving senators of the Fifth Republic. And should they see out the end of their terms of office in 2014, Luart and Poncelet will also have served 37 years. Even so, Poncelet will not catch his predecessor Alain Poher, whose career in the upper house spanned 49 years, from 1946 to 1995, though with a spell away from 1948 to 1952. And he will still be short of the 47 years service by Geoffroy de Montalembert, who entered the upper house in late 1946, as one of the National Assembly's nominees for the Parti Républicain de la Liberté. In 1948 he was elected as an Independent, for the department then known as Seine-Inférieure, now Seine-Maritime, and would be re-elected on a further six occasions. In 1992, when he presided over the election of Monory as Poher's successor, it was the sixth time since 1977 that Montalembert had acted as *président d'âge*. When he died, in 1993 at the age of 94, he had set the all-time record for continuous service, beating the previous best by Charles de Freycinet, senator for Paris from 1876 to 1920. Such cases are, however, exceptional and average Senate careers last barely one-quarter the length of Montalembert's.

From a *chambre d'agriculture* to the *République des professeurs*

Historically, the Senate has been seen as an enormous *chambre d'agriculture*, the chamber of barley and chestnuts (in the south), or wheat and sugar beet (in the north). This was not simply because it was populated by landowners and farmers but also because of its concern for rural affairs, reinforced by the link between the electoral colleges and *la France profonde*. Like the myth of the Senate as an assembly of old men, there is a grain of truth in this image: in 1959, 24 per cent of senators were defined as *agriculteurs*, the same proportion as in 1876. No other single category (using the Senate's own criteria) came close (see Table 6.8 below). A gradual decline set in during the 1970s, though even as recently as 1986, agriculture and landowning still accounted for 15 per cent, on a par with industry, the medical professions and the broadly defined category of employees. By 1995, less than 10 per cent of senators described themselves as *agriculteurs*. Business, another mainstay of the Third and Fourth Republics has witnessed a comparable decline, despite the presence of the likes of Dassault. This does not mean, of course, that the agricultural lobby's leverage has disappeared. No senator from a department with significant agro-industrial interests can ignore them. But the symbolic shift is a significant one.

The decline in the number of *sénateurs-agriculteurs* has been matched by an equally striking rise in the number of men and women from the teaching professions. The 29 *sénateurs-enseignants* in 1959 were almost all from higher education. By 2004 that had changed: of 85 *enseignants,* 20 came from tertiary education, 36 from secondary education, 13 from the primary level, with 8 others and 8 retired teachers. The *grande chambre de l'agriculture* has given way to the *République des professeurs* and arguably, as the table shows, civil servants, or rather *hauts fonctionnaires* (often from local government) who provide 28 of the 47 senators in that category. The tradition of *médecins-légistes* has held up pretty well, as has the representation of legal professionals.

Table 6.8 - **Socio-professional composition of the Senate 1959-2008**

	1959	1968	1977	1986	1995	2008
Agriculture	65	72	60	49	31	23
	24.9%	25.4%	20.3%	15%	9.7%	6.7%
Trade/Industry	44	34	46	46	26	28
	17%	12%	15.6%	14%	8%	8.2%
Employee	34	17	36	49	30	50
	8%	6%	12.2%	15%	9.3%	14.6%
Medicine	21	22	30	48	41	38
	8%	7.7%	10.1%	15%	12.8%	11.1%
Law	46	75	56	43	19	43
	18%	26.5%	19%	13%	5.9%	12.5%
Education	29	27	29	35	53	92
	11%	9.5%	9.8%	11%	16.5%	26.8%
Civil Service	22	34	33	34	25	57
	7.5%	11.3%	11.2%	11%	7.8%	16.6%
None declared	1	2	5	15	19	12
	0.3%	0.7%	1.7%	5%	5.9%	3.5%
Retired	N/A	N/A	N/A	N/A	69	N/A
					21.4%	
Other	N/A	N/A	N/A	N/A	9	N/A
					2.8%	
Total	262	283	295	319	321	343

Sources: Chevalier, p. 336; Sénat, Service de la Séance

One figure that looks rather surprising is the number of senators who declared themselves retired in 1995. The figures were not presented in the same way as in previous or subsequent years, but the number of *retraités* is still strikingly high. In 2004, only 25 senators described themselves as retired.

Senators for French expatriates

The major differences between AFE senators and their colleagues lie in their professional and political backgrounds. The 35 senators who have represented French expatriates have mostly come from four professional backgrounds: trade and industry (9), secondary or higher education (5), the law (6), and journalism or broadcast media (5). There have been three *ingénieurs* and two civil servants, but just one *agriculteur* and one retired general. The first four groups were, of course, the very ones that agitated for expatriate representation in

1946 and that one would expect to find claiming a prominent role in representing the interests of an expatriate 'community' (insofar as such a thing exists) and promoting the interests of French industry and culture abroad. Some have enjoyed a higher profile among expatriates than others: Jacques Habert was an academic and the editor of *France-Amérique*, the North American edition of *Le Figaro*. In 1975 he became the first chairman of the Association Nationale des Écoles Françaises de l'Étranger. Another North American representative was André Maman, professor of French language and *civilisation* at Princeton from 1958 to 1993. Senator from 1992 to 2001, Maman remained an active emeritus professor and Princeton students enjoy the benefits of an André Maman Fellowship, an internship at the Luxembourg Palace. Perhaps less well known, but no less productive than either Habert or Maman has been Robert Del Picchia (since 1998), whose career as a radio journalist stretches back to the late 1960s and whose credits involve work for RMC, RTL and France Inter.[25] From 1973 he was the French editor for various Austrian radio stations and in 1988 became the CSFE delegate for French nationals in Austria as well as being a member of the Franco-Austrian chamber of commerce. In the Senate, Del Picchia has been a strong advocate of the introduction of on-line voting to improve rates of participation among expatriates. Others have made their reputations in the promotion of French trade. Michel Guerry was a member of the CSFE for the Athens constituency, a foreign trade adviser to the French government and an honorary president of the Franco-Hellenic chamber of commerce when he was elected in 2001. Louis Duvernois is an engineer by profession, and adviser to the chairman of the Forum Francophone des Affaires, an organisation set up at the Versailles Francophone summit in 1987. He was elected in 2001 to represent expatriates in Quebec.[26]

Where AFE senators differ most obviously from their departmental peers is that they do not hold a local mandate. Guy Penne was unique among the group as being a mayor, for the commune of Sainte Cécile-les-Vignes in the Vaucluse.[27] The reason for this is that, naturally, most are expatriates themselves. Though their calling may be different and profiles lead them to membership of particular standing committees or other Senate bodies, AFE senators are not viewed as a group apart. They have served as secretaries or vice-presidents or as chairs of standing committees: Xavier de Villepin, who stood down in 2004 after 18 years in the Senate, chaired the foreign affairs and defence committee for a number of years, which must have made for a family atmosphere when son Dominique was in charge of the Quai d'Orsay. Unlike their peers, however, expatriate senators are not generally called to government.

Although they are small – around 150 members in each - the colleges that elect the expatriate senators are no more malleable than their departmental counterparts and electors do not like parachuted candidates, as Dominique Paillé, found to his cost in September 2008. An advisor to Nicolas Sarkozy and a UMP spokesman, in 2007 Paillé lost his seat in the National Assembly for the Deux-Sèvres, the heart of Royal territory. He had no more good fortune now, as delegates preferred to elect a Socialist vice-president of the AFE (Claudine Lepage), two sitting UMP senators and a non-aligned right-wing president of the Union des Français de Monaco. Paillé's list polled only 16 votes (10.6 per cent) of the 151 cast and though he claimed that just five more votes cast his way would have secured the seat, this was in fact inaccurate.[28] The Socialist list, which had secured 47 votes, would have taken a second seat with a higher remaining average.

Senate elections and the Constitutional Council

All senators have to be ratified by the Constitutional Council. The Council's role has evolved over the years from simply acting as a watchdog, ratifying elections and hearing complaints, towards that of active commentator on all aspects of electoral processes. In the specific case of the Senate, for example, repeated expressions of concern regarding the accreditation of supplementary and replacement delegates led, in 2004, to delegate elections being moved to earlier in the summer, to try to ensure a more thorough and transparent process of verification.

Senators take their seats by right and await the Council's pronouncement. Only candidates or members of the electoral college can petition the Council and on the whole the volume of petitions concerning the upper chamber has been modest: 2004 was a record year for complaints, with 20 presented concerning 14 departments, compared to 14 complaints regarding eight in 2001. The previous worst was 1983, with 19 referrals and 7 decisions. Nine of the 2004 referrals were thrown out. In 2008 three elections were contested. Those in Polynésie Française and the Aube were straightforward, but in the Ardèche, Jacques Genest (UMP) raised an objection after to failing to get elected by just six votes, just as he had in 1998. The Council rejected the objection on 8 January 2009.

Only five Senate elections have been annulled since 1959: the figure for the National Assembly to 2002 was 55.[29] The first Senate annulment came in April 1959, when an elector for the canton of Nontron (Dordogne) complained at the intimidating nature of electoral propaganda circulated by the local chamber of agriculture in favour of the Radical candidate, Charles Sinsout, who was duly elected in the re-run. The Senate then went through four full electoral cycles before the next two cancellations, following the 1995 *renouvellement*. The first, in Bas-Rhin, concerned a complaint that the *suppléant* to one of the candidates, Joseph Ostermann (RPR), was ineligible. Ostermann was elected in the re-run in February 1996. The second concerned the Vaucluse, where the election of Claude Haut (PS) was annulled due to the loss of one of the official attendance sheets and the closeness of the result: he was just one vote ahead of the RPR candidate who lodged the complaint. The complexities of the case took rather longer to unravel than the Bas-Rhin case, and it was not until June 1996 that Haut was vindicated.

It was also the closeness of the result that brought about the cancellation of a by-election in Haute-Saône in September 2002. In June 2002, UMP senator Alain Joyandet had successfully stood for the National Assembly, having reasoned that the previous year's local election results had put his re-election to the upper chamber at risk. The UMP's candidate to replace him was Christian Bergelin, himself 21 years a deputy. Bergelin had been minister for youth and sport under Chirac from 1986-8 and became president of his departmental assembly in 1989. The left made significant inroads, however, in the 1998 *cantonales*, creating a hung assembly.[30] The 2001 municipal elections gave the left further reason to hope that they might take both the department's seats come 2004. Joyandet's resignation gave them an early chance to test their position. Bergelin won by just one vote, but the beaten Socialist and chairman of the *conseil général*, Yves Krattinger, lodged a complaint, alleging that a number of delegates had been absent from the ballot without good reason ('sans justificatif adéquat') and that the votes cast by their *suppléants* were invalid.[31] The Council agreed. Krattinger won the re-run by a dozen votes.

Bas-Rhin proved contentious once more in 2004 and again it was a question of *délégués suppléants*. Daniel Hoeffel refused to accept third place on the UMP list, behind fellow *sortant* Philippe Richert and Fabienne Keller, mayor of Strasbourg. Instead Hoeffel set up his own dissident list and came within two votes of beating the UMP to the department's fifth seat.[32] Hoeffel complained that three *délégués suppléants* were not the right ones: delegates further up the list of stand-ins had been passed over. The closeness of the vote made the petition impossible to ignore, but Hoeffel, curiously, decided not to stand and the outcome was the same.

Although senators retain the right to hear requests to lift a colleague's parliamentary immunity, the Constitutional Council formally declares the deposition (*déchéance*) of a senator. This seldom happens in either house. The Council has heard only 18 cases since 1959, 15 of which it has confirmed, seven affecting the Senate. Two of these have been for personal reasons: in February 1983 Paul-Yves Lavolé, *suppléant* to the Louis Le Montagner in 1974, informed the Council that he was unable to take over the seat for Morbihan vacated by the latter's death.[33] And in December 2004, the Council declared the *déchéance* of Henri d'Attilio (PS, Bouches-du-Rhône), whose deteriorating health (Alzheimer's disease) had led to him being placed under legal guardianship, although Claude Lévy suggested that the PS dragged out the examination of d'Attilio's case in order to retain the seat. Elected in 1998, d'Attilio took no part in public life from 2001, but his *suppléant*, Jacques Siffre was ineligible after being found guilty of misuse of public funds, while the next candidate on the left-wing list was a Communist. Rather than allow the PCF to gain a seat they would hold until 2007, the PS group obfuscated and it was not until late 2003 that the *bureau* finally brought the case to the Council. By the time the decision was published in 2004, Siffre was eligible once more.[34] The other instances are all linked to misuse or misappropriation of public funds.

The speaker can also exercise his prerogative to ask the Council to confirm the eligibility of a senator. In 2004, the opposition claimed that his involvement in a number of companies holding important government contracts made Serge Dassault, ineligible under the incompatibility laws. Speaker Poncelet asked the Council to examine the case. The *sages* ruled that there was no impediment to Dassault continuing as a senator for the Essonne, largely on grounds of precedent: in the face of similar criticisms, their forerunners had confirmed the election of his father Marcel Dassault as deputy for the Oise in 1977.[35]

7

Being a senator

The very first task facing senators, old and new, after a *renouvellement*, is to elect their speaker. Until 1989 this was a largely uncontroversial matter. Indeed, the long presidencies of Gaston Monnerville and then, especially of Alain Poher, created a general indifference among outside commentators. The election of the speaker, it was said, was 'l'affaire des sénateurs'. Since 1992 and the election of René Monory, the post of speaker has been anything but a matter of indifference. The election has become the subject of growing media attention, culminating, in 2008, in the longest and most heavily publicised campaign in its history (beginning, arguably, in 2004). Paradoxically, a large proportion of the electors, the new senators, are exposed to the intensity of the campaign only at the last minute and with very little idea of what to expect. Candidates have to be careful, therefore, not to declare themselves officially too soon. But whatever the other considerations, no-one could argue with much conviction that the elections of Christian Poncelet in 1998 and still less that of Gérard Larcher in 2008 were no-one else's business.

After a *renouvellement*, the Senate reconvenes under the aegis of a provisional *bureau d'âge*, comprising the eldest member of the Senate (the *doyen d'âge*) in the chair, assisted by the six youngest senators. (The appointment of a *bureau d'âge* at its first meeting is common to all elected bodies in France, from parliament to the smallest commune.) No debate can be held while the *président d'âge* is in the chair, but he or she is accorded the privilege of addressing the house. Such speeches tend to follow a pattern. First, new members are welcomed and any who have just made the transition from the lower chamber are reminded, lest they be in any doubt, that they have come to an assembly were calmness and serenity of action, clarity and precision of thought are the watchwords. The president will then situate the Senate within the institutions of the Republic and its unique composition and role, before linking this to a topical theme. Marius Moutet, *président d'âge* in 1959, 1962 and 1965, made a particular point of upholding the rights of the Senate. Geoffroy de Montalembert, who fulfilled the role on six occasions between 1977 and 1992, became a master in the art. And in September 2001 Paulette Brisepierre emphasised her position representing French nationals abroad to underline this specific and then unique aspect of the Senate before expanding into the wider role of France abroad as a force for good. Referring to her own albeit temporary position and the presence of three other women in the *bureau d'âge*, she exclaimed that 'parity is here', to ironic murmurs from the left.[1] In 2008, Serge Dassault used the platform to make a provocative speech calling for greater freedom for French industry.[2]

The *président d'âge* then draws the names of six senators who will act as tellers, declares the election open and draws a letter from a green marble urn to decide from what point in the register voting will begin. This can produce some neat ironic twists too: in 1998, in the ballot to decide between Monory and Poncelet, the letter 'U' was drawn and so the vote began with Maurice Ulrich, one of Chirac's closest intimates. Senators vote at the tribune. The election is a three-round majority-majority-plurality vote. In the event of a tie, in common with all elections in France, the elder candidate is declared the winner. Once a victor has emerged, the presidential chair on the *plateau* is handed over immediately and the speaker makes a brief speech of thanks. The full inaugural address comes only once the whole *bureau* - the executive presidium - has been elected and the political groups and commissions have been settled. In 2008, for example, Gérard Larcher was elected on 1 October, but his colleagues had to wait until the 14th to hear his programme (though they already had a good idea of the content).

Président de tous les sénateurs - the speaker of the Senate

In his study of the speakers of France's assemblies, Arnaud Martin differentiates two presidential types: 'individual' and 'collective'.[3] In the first category, where authority is exercised individually (albeit with substitutes to stand in at need) he places the speakers of the British, US, Canadian, and Irish parliaments, as well as the president of the Dutch lower house. The Dutch upper house, along with most other advanced democracies, Martin places in the second 'collective' category by virtue of the fact that the speaker works within a larger presidium. Given that Martin accepts that, even within collective systems there is always a nominated president, perhaps a better rendering would be 'collegial'. Notionally, the speaker of the French Senate falls into the collegial group, not once, but twice over: he (and it has always been a man so far) chairs the *bureau*, but also the *conférence des présidents*, which establishes the Senate timetable. (Explanations of the roles of the *bureau* and the *conférence* are provided below.) The president of the Senate is, then, an independent and impartial chair with ultimate responsibility for all that goes on within the confines of the Luxembourg Palace; he guarantees that the Senate is able to conduct its business in a proper manner; he ensures that senators are able to fulfil their roles as freely elected parliamentary representatives; and he exercises an external role as representative of the Senate and, by virtue of his role as interim President, as the *deuxième personnage de la République*. (In the real order of things, the speaker is third, behind the prime minister.)

Despite the collegial nature of the office, however, speakers are pre-eminent in so far as they are chosen before the other members of the *bureau*, are elected on an individual programme and, at least since 1992, have sought to impress their particular stamp. What is more, because the French parliament lacks the discipline of a British-style whipping system, the speaker is sometimes called upon to act as leader of the majority: witness Poncelet's dressing down by Chirac over parity legislation. The long presidencies of Monnerville and Poher blurred the nature of the speakership, but it has become clear, since Monory's election, that the post is part of the inter- and intra-party game.

An independent, internally elected speaker was an innovation of the modern Republic. Under the Directory, the Council of Elders adopted the system of monthly rotation used by the National Assembly in 1789. The Consulate gave senators the right to elect their own speaker, but the *sénatus-consulte* of Year X (1802) handed that privilege to the First Consul, a right Napoleon was hardly likely to relinquish on becoming Emperor. Under the Restoration and the July Monarchy, the Chancellor of France, who also served as minister of justice and keeper of the seals, was speaker *ex officio*, in obvious imitation of the House of Lords. The Second Empire revived the practice of the First, though from 1869 the speaker was appointed by the Emperor from a list of internal nominees. The National Assembly of 1871 took as its organisational model its 1848 predecessor, which had elected its own president assisted by a *bureau* of vice-presidents, *questeurs* and secretaries. In 1876, both the Senate and the Chamber of Deputies adapted this model, with an election at the beginning of each parliamentary session in January.

The differences between the two assemblies very quickly imposed marked distinctions on the offices of the two speakers, distinctions still evident today. Under the Third Republic, where majorities easily fragmented and governments seldom lasted six months, speakers of the Chamber could be called upon to form a cabinet, on the grounds that their office meant they enjoyed the confidence of the lower house. Sometimes they were caretakers, holding the fort while the Chamber found its majority, but at other times politicians used the *perchoir* (a nickname applied *only* to the chair of the lower house) as the platform for their own ambitions. The Senate's role, its traditions and its culture came to militate against the presidency of the upper house being used in the same way. Elevation to the *plateau*, the term used to refer to the raised area at the front of the debating chamber, taken as shorthand for the presidency, was usually the crowning accolade in a career of long public service, unless the Elysée beckoned. Since 1876 there has been only one exception to this rule: in 1882 Léon Say gave up being speaker to become minister of finance.

These patterns of behaviour were, to a certain extent, handed down to the Fifth Republic. Some of the occupants of the Hôtel Lassay, official residence of the speaker of the Assembly, have been household political names; Jacques Chaban-Delmas, Laurent Fabius, Philippe Séguin and Jean-Louis Debré. Chaban became prime minister in 1969, after nearly 11 years as speaker (and took the office twice again, in 1978-81 and 1986-8). Fabius did things the other way around. Prime minister in 1984, he lost the election in 1986 and saw his position within the PS undermined by the rise of Michel Rocard. Mitterrand had wanted to install Fabius as general secretary of the PS, but the party resisted and Fabius settled instead for the *perchoir*, which he used to play the role of the *anti-Rocard*. The crushing victory of the right in the 1993 election saw Séguin take over, putting him in the box seat, so to speak, to assume the leadership of the RPR when the decision to dissolve the Assembly backfired. Fabius resumed the duties of speaker between 1997 and 2000, this time as the *anti-Jospin*.

One might point out, however, that a turn as speaker of the National Assembly has seldom brought good fortune. Although he went from being speaker to prime minister, Chaban's reformist instincts were at odds with reactionary tone of the majority elected in 1968 and he was replaced in 1972 rather than be allowed to prepare the general election the following year. He then found himself abandoned by a large part of the Gaullist party in the 1974 presidential election. Chaban's re-election to the *perchoir* in 1978 was largely a gesture of reconciliation on Chirac's behalf. Séguin's ambitions to rebuild the RPR after 1997 were undermined by 'the prisoner in the Elysée' and in early 1999 he resigned. Fabius's Elysian aspirations also came to nought. Though he backed the 'no' vote in the 2005 referendum on the European constitution and tried to reach out to the far left through the good offices of the then Socialist senator and former Trotskyist Jean-Luc Mélenchon, his overtures were rebuffed and his presidential chances derailed by Ségolène Royal. Jean-Louis Debré had no such ambitions and was rewarded for steering the UMP majority through the 12th legislature with appointment by Chirac to the chair the Constitutional Council created by his father nearly fifty years before., He then had to look on as Balladur (whom he defeated to become speaker in 2002) set about reconditioning the regime.

Vingt-deux ans de présidence

Speakers of the Senate have been cut from a very different political cloth. Monnerville, deputy for Guyane under the Third Republic and in the two Constituent Assemblies, became a senator almost by accident. Defeated in the election to the National Assembly in 1946, he was contemplating returning to his legal practice when news came from through from Cayenne that he had been elected to the Council of the Republic. There was nothing accidental, however, about the rest of his career in the upper house. Elected vice-president, his elevation to speaker on the death of Champetier de Ribes in March 1947, owed itself to the several factors: he was a Radical and the party provided the pivot of the majority in the upper house: he was an overseas representative whose success in France reflected a certain vision of the union of *métropole* and *outremer*; he could unite the centre-right, centre left and left against the Communists; but above all he was committed to pushing the upper house to the limits of its constitutional role and beyond between 1947 and 1958.

The part played by Monnerville and his colleagues in the short weeks in which the constitution of the Fifth Republic was drafted, has already been described above in Chapter 2. The success of the delegation in securing an enhanced role for their assembly, coupled to the failure of the Gaullists in the Senate elections of April 1959, made any challenge to Monnerville inconceivable. While the National Assembly marked the passing of the old regime by electing Chaban speaker rather than the veteran Paul Reynaud, Monnerville's unopposed re-election signalled that the upper chamber intended to uphold the traditions of the parliamentary Republic to the best of its ability.

Table 7.1 - **Presidents of the Senate 1958-2008**

President	Term	Re-elected
Gaston Monnerville Gauche Démocratique	1958-1968 Retired	1959, 1962, 1965*
Alain Poher Union Centriste	1968-1992 Retired	1971, 1974, 1977, 1980, 1983, 1986, 1989*
René Monory Union Centriste	1992-1998* Defeated	1995
Christian Poncelet (RPR/UMP)	1998-2008 Retired	2001, 2004*
Gérard Larcher (UMP)	2008	
* indicates election in which the incumbent faced a challenge		

The very different readings of the constitution between the Elysée, Matignon and the Luxembourg Palace made a collision likely and the differences of opinion over the standing orders, as well as various noises from within the Gaullist movement about reform of the Senate, made relations difficult. Nevertheless, all out hostilities were only engaged with de Gaulle's announcement that he intended to bypass parliament by invoking Article 11 to ask the people to approve the future election of the head of state by universal suffrage and by Monnerville's forthright response at Vichy. Senators stood by their speaker by re-electing him unopposed but defeat in the referendum was followed by a general election which gave the government a solid enough majority. And despite de Gaulle's soothing words at the beginning of 1963, Monnerville endured a long period of ostracism from official functions, while Pompidou observed a total boycott of the Senate and his ministers a partial one.

Although his *bureau* showed solidarity with their speaker, by 1965 some sections of the majority came to believe the time had come to find someone better placed to negotiate with the government. One view was that Edgar Faure might be the man, while the Christian Democrats André Colin and Jean Lecanuet were certainly interested. It was not easy, however, for potential candidates to declare themselves openly. A stalking horse had to be found. Failure to be re-elected outright in the first round would force Monnerville to withdraw and then the real candidates could enter the fray. Georges Portmann, Independent senator for the Gironde under three Republics, accepted the challenge.

The choice before senators was not altogether straightforward. De Gaulle looked certain to be re-elected to the Elysée, while Pompidou had stamped an impressive authority on the prime ministerial office and asserted his position as *chef de la majorité*. Government leaks certainly encouraged the view that a change of speaker might pave the way to warmer relations. With 250 votes cast in the first round, Monnerville needed 126. He obtained 127 to 81 for Portmann.[4] The challenge had failed, but only by a whisker and Monnerville knew it. His response was to offer the government reform - but on the Senate's own terms: *autoréforme*. He asked Marcel Prélot and Edouard Bonnefous to come up with suggestions, which proved to be both imaginative and inventive. But they were never likely to win favour, especially when the 1967 general election went so badly for Pompidou, who resorted to what amounted to government by decree. Institutional reform was far from anyone's minds. The events of 1968 changed all that.

From Poher to *pohérisation*

Faced with the wave of social unrest that swept France in May 1968, de Gaulle's initial response was to promise a referendum. Pompidou counselled in favour of a snap general election in late June, which the Gaullists won by a landslide. De Gaulle then decided to replace Pompidou with the more pliant Couve de Murville and appointed cabinet ministers whose function was to prepare reform of the regions and the Senate, with a view to a referendum as soon as possible. Faced with the prospect of fighting another referendum and aware that in any case, the political balance in the upper house had decidedly shifted away from his Gauche Démocratique group towards the Centre, Monnerville announced he would not seek re-election. His departure had in part been prompted by the announcement by André Colin, leader of the Centrists that he intended to run for speaker. The Centrists took the presidency, but Colin did not.

Five candidates went into the first round. Colin, the Independent Pierre Garet, Socialist André Méric, Communist Georges Cogniot, and the Radical Etienne Dailly. Garet held a narrow lead after the first round. Dailly and Cogniot withdrew, but their votes did not split as expected in the second ballot. Cogniot's swung in behind Méric, Dailly's votes split between Méric and Garet. However moderate they might be, anti-clerical Radicals were not prepared to vote for the Christian Democrat Colin and the Socialists even less so. If the Centre wanted to secure the presidency they would have to come up with another candidate.

Table 7.2 - **Presidential election 1968 - first and second rounds**

Name	Group	First	Second
Pierre Garet	Indépendants	64	110
André Colin	UCDP	58	62
André Méric	Socialiste	53	83
Etienne Dailly	Gauche Démocratique	37	/
Georges Cogniot	Communiste	18	/

Monnerville played a significant role in brokering the solution. For several days he had been sounding out opinion on behalf of the senator for Val-d'Oise, Alain Poher. A Centrist, but more conciliatory than Colin, Poher was able to rally the Radicals and Socialists, and defeated Garet by 125 votes to 107.[5]

Speakers of the Senate may well be considered first among equals, but they are also expected to provide a clear theme or character to their terms of office. For Monnerville the task in his first two terms was easily defined: ensuring the upper chamber's rights as a parliamentary assembly were respected. All his successors have re-stated that position. But ever since 1965, speakers have chosen to lay out the themes that they want the upper chamber to pursue under their stewardship. For Poher, the imperative was to restructure the Senate in two ways: through reorganisation and streamlining of its committees to cope with the growing volume of legislative work and, later, through the renovation of the material fabric of the Luxembourg Palace. Poher would go on to serve 24 years as speaker, overtaking the total period accumulated by Monnerville between 1947 and 1968. But what began as a streamlining presidency in the 1970s and one of defiance in the early 1980s, ended as one of frustration and disappointment.

In September 1986, the Senate was settling into the first period of cohabitation. After that year's *renouvellement*, the chairs of the Union Centriste, the Gauche Démocratique and the RPR group visited Poher to inform him that if he sought a seventh term, he would have their support. He was easily re-elected. Although the RPR had become the largest group, it was not in a position to take the presidency and it suited its leaders to leave Poher alone. Three years later, however, the situation had changed significantly. The failure to defeat Mitterrand in 1988 caused deep rifts in the RPR, where Chirac's incapacity to land the big prize provoked more or less open revolt. At the same time the UDF was in danger of fragmentation. Against this background, Poher made a decision that while politically expedient did neither himself nor the Senate any favours. On 24 September 1989, as the results of the *renouvellement* were arriving, he summoned the chairs of the three main majority groups to his office and informed them that he would seek an eighth term.

Paradoxically, the only chairman to offer his immediate support was Pasqua. The *renouvellement* had brought his party 14 new seats, completing a triumphant cycle of elections that had seen them expand from 41 in 1980 seats to 91. The UDF groups still held more than 130 between them, however, and it was premature to hope the RPR would mark the twentieth anniversary of de Gaulle's defeat by taking the Petit Luxembourg. Pasqua, moreover, feared the emergence of a relatively young UDF candidate would dent his own ambitions. Three years was not so long to wait.

The UDF groups were, however, profoundly opposed to Poher's re-election, none more so than his own Union Centriste. The future of the Senate, which the UDF regarded as 'their' assembly, did not seem to lie in the hands of a man who would very soon be celebrating his 80th birthday. But unable to find a single candidate to challenge Poher, they sent three into the first round to test opinion. The results were inconclusive. Poher polled 115 votes, mostly from the RPR, while Philippe de Bourgoing (URI) took 50, Jean Arthuis (UC) 40 and Jean François-Poncet (RDE) 21. Daniel Hoeffel, chair of the UC, invited the URI and RDE to a joint meeting, but they refused. Instead the UC held an internal election and chose René Monory ahead of Hoeffel and Lecanuet. The Independents selected Pierre-Christian Taittinger. In the second ballot, Poher still led, though his 108 votes were fewer than the combined totals of Taittinger (66) and Monory (57). Monory withdrew and the UC was now faced with the choice of keeping Poher in office or losing the presidency to the Independents. The group voted internally for Taittinger. As the third round approached, Pasqua, of all people, appeared to lose his nerve and visited Poher, suggesting he should stand down in favour of Maurice Schumann or the chair of the finance commission, Christian Poncelet. Poher was resolute and vindicated as he took 127 votes to 111, with a small group of Centrists and the RDE rallying to him.

Poher promised his colleagues that his new term would usher in a period of review of the way the Senate went about its business and there were indeed some changes. But this was nothing like the sort of progress envisaged by the *rénovateurs* whose influence was beginning to be felt in the corridors and committee rooms. Worse was to follow. Poher became less visible and critics began to suspect the Senate was being run by his personal staff. The speaker, and by association his assembly, appeared to be fumbling and out of touch, a process someone described as *pohérisation*. His final term of office had become 'un mandat de trop' - one too many. When his successor, René Monory, fell from office in 1998, it was, according to some, because he in turn had become *pohérisé* and colleagues would not chance a term too far.

France's no.1 car dealer

Monory's success in 1992 was due to the lessons of 1989: if the UDF wanted to retain the presidency, it would need every vote it could muster. The need for unity was made doubly clear by Pasqua's unilateral announcement that he would be standing (much to the annoyance of would-be candidate, Poncelet). The UDF had good reason to dislike Pasqua: he was, after all, the principal architect of the RPR's extraordinary rise in the upper house. The pro-European UDF was, moreover, determined that, just one week after the referendum to approve the Maastricht Treaty, one of its most vociferous critics should not become speaker. This time the result of 1989 primary was reversed: Monory beat Taittinger by 66 votes to 60. In the meantime, Socialist senators debated whether they should, *in extremis*, vote tactically to prevent Pasqua becoming speaker. That danger never materialised. Pasqua announced that if there were a majority candidate ahead of him in the first round, he would withdraw. Monory gained 125 votes to 100 for Pasqua and the second ballot was a formality: 'le premier garagiste de France' became *le deuxième personnage de la République*. The media were disappointed. 'We came expecting Clausewitz', wrote *Le Monde*, but 'got the Comtesse de Ségur'.[6]

Monory was not a young man when he was elected - 69 compared to Pasqua at 65 - and had been a senator since 1968, although his time in the upper house was punctuated by turns finance minister under Barre (1977-81) and education minister under Chirac (1986-88). He had also been the moving force behind Futuroscope, in his Vienne fiefdom. Who better to modernise the Senate? That was Monory's theme: modernisation of the Senate's methods and structures, and openness. 'When the Senate is invited, we should be present', he told one interviewer and for his part he was indeed present.[7] Unlike Poher, Monory did not limit himself to his institutional role. If anything he was more active than ever in his party, the Centre des Démocrates Sociaux (CDS), and as an active and vocal figure within the parliamentary majority. He became a regular in opinion polls and enjoyed ratings not achieved before or since by a speaker. As the 1995 Presidential election loomed and the UDF failed to find a candidate, it was even suggested Monory might stand. Unlike most of the CDS, he backed Chirac against Balladur.

Despite the potential shortcomings of his rhetoric, Monory achieved his goals. It helped that the right won a landslide in the 1993 general election and that Séguin was similarly inclined to streamline his chamber's affairs. Monory opened the doors of the Luxembourg Palace to the outside world and brought *rénovateurs* into key positions. If he was not the speaker who anticipated the Senate's future as the *chambre de la décentralisation*, he certainly laid the foundation. The modernisation of communications, the introduction of the latest technology into the chamber's infrastructure and, above all, the very clear restatement that the Senate's voice must be heard and heeded, were his legacy. Outwardly, Monory's re-election in 1995 did not seem to be in doubt. He had backed the right horse in the Presidential campaign and was easily re-elected in his department. Within the UDF family, however, the CDS had lost seven seats. According to some versions of events, Monory was saved by Chirac's intervention behind the scenes, but this is uncertain. The UDF was in a bad way in 1995, but it was not yet at the point of disintegration. That did not come until the dissolution of 1997.

A modest speaker for an ambitious Senate

The right might well have lost the general election anyway had the tenth legislature gone the full term, but having thrown away control of the Assembly and with a lame duck in the Elysée, the RPR turned its attention to squeezing the UDF out of the Petit Luxembourg. When Jospin called the Senate an 'anomaly', Monory's response was muted and rambling (he was not the most lucid orator at the best of times) and the word *pohérisé* was even muttered in some quarters. This was not the real cause of Monory's downfall: the RPR had decided the time had come to take control and in Christian Poncelet had a candidate capable of winning.

Unlike Monory, Poncelet ended his short ministerial career when he entered the Senate in September 1977, alongside Pasqua and a dozen other new Gaullist senators who were to provide the nucleus behind the transformation of the RPR's fortunes. Nine years later, when the RPR became the largest group, Poncelet was eased into the chair of the finance commission, arguably the second most important position in the Senate because its holder also manages the upper chamber's impressive budget. Poncelet quickly gained a cross-party reputation for good management and even-handedness. As early as 1989 he was seen as a future speaker and he would have stood in 1992 if Pasqua had not blocked his path. Circumstances were unfavourable in 1995, but three years later everything fell into place. The leaders of the UDF were at loggerheads about the future of their movement. If Poncelet could dislodge just a few votes, the *plateau* would be his.

Monory did not play his hand well. Jospin's intervention had not helped and rumours of a challenge had begun to circulate when, in June, Monory claimed that the chairs of the three majority groups had asked him to stand again.[8] Two of the men concerned, Josselin de Rohan (RPR) and Henri de Raincourt (URI) separately announced that their groups would make no formal decision until after the *renouvellement*. In July the name of the challenger was common currency, but it was September before Poncelet formally announced his intention to stand with the publication of a manifesto. *Propositions pour une rénovation du Sénat. Une présidence modeste pour un Sénat ambitieux* repeated the usual mantra of upholding the Senate's role and carrying forward the modernisation agenda, but at its centre was a promise to re-centre the upper chamber around its vocation as the *chambre des collectivités locales*. The manifesto also included a promise only to seek a six year term. The coded reference to *pohérisation* was easy enough to decipher.

Monory was desperate and turned to the Elysée, hoping to cash in his support for Chirac in 1995. The reply was that he should not embarrass the President who had, it was claimed, protected Monory already three years before. The three men were seen together in public on only one occasion during the campaign, in early September at the launch of an exhibition at the Musée du Luxembourg entitled 'Sénat Média'. Planned months in advance, the exhibition underlined the strides the upper house had made under Monory in making its work accessible to the public and as a platform to stake his claim to three more years. But this celebration of Monory's Senate went badly wrong. On his arrival, Chirac first shook the speaker's hand as protocol demanded, before turning to the chair of the finance commission and purring, 'Christian, tu vas bien?'[9]

A good result for the Centrists in the *renouvellement* might have rescued Monory, but they lost more seats, while the RPR and the URI made gains. Only now did Raincourt call on his troops to rally to Monory. If the UDF had held together, Monory would have won 120 votes in the first round to 100 for Poncelet, but in fact the scores were reversed: 118 for Poncelet to 102. Monory withdrew: 'They found me too old' he said to one colleague, but he also blamed Chirac for not getting involved and others (Raincourt?) for rallying too late. The Centrists and Independents hastily arranged a meeting to find a challenger and Hoeffel beat Raincourt. Hoeffel did better - 109 votes - but so did Poncelet with 125. He was elected in the third with 189 votes, as 37 majority senators spoiled their ballots.

During the feverish negotiations, Philippe Séguin, then chair of the RPR, had repeated the old adage that the election of their speaker was nobody's business but that of senators. No-one really believed that. 'We are losing the Senate', exclaimed Hubert Falco (URI), 'and not one of our leaders is here'. *Le Monde*'s headline the following day was unambiguous: 'Chirac seizes the Senate' ran its front page.[10] In fact, Chirac had little time for the senator for the Vosges, but he recognised the blow that had been dealt to the UDF.

Poncelet's first term can be characterised by two strands. On the one hand he had to steer a course between a fractious majority, a demanding President and a hostile government. On the other, he pursued his manifesto pledge to 'renovate' the Senate (the word appeared no fewer than three times in his inaugural address) and make it the *chambre de collectivités locales*.[11] He managed both with reasonable success. Parity and *décumul* legislation passed on the Senate's terms and the government's reforms of the upper house were kept to a minimum. There were major conflicts over the 35-hour week and the PACS, but they passed on the Assembly's last word. At the same time, while the government appointed a commission, chaired by Pierre Mauroy, to examine the way forward with decentralisation, Poncelet launched a parallel Senate committee. The result was *Pour une République territoriale*, a report that later provided the Raffarin government with a blueprint for reform. At the same time, under the guidance of the Senate's director of communications Alain Delcamp, the modernisation agenda and the determination to lead the way on local government reform were rapidly transforming the upper chamber into an information hub for France's local *élus*. Re-elected in 2001, Poncelet floated the idea of establishing an Observatoire de la Décentralisation, based at the Luxembourg Palace, though it remained on the drawing board until 2004. Between September 2001 and April 2002, the Senate majority was focused on preventing Jospin from getting to the Elysée, but in the end he did the job for them.

The sense of shock that Jean Marie Le Pen would go through to the second round was balanced with an equally profound sense of satisfaction that the hubris-drenched 'Monsieur Anomalie' had met his nemesis. The appointment of Raffarin as prime minister strengthened the institution's sense of well-being and the constitutional revision of 25 March 2003 marked a moment of triumph for speaker and assembly, when the principle that the Senate should have first sight of all legislation concerning local government was enshrined in the constitution (Article 39-2).

In fact, the hard work had only just begun. Raffarin set himself a target of 150 days to decentralise France and despite comfortable majorities in the two chambers, met with reservations in both, in the end resorting to Article 49-3 to push his plans through before the 2004 summer recess. Among those most critical of some of the content and the speed of the reforms was Poncelet.

In the meantime, the speaker had also been at work reforming the Senate. Chirac's re-election and the elevation of Raffarin had led some sections of the majority to think they would be spared any changes. Poncelet was summoned to the Elysée and told in very firm terms that the introduction of the *quinquennat* rendered the Senate's nine-year term untenable and that Chirac expected the upper house to make an effort. The upshot was the *loi Poncelet*.

Un mandat de trop?

Six years after his election, Poncelet had achieved the goals he had set himself: the Senate had been reformed, its pre-eminence over local government legislation had been established and the process of decentralisation had moved into new territory with subsidiarity and the right of experimentation inscribed in the constitution. A third goal, to assert the Senate's identity within the Republic by putting itself at the forefront of international bicameralism - through the organisation 'Sénats du Monde' for example - had seen the upper house raise its profile at home and abroad. The *loi Poncelet* had been enacted and the creation of a single UMP group had been negotiated relatively smoothly. In 1998, Poncelet had said he sought election for only six years and he could look back at a job well done.

As the 2004 spring session opened, however, Poncelet looked anything but a speaker preparing to step down. On the eve of the summer recess he wrote to UMP senators informing them of his decision to stay on. He made no attempt to worm his way out of the promises of 1998. Instead, he argued that the changes wrought since then called for continuity of leadership and asked to be allowed one more term. Another reason was that his potential successors were otherwise occupied. It was no secret that prime minister Raffarin aspired to be speaker one day and Gérard Larcher, labour relations minister, harboured similar ambitions. There were other potential candidates too for whom 2004 was too soon and who preferred a third Poncelet term to the election of a new, relatively young speaker, in much the same way as it suited Pasqua to keep Poher in office in 1989. Poncelet may have been very willing to stay on, but the fault for seeking a further term was by no means his alone.

Not all UMP senators agreed, and there was a challenge in the shape of Alain Lambert, maverick senator for the Orne. First elected as a Centrist in 1992, Lambert went straight to the finance commission, where he became *rapporteur général* in 1995 before succeeding Poncelet in the chair in 1998. Lambert was also known to harbour ambitions to be speaker, but in May 2002 Raffarin made him budget minister, which he remained until a reshuffle in March 2004. He returned to the Senate in a by-election in September and had hardly had time to build a platform, but he felt that there should at least be a contest. Lambert campaigned on refocusing the Senate on its parliamentary role and countering the feeling shared by many senators that the Luxembourg Palace had become a high-end conference centre. Committing himself to no more than a six-year term, Lambert piquantly reminded colleagues of Poncelet's promise. Poncelet won a UMP primary 95 to 49, but Lambert's score was honourable enough.

It was not long before disquiet resurfaced within the majority. In the summer of 2005 both *Le Monde* and *Le Canard enchaîné* published stories regarding Poncelet's financial affairs that did not reflect well on either speaker or Senate, though he naturally denied the allegations flatly.[12] Nevertheless, the whiff of scandal was a setback. Already, critics within his own party had begun to suggest that, like Poher before him, Poncelet was leaving the running of the chamber to his chief-of-staff, Alain Méar.[13] In the autumn of 2004, the *bureau* had postponed appointing a new general-secretary to the Senate and now, in June 2005, Méar was passed over in favour of Delcamp.[14] By July 2005 Patrick Roger, *Le Monde*'s Senate commentator was writing about an *fin de regne* ambiance in the Luxembourg Palace.[15]

Then, in the autumn, parliament had to decide what to do regarding the electoral calendar. With presidential, legislative and municipal elections due in the spring of 2007, to be followed by a *renouvellement* in September, the schedule looked too crowded. The Villepin government proposed leaving the two national elections in 2007 and putting the municipal elections back to March 2008, with the *renouvellement* to follow. There were some forthright objections to moving the Senate elections, but if the municipals were to move, leaving the *renouvellement* in 2007 made no sense. Adding an extra year to Poncelet's term was not, however, at all what some wanted and the *rentrée parlementaire* for 2005 was marked by various stories that the speaker had become *pohérisé*.[16] The elections of Sarkozy and the new majority in the lower house, together with new accusations against Poncelet, led to claims in the summer of 2007 that a palace coup was fomenting.[17] Quite who was behind this talk was never made clear. Each of the pretenders was discretion itself and none could hope to derive much benefit, unless Poncelet could be persuaded to resign early, which was always very unlikely. Then, during the summer of 2008, advanced publicity for a book by two journalists investigating the Senate's finances revealed that after retirement, Poncelet would enjoy the privilege for life of a luxurious Parisian apartment.[18] The reality was rather that Poncelet had, since 2004, lived in an apartment near the palace, not the Petit Luxembourg itself and he was at pains to insist that the lodging was not for life but until the end of his senatorial mandate in 2014.[19]

Mon bon Gérard

Le Sénat - Enquête sur les superprivilégiés de la République, by Robert Colonna d'Istria and Yvan Stefanovitch, was finally published in September 2008, just as the most publicised presidential election in the history of the Senate was reaching its climax. It was a campaign quite unlike any other. In the first place, the names of the principal candidates were public knowledge, not just a *secret de palais*, years in advance. Dismissed from office in May 2005 after the referendum over the EU constitution, Raffarin had returned to the Senate the following September and, as most pundits expected, began to prepare the ground for a tilt at the presidency, though he was careful to distance himself from any talk of an early push to replace Poncelet. The main threat to Raffarin came from Gérard Larcher, mayor of Rambouillet and senator for the Yvelines from 1986 until 2004, when Raffarin had brought him into government. Retained by Villepin but not by Fillon, Larcher's candidature was being talked about months before he returned to the Senate in October 2007. The networks he had built up as a vice-president of the Senate, as chair of the economic affairs commission and as an energetic and industrious member of countless other committees over nearly 20 years (compared to eight, all told, for Raffarin) made him a very serious obstacle to the former prime minister.

In time two other candidates emerged. In February 2008, and with the election of a new speaker as their *raison d'être*, five senior senators – the Centrist Arthuis, Lambert, Hubert Haenel (UMP, Haut-Rhin), Dominique Leclerc (UMP, Indre-et-Loire) and Philippe Marini (UMP, Oise) - set up 'Un nouvel élan pour le Sénat' to organise a series of workshops examining the Senate's responses to a range of issues. More than 70 colleagues contributed to the various fora, from which a candidate emerged in the shape not of Lambert, but of Marini, mayor of Compiègne and *rapporteur général* to the finance commission. Marini hoped to build a broad consensus within the majority and to overcome the RPR/UDF division that appeared to be re-emerging with the Raffarin-Larcher stand-off.[20] He even went as far as to suggest a primary of the whole majority including the UC and pro-government members of the RDSE. Finally, Jean-Claude Gaudin, first vice-president, mayor of Marseille and one of the few UMP success stories of the municipal elections, refused to rule out standing.

'Un nouvel élan pour le Sénat' (Marini); 'Pour un Sénat libre et moderne' (Raffarin) ; 'Nouveau cap [course] pour le Sénat' (Larcher). The manifestoes told their own story. The content did not differ very greatly from one to the other, but they underlined, individually and collectively, how anxious UMP senators had become by the time they met on 24 September 2008 in the salle Clemenceau to close the Poncelet chapter. There were, in the end, just three candidates. Gaudin could not stand if Raffarin did – they would cancel each other out and he had far too many commitments in Marseille, though he only took the final decision on the eve of the ballot. The contest between Raffarin and Larcher was expected to be tight: UMP senators for the brand new *collectivités* of Saint-Martin and Saint-Barthélemy were even flown in. Marini remained an outsider, but looked to win enough votes in the first round to play kingmaker in exchange, perhaps, for the chair of the finance commission.[21] In fact, the contest was over in the first round. Larcher took 78 of the 152 votes cast, giving him an absolute majority. Raffarin's 56 votes and Marini's 17 became purely academic.

There are various explanations for Larcher's triumph, though the simplest and most convincing is that the old RPR had no intention of letting the *plateau* slip from its grasp. That was certainly Poncelet's view: 'I didn't expect everything to be settled in the first round. The Gaullist vote must have gone with Larcher'.[22] This was always going to be Raffarin's main stumbling block. As early as January 2008, Patrick Roger, *Le Monde*'s Senate correspondent, suggested that Raffarin, who had done so much to make the UMP a reality, might find the old RPR insurmountable. Raffarin's problems began, Roger suggested, on 16 December 2007, with the death of Serge Vinçon, UMP senator for the Cher and chairman of the foreign affairs commission. He was replaced by Josselin de Rohan, the veteran Chiraquian chair of the UMP and before that of the RPR group. His place at the head of the UMP went to Henri de Raincourt, formerly an Independent. Outwardly this might seem to suit Raffarin, but as Roger pointed out, it was unlikely the old RPR majority within the UMP would allow the old URI to hold the presidency of the Senate and the chair of the group.[23] After the election, Raffarin made no secret of the fact that he suspected Raincourt of secretly supporting Larcher in safeguard his own position.[24] The Raffarin camp also accused other senior majority figures, keen to maintain their positions in the chair of this or that commission, of backing Larcher: change at the top was not reflected elsewhere.[25]

For some, the former prime minister was too much in the public eye. For others, he spoke too often and too openly of his relationship with Sarkozy: fiercely defensive of their independence from outside interference, some senators feared Raffarin might be too willing to toe the Presidential line, despite his own claims to the contrary. That argument might appear outwardly difficult to square with the very strong and credible rumour that Larcher was the Elysée's preferred candidate: 'mon bon Gérard' as Sarkozy called him. The two men were close enough, in 2002, for Sarkozy to sound Larcher out about a ministerial portfolio, had he been called upon to form a government after Chirac's re-election. According to Henri Guaino, one of Sarkozy's closest advisors at the Elysée, 'Gérard knows Nicolas better than he lets on.' During his difficult moments with Fillon, the President could be heard to say, 'In any case, there's always Gérard'. But Larcher also knew how to say no without causing offence. When Sarkozy thought of appointing him minister of agriculture, Larcher's reply was to the point: 'If you have got something against me running for speaker of the Senate, then say so'.[26] And if the President showed no outwards signs of favouring one or other candidate, the prime minister certainly pushed Larcher's case.[27] The senator-mayor of Rambouillet remained discrete about his relations with both the Elysée and Matignon. An ability to appear all things to all men, and yet remain his own master was not the least of Larcher's qualities.

Still, the sense that the RPR had rallied to their man caused anger in the UMP. Lambert expressed his fury that the old RPR would add the Petit Luxembourg to the Hôtels Lassay and Matignon and the Elysée, though one also sensed a thwarted ambition. He had already spoken, before the primary, of running in the official election and he restated his intention afterwards too.[28] In the event, Lambert withdrew on the morning of the election. Michel Mercier announced his candidature at midday on 1 October, only to withdraw it again an hour before the sitting began, amid claims from the left that the he had been bought off with the promise of a vice-presidency for the UC. In response, the CRC withdrew their candidate, allowing Jean-Pierre Bel a clear run. Larcher was elected in the first round with 173 votes to 134 for Bel, but there were 19 votes cast for non-candidate and *questeur* René Garrec two for Raffarin and 11 spoilt or blank papers.

The executive *bureau* and the *conférence des présidents*

Although the president of the Senate has ultimate responsibility for all that happens within the Luxembourg Palace, he is assisted by two groups of senators: the *bureau* and the *conférence des présidents*. The function of the *bureau* is to oversee the administration of the Senate and to ensure that legislative business is conducted smoothly. It comprises 26 senators: the speaker, eight vice-presidents, three *questeurs* and 14 secretaries. Like the speaker, the *bureau* is elected after the *renouvellement* for a three-year term. The vice-presidents and the *questeurs* are elected in public session, at the tribune and by secret, multi-name ballot. The nomination of the secretaries is different in character and intent and is described below.

The principal function of the vice-presidents, as their title suggests, is to replace the speaker when he is otherwise preoccupied or indisposed: it is not unusual to see the chair change three or four times in the course of a sitting. Vice-presidents are usually prominent, long-serving members of the Senate, but the position has seldom been used as a platform for direct election to the presidency, though Larcher was a past vice-president. There were originally four, and then six after the election of Monory, an increase the opposition anticipated would result in each group being allocated a vice-presidency. They were most indignant when this did not happen. The increase to eight followed Larcher's election and gave some credence to the suggestions that Mercier had stood down on the promise of a vice-presidency for his group.

Table 7.3 - **Vice-presidential elections 2008**

7 October 2008	Group	Votes (335)
Catherine Tasca	Soc	278
Monique Papon	UMP	274
Roland du Luart	UMP	257
Jean-Claude Gaudin	UMP	254
Roger Romani	UMP	247
Bernard Frimat	Soc	234
12 November 2008	**Group**	**Votes (320)**
Jean-Léonce Dupont	UC	222
Guy Fisher	CRC	187

The vice-presidents are elected at the next sitting following the election of the speaker. In 2008 this fell on 7 October and the groups made a determined effort to achieve a consensus. There were only six candidates for the posts and by careful planning two *sénatrices* were elected first and second vice-presidents. The expansion was completed in November 2008, with an amendment to the standing orders and it was no surprise that the UC and the Communiste, Républicain et Citoyen group (CRC) took one each.

The role of the *questeurs* is to oversee the general management of the Senate on behalf of the *bureau*. They take responsibility for the assembly's space, the allocation of offices and the important matter of who sits where in the *hémicycle*. They are responsible for all services within the Senate and administer the disbursement of grants agreed upon by the finance commission and applications for funding for commissions of enquiry or *missions d'information*. The *questeurs* share responsibility with the speaker for the policing of the Palace precinct. On the whole, they are regarded as the bulldogs of the *bureau* and no senator looks forward to being summoned to their office. The three posts are generally split 2:1 between the majority and the opposition and since good *questeurs* are hard to find, they often serve two or more terms.

The standing orders require that all political groups, including the *réunion des sénateurs non-inscrits,* should be represented within the *bureau*. The group chairs meet to ensure that the allocation of the secretarial posts completes this requirement before the candidatures are formally put to the assembly for ratification by a proportional system. Table 7.4 below details the distribution of posts in February 2009. The representation on the *bureau* is a reasonable match up to each group's proportional size in the Senate, though the UMP has a clear preponderance of the more senior posts. Although it is not a requirement, it is also practice to use the secretarial posts to represent different categories of senators: thus, among the secretaries in 2009 there was a senator for French expatriates and two from the overseas departments.

Table 7.4 - **The Senate *bureau*, February 2009**

	P	V-P	Q	S	Total
UMP	1	4	2	4	11
UC-UDF	/	1	/	1	2
RDSE	/	/	/	1	1
Soc	/	2	1	6	9
CRC	/	1	/	1	2
NI	/	/	/	1	1

The secretaries' principal role is to provide administrative support during public sittings and ensure business is carried out as smoothly as possible. They oversee voting procedures, production of the parliamentary record and countersign, with the speaker, the formal record of debates. The standing orders require a minimum of two to be present at the tribune at any given time, but if this condition cannot be fulfilled, the speaker may call on the two youngest senators present. Being a secretary carries some prestige, but it is hard work and few seek a second successive term. On the other hand, there is no better means of getting to understand the ways of the house and many senators with ambitions to go further in the *bureau*, in one of the commissions, or within their group signal their intentions by serving as a secretary.

While the *bureau* handles the administrative side of the Senate's operations, the *conférence des présidents* is responsible for the daily agenda, the time allotted to each group and speaker in debates, the general timetable and monitoring the progress being made by commissions. First established in 1921 (ten years after the Chamber) its function was to assist the speaker in coping with the weight of legislation. Although the 1958 constitution handed control of parliamentary time over to the government, the *conférence* was not abolished, though it met infrequently: the standing orders do not stipulate how often the *conférence* should meet, only that it may meet once a week when parliament is sitting. At times under Poher, who preferred to run business through his own office and the *bureau*, the *conférence* barely met every six months. Under his successors, however, meetings have become frequent and cooperation between the *conférence* and the *bureau* is much closer within the Senate and with their counterparts in the National Assembly.

The *conférence* is a hybrid, *ex officio* body. It is chaired by the speaker. The vice-presidents are members, along with the chairs of the six permanent commissions, the *rapporteur général* of the finance commission, the presidents of the political groups (including a delegate representing the *non-inscrits*), and the chair of delegation to the European Union. The *conférence* can also invite the chair of any special commission whose contribution might be pertinent to join its deliberations.

The *conférence*'s principal function is to examine the order in which the government wants legislation to be discussed and to fix the timetable accordingly. To facilitate the task, the government may send a representative to meetings, but only one. On occasion, prime ministers have found the time to attend (e.g. Rocard in 1988, Balladur in 1993), but generally the minister responsible for relations with parliament fulfils this task. Most of the *conférence*'s deliberations are spent deciding which senators will speak and for how long in which debate. Time for debate, being precious, is allocated to groups according to a formula that ensures they each have a fixed minimum and that any remaining time reflects their size, but the running order of speakers is not always the same: the Senate observes a practice whereby the group whose senator spoke first in one debate goes last in the next and then moves up the running order accordingly. The *conférence* also has responsibility for deciding which sittings will be set aside purely for the discussion of private bills.

The Republic of committees

Few senators reach the giddy heights of the *bureau* or the *conférence*, but all serve on one or other of the Senate's permanent commissions, which, as any senator will freely tell you, is where the real work is done. The choice of the term *commission* dates from the early Third Republic and reflects the dislike of the word *comité*, with its overtone of permanence and its echo of the Revolutionary Committee of Public Safety, but the idea that the commissions were temporary was pure fiction from the outset. The core commissions very quickly became permanent *de facto* and membership changed only slowly. With governments turning over regularly, commissions became enormously powerful, provided stability and served as the nursery for potential ministers. The Senate was the first chamber in the 1870s to provide permanent accommodation for its commissions and even before the decision had been taken in 1879 to move parliament back to Paris, some Senate commissions were meeting in the capital to be close to the ministries.[29] In 1921 the standing orders were reformed to meet the requirements of the huge increase in the volume of legislation. Commissions were divided into two categories: *générales* (i.e. permanent) and *spéciales*. At the beginning of the Republic commissions had a chairman, a secretary and a *rapporteur*, but the reform expanded this by two vice-presidents and a second secretary, as well as a staff of increasingly specialised civil servants. Until 1921 the size of the commissions varied according to their importance but now the permanent ones were fixed at 36 with each senator limited to just two each. Presidents of the permanent commissions came to carry enormous influence and several used these as the springboard to other things. Clemenceau, for example, chaired both the defence and the foreign affairs commissions before becoming prime minister in 1917.

The Fourth Republic replicated the system and by 1958 the Council of the Republic had 19 permanent commissions, to say nothing of the various sub-committees. Debré wielded the axe. Article 43 of the constitution imposed a limit of six on each assebmly, but left it up to members to decide how the responsibilities would be divided up. The Senate's commissions are detailed below in Table 7.5 in the order they appear in the standing orders. The Fifth Republic also limited each senator to one commission.

Table 7.5 - **Senate commissions and membership, February 2009**

Commission	
Cultural Affairs	56
Economic Affairs and National Planning	78
Foreign Affairs, Defence and the Armed Forces	56
Social Affairs	56
Finance, Budgetary Control and National Economy	48
Constitutional Laws, Legislation, Universal Suffrage, Standing Orders and General Administration	48

The size of each commission is a function of the range of delegated responsibilities: the cultural affairs commission, for example, covers not only cultural policy, but education, *la francophonie* and the media: it is no surprise, then, that Pasqua headed there when he first became a senator in 1977. Each commission elects its own internal *bureau*. Like the Senate itself, the first meeting of each commission is managed by a *bureau d'âge*. In theory, the commissions are free to elect their own chairs, but these are always decided in advance between the majority groups and there are seldom any surprises. The number of vice-presidents varies from one commission to another. Most have seven, though the finance commission has eight, despite being one of the smallest. It is also the only commission to have a *rapporteur général*. The commissions also have a number of secretaries: one per group of ten commissioners. Apart from the chair (and the *rapporteur général*) other posts within the commission are distributed across the groups. Until the mid-eighties, it was a tradition to allocate the chair of one of the commissions to the opposition. This changed, however, with the *RPR-isation* of the upper chamber. Unable to take the post of speaker, in 1986 the RPR insisted that it should, however, have the chairs of two commissions. To accommodate these demands, Poncelet took the chair of the finance commission, while the Socialist Léon Eeckhoutte was removed from cultural affairs and replaced by the redoubtable and emblematic figure of Maurice Schumann. At the time of writing, four of the chairs are held by the UMP, two by Centrists (Arthuis at finance and Nicolas About at social affairs).

The two most prestigious commissions are also the two smallest; finance and legislation. They are important not only in the broad legislative sense, but also have significant roles to play in the organisation of the upper house. The weight and influence of the chair of the legislation commission, which oversees the standing orders is self-evident. What is less generally known is the role of the finance commission as the body responsible for managing the Senate's impressive internal budget. Its chair wields influence not only over discussion of the national budget, but also over the disbursement of grants, applications for subventions, internal auditing and the presentation of the Senate's accounts. At the height of his campaign for speaker in 1998, Christian Poncelet, then chairman of the commission, was heard to joke that he had no money left with which to bribe colleagues. It *was* a joke of course, but a decade later, amid allegations of corruption and a lack of transparency, the joke had a different resonance. Given the UMP's reliance on the UC for a majority, Marini's attempt to use his campaign for speaker to lever himself into the chair of the finance commission, if that is what it really was, looked doomed. Had that happened, the UC would have demanded a far higher price for their co-operation than just a vice-presidency.

Elections to the commissions are held after every *renouvellement*, using a proportional formula that ensures that each group is represented on each commission. These elections can be a real headache for the group chairs, as they try to reconcile each individual senator's wishes with his or her field(s) of expertise, to ensure that more experienced members retain their seats where they can be most effective, respect the proportional balance of the groups within the assembly and fulfil promises made for services rendered.

Political groups and political balance

The political groups have not been officially established when the speaker is elected, but the rest of the *bureau* and the commissions cannot be constituted until lists of members have been formally drawn up. This is why there is often a gap of a week between the election of the speaker and the rest of the *bureau* and of the appointment of the commissions, while a whole series of complex negotiations take place within and between the groups.

Political groups are freely constituted within the Senate, but must have a minimum of 15 members and no senator can be a member of more than one. Senators may be full members of a group or they may become either *apparentés* or *rattachés* individually or as sub-groups.[30] The distinction between these two is not altogether clear, even to insiders, though *apparentés* are closer than *rattachés*. In any case, when it comes to calculating the numbers of members of the *bureau* or commissions, these two sub-categories are included and of course therein lies the advantage to both parties. Unlike the standing orders of the National Assembly, where the minimum for a group to be officially recognised is 20 without *apparentés* or *rattachés*, in the Senate, these can help a group to survive. Senators who prefer to preserve their independence are described as *non-inscrits*, but even they are recognised as a *réunion*, with a delegate to the *conférence des présidents* to ensure that their interests are represented and that they obtain seats on the commissions.

When he complained that the Senate was an anomaly because there was no chance of political *alternance* between majorities, Jospin was expressing his exasperation at having to deal with an upper house whose right-wing majority looked impregnable. But Jospin himself might also have reflected on how it was that the right, rather than the left, had taken control of the Senate in the 1980s. The Socialists (then known as the SFIO) were anything but senatophobic in the early years of the regime. As we have already seen in Chapter 2, in the 1960s the Senate looked like a relic of the Third Force politics, with the Gauche Démocratique as its hinge. This balance hardly changed in the course of the first electoral cycle, except that the Gauche Démocratique went into steady decline, while the Centre Démocrate developed as the dynamic force within the majority bloc, leading to Poher's election in 1968.

Table 7.6 - Political groups 1959-68

Group	1959	1962	1965	1968
Communiste	15	15	15	18
Socialiste	60	52	52	52
Gauche Démocratique	66	50	50	43
MRP/Centre Démocrate/UCDP	34	35	38	47
Indépendants/URI	73	65	64	54
CRARS/RIAS	20	20	17	19
UNR/UDR/RPR	37	32	30	36
Non-inscrits	6	6	9	14

Nine years later the balance did not seem so very different. The Socialists, (now reinvented as the PS) and the Communists had rediscovered the secret to winning seats in the upper chamber. By then, of course, politics had moved on. From 1972 the PS and PCF were allied under the Common Programme, which the Communists tore up on the eve of the 1977 *renouvellement* but which still brought benefits to both, to the point where the Socialists became the largest single group. In response Radicalism had split in two, with the Mouvement des Radicaux de Gauche (MRG) stepping to the left, while the Radical Party fell in behind the governing majorities under Pompidou and Giscard. The Gauche Démocratique, however, never did split, so that it and its present day heir, the Rassemblement Démocratique et Social Européen contains senators of the majority and the opposition. In 1978, the Radical Party joined the Centrists and the Independents under the UDF umbrella, but the three components continued to exist separately. The Independents and their CRARS/RIAS allies had continued to decline against the Centrists. And despite a brief upsurge in 1968, when the new seats created by the reorganisation of the Paris region came on-stream, Gaullism remained a marginal force.

Table 7.7 - **Political groups 1971-7**

Group	1971	1974	1977
Communiste	18	20	23
Socialiste	49	51	62
Gauche Démocratique	38	35	40
MRP/Centre Démocrate/UCDP	46	54	61
Indépendants/URI	59	58	52
CRARS/RIAS[31]	16	15	15
UNR/UDR/RPR	38	30	33
Non-inscrits	19	19	9

The situation by the end of the third cycle (1980-1986) could hardly have been more different. The roots of the transformation of Gaullist fortunes in the Senate can be traced to the 1977 *renouvellement* and personified by one man: Charles Pasqua. A Gaullist activist since the 1940s, Pasqua set aside any dislike of the Senate that still hung over from 1969, recognising the platform the upper chamber could offer the right if the left got into power, which looked a very strong possibility on the eve of the 1978 general elections. To this end, when the RPR, was launched, he insisted that the chairs of the party groups in the National Assembly and the Senate should be *ex officio* vice-presidents of the party and took over the latter post himself in October 1981. At the same time, he launched an offensive aimed at supplanting the Centrists and Independents as *the* party of the notables. While Chirac, the old Radical-Socialist *manqué* charmed the local *élus*, Pasqua placed an electoral machine at their disposal.

Table 7.8 - **Political Groups 1980-6**

Group	1980	1983	1986
Communiste	23	24	15
Socialiste	69	70	64
RDSE	37	38	35
Union Centriste	67	72	70
URI	52	49	54
RPR	41	58	77
Non-Inscrits	13	5	4

The impact was remarkable. Although the presidential and general elections in 1981 were a disaster for the right, cantonal elections to half France's departmental assemblies in 1982 showed that the electoral tide that had flowed towards the Socialists for much of the 1970s had turned. Municipal elections the following year confirmed the trend. Chirac's RPR-UDF alliance completed a grand slam of all 20 Parisian *arrondissements* and elsewhere in France's 220 largest towns (more than 30,000 inhabitants) the right won control of 39 councils and lost just 4, bringing it to within eight of the left's total (114 to 106). The RPR overtook the UDF as the predominant right-wing party in France's 36,000 *mairies*.[32] This success translated quickly and impressively to the Senate. By 1986 the RPR had overhauled the Socialists and the Centrists. Despite only a moderate performance in the 1989 municipal elections, the RPR's expansion continued unchecked, with another 14 seats gained.

The growth of the RPR can partly be accounted for by the availability of new seats, but it was also in part due to the decline of the Radicals and the Communists in France's town halls. Once the pivot of the upper house, by 1989 the Gauche Démocratique had fewer than two dozen members. In an attempt to modernise its image the group changed its name to the Rassemblement Démocratique Européen (RDE), later becoming Rassemblement Démocratique et Social Européen (RDSE) to please its MRG members, but in 2004 the group nearly disappeared altogether. As for the Communists, its brief renaissance at the end of the 1970s and the beginning of the 1980s came to a dramatic end in the 1986 *renouvellement* of series C, which included most of its Francilian heartlands. By 1992 the group relied on a *rattaché* for its continued existence and three years later changed its name to Communiste, Républicain et Citoyen (CRC) to acknowledge that it now recruited members from outside the party. The change paid dividends. Six years later the CRC overtook the RDSE and has maintained a steady level since. At the end of the 2008, the group modified its name to reflect the recruitment of Jean-Luc Mélenchon, who left the PS to found the Parti de la Gauche.

Table 7.9 - **Political groups 1989-98**

Group	1989	1992	1995	1998	2001
Communiste/CRC	16	15	15	16	23
Socialiste	66	70	75	78	83
RDSE	23	23	24	23	19
Union Centriste	68	66	59	52	53
URI	52	47	46	47	40
RPR	91	90	94	99	96
Non-Inscrits	5	10	8	6	6

The Socialists stood still during the 1980s, but the 1992 *renouvellement* proved to be a turning point. Given that it was based on the same municipal elections as 1989, it seems strange that the RPR should have lost seats, but this is where the geographical distribution of the series (B in this case) came into play and favoured the PS, who despite facing general election defeat climbed back to their own high water mark of 70 seats in the Senate, previously achieved in 1983 in the same series. After the general election in March 1993, there were more senators than deputies in the parliamentary party.

The 1995 *renouvellement* was rather paradoxical. The right was riven by the fallout from the Chirac-Balladur contest for the Elysée. Gaudin, who was put in charge of trying to reconcile the factions, did his best, but the UDF continued to lose seats. The RPR, on the other hand, demonstrated as it had in 1992 over Maastricht and would again after the 1997 dissolution, that it was rather more robust. Further RPR gains in 1998, losses for the UC and the near collapse of the UDF meant that the time was right at last to take the *plateau*, albeit with the help of a couple of dozen Independents.

The *gauche plurielle*'s attempts to reform the Senate are detailed in Chapter 4 above. In the end the only change that took place was the reduction of the threshold for PR. However modest the change, it yielded results for the left in 2001. And, as Table 7.10 overleaf shows, even though the threshold was raised again for 2004, the CRC held steady while the PS expanded at a faster rate than even the RPR managed in the 1980s, gaining 14 seats in 2004 and 20 in 2008. Some of those gains have been made due to the increase in the number of seats following the *loi Poncelet*, but the increases also helped the right to restrict their losses.

Victory for Jospin in the 2002 Presidential election would have ushered in a fascinating phase for the Senate. Instead Chirac was overwhelmingly re-elected and used the subsequent general election to create an electoral coalition, the Union pour une Majorité Présidentielle, which duly metamorphosed into a party, the Union pour un Mouvement Populaire. In the Assembly it was only natural that there should be a single UMP group, given that so many deputies had relied on government endorsement for their seats, but in the upper chamber, untouched but not unaffected by events, majority senators saw no real reason to abandon their traditions and practices. There was already an unofficial majority *intergroupe* chaired by Raincourt. Things were not viewed, however, the same way by Chirac nor by Raffarin. Raincourt, Poncelet and RPR chair Josselin de Rohan were instructed to set up a single entity, though it was December before the UMP group made its official debut in the Senate. All 94 RPR senators joined and 40 of the 41 Independents. Only 29 of 54 Centrists switched, four of the 21 RDSE senators and one *non-inscrit*. For the first time since before the First World War, one group held an absolute majority in the upper chamber. Rohan became chair.

Table 7.10 - **Political groups 2003-2009**

Group	2003	2004	2008	2009
CRC-SPG[33]	23	23	23	24
Socialiste	82	96	116	115
RDSE	17	15	17	17
Union Centriste	27	33	29	29
UMP	166	154	151	151
Non-Inscrits	5	7	7	7
Total	**320**	**328**	**343**	**343**

The UMP's position did not survive the 2004 *renouvellement*. Despite their moderate performance in the 2001 municipal elections, the fact that the PR threshold had risen again and that there were more seats available, the Socialists could be delighted with the outcome. Henceforth the UMP would have to rely on the Centrists support, though the chairs of two commissions and other posts secured that quite easily.

One of the paradoxes of elections in France in the period 2002 to 2008 was the ability of the right to win impressive victories at the national level, but to lose local elections. Raffarin discovered, in regional and departmental elections in 2004, that while most people in France think decentralisation is a good thing, no one will vote for it. Then, after Sarkozy's comfortable win over Royal and the equally straightforward victory in the general election, in March 2008, the government performed poorly in the municipal elections. The effect was bound to be felt in the Senate, where an extra twelve seats came on stream. Officially, the PS reckoned they might gain ten or a dozen, though their analysts knew the figure might well be double that. The majority was clearly worried and Alain Marleix, minister for state reform and local government and UMP elections officer, was hard put to limit the damage. On paper he appeared to have managed the process quite well. The UMP returned only three senators down. In fact the new seats masked a catastrophic performance and a little more discipline among the opposition might have made it worse.

La gauche au pouvoir?

Interviewed by *La chaine parlementaire-Public Sénat* in the salle des conférences on the afternoon of Larcher's formal election, Jean-Pierre Bel was asked if he expected that, three years later, it might be him or a colleague whose elevation was being anticipated. Bel commented simply that, in politics, tomorrow's promises count for nothing. His caution was understandable but also partly rhetorical. Until it really does win a majority in the Senate, the left will continue (rightly) to underline the democratic deficit in the upper house, the imbalances between and among the electoral colleges and the disparities of representation from one commune to another. Bel was simply repeating the same mantra that his colleagues had been chanting since March 2008, deliberately underestimating likely gains in order to underline the iniquities of a system where the PS, with or without its allies, controlled 20 regional assemblies, a majority of departmental ones, had taken an impressive number of seats on municipal councils, and yet would not break the grip of the right on an assembly supposed to represent local authorities.

The possibility of a Socialist victory in the 2011 *renouvellement* is beset by imponderables. It will be the first time that the new series will function. *Série 1* features 170 seats: 165 outgoing and the last tranche of the new ones created in 2003. Of these, 108 will be elected by PR, 53 in the Ile-de-France, 18 in the Nord-Pas-de-Calais. Superficially, given the progress made by the left in 2004, the distribution of departments in *série 1*, set against the results of the 2008 municipal elections, it is perfectly possible that the Socialists will become the largest single group in the Senate. For opposite reasons to the PS, the UMP tell anyone willing to listen that this is not only possible but inevitable.

Table 7.11 - **Sortants in 2011 by group**

Group	Seats in Series 1	Total
CRC-SPG	19	24
SOC	48	115
RDSE	5	17
UC	19	29
UMP	71	151
NI	3	7

The Socialists will go into the election in good shape and with the most to gain. Their 48 seats (*rattachés* and *apparentés* included) represent less than half of their complement and although some of the seats they took in 2001 came thanks to the temporary lowering of the PR threshold, they can certainly hope for a similar return to 2008. The UMP has the most to lose, with 71 seats up for election.

The unknowns of the contest, however, will be the UC, which comprises members of both Bayrou's Mouvement Démocratique (MoDém) and Hervé Morin's Nouveau Centre, and the various components of the CRC-SPG group. Both are very vulnerable, with 19 *sortants* in the *renouvellement*. Deals will probably be made on a department-by-department basis, but all the parties will be trying to anticipate the post-electoral impact on the balance of the upper chamber. It is not impossible to imagine a Senate where the UMP and Socialist groups cancel each other out, leaving the Centrists and the CRC-SPG, or even the RDSE if it survives, to hold the balance. Relations between the PS and the parties on its left are volatile and a great deal may depend on relations in the run-up to the Presidential and general elections in 2012. Would the left really spurn the opportunity to seize control of such a 'formidable war machine'? Left-wing *sénatophobie* can surely be no more deep-rooted or strategically inept than that of the Gaullists in the 1970s. Bel is right, nevertheless, to err on the side of caution. *Alternance* is a possibility, but by no means a certainty.

Conclusion

A quoi sert le Sénat?

President Larcher delivered his inaugural address to colleagues on 14 October 2008. It contained no surprises. Indeed, one would be hard-pressed to find a finer précis of the Senate's *structures structurantes*. All the themes of his election manifesto were reprised and in his opening comments he repeated the necessity to set a new course for the Senate, though on close examination, it looked like the old course repackaged. The 'nouveau cap', he stressed, would be fixed on two points: restating the pre-eminence of the national and local *élu* in politics and asserting the Senate's autonomy of thought and deed. Larcher's *feuille de route* (road map) for the next three years broke down into three parts. In the first, he outlined how he intended to reshape the Senate internally; in the second he focussed its place in the wider political process and thirdly he outlined the necessity to improve the Senate's public image.[1]

Larcher reiterated his commitment to being the president of all 343 senators, insisting on collegial consensus as his management model through better co-ordination of the work of the *bureau* and the *conférence des présidents*. This sort of pious wish was not so very different from those expressed by his predecessors at the beginning of their terms. Larcher added an extra layer, promising to give greater status to the opposition, through the distribution of chairs and *rapporteur*-ships on commissions of enquiry and *missions temporaries*, though not, it should be noted, on the permanent commissions. At no point did he suggest a return to the *status quo ante* 1986.

The broader challenges facing the Senate were not difficult to anticipate. With the formal appointment of the second Balladur committee just days away, Larcher announced the creation of a cross-party *mission temporaire* to examine the organisation of local government. He restated the Senate's commitment to its work with the EU as well as its role in continuing the dialogue among second chambers around the world, an initiative for which he saluted 'mes prédecesseurs'. (There was no applause at this point, though the cameras of the parliamentary television channel picked out Poncelet, who remained unmoved. An equally eloquent silence had accompanied Larcher's thanks to Poncelet in his brief speech following his election.) But above all, the 2008 revision of the constitution presented a number of challenges for the Senate and Larcher undertook to head a committee (the *conférence des présidents* under a different title) that would examine how the upper chamber should respond to the new balance between institutions, especially with regard to the raised status of the commissions and to the first block of organic laws putting the reform into action, due to be debated in the forthcoming session.

Larcher did not mince his words with regard to the shadow of sleaze hanging over the house. There must be transparency, and while he insisted on the Senate's right to autonomous management of its finances, he promised a freeze on the budget for 2009 and that, in the course of the year, the upper chamber's accounts would be subject to external audit. At this point the cameras picked out a rather stern-looking Jean Arthuis. Larcher also touched, briefly, on the possibility of *autoréforme*, but left the question hanging tantalisingly in mid-air. Whether this was simply a reference to according a greater role to the opposition or to pursuing reform of the electoral colleges was not made clear.

The Senate's legitimacy, Larcher concluded, lay in its role as a parliamentary assembly acting autonomously as a *chambre de législation* and a *chambre de contrôle*; it must renew its relationship with citizens and local *élus* through direct communication and not allow others to misrepresent its work and he demanded that his colleagues attack the task with energy. 'In three years time' he concluded, 'I want it to be impossible for anyone to ask – "what does the Senate do"?'

La chambre de tous les dangers

No-one doubted that the new speaker would tackle the task energetically. A notorious *gourmand*, Larcher is renowned among friends and opponents alike for having an equally voracious appetite for work. 'Heavily built but agile, like a wild boar', is how one commentator described him.[2] Larcher's energy and his preference to get the day off to an early start was a shock to some of his collaborators, but perhaps goes back to his days as a veterinary, specialising in equine medicine, being called out early to the gallops. In any case, from the outset Larcher's Senate proved to be a more difficult partner than the government might have anticipated. On the day of his inaugural, he welcomed to the *hémicycle* Christine Boutin, the controversial and enigmatic housing minister, who like Larcher comes from the Yvelines. Boutin had come to participate in the debate over measures to tackle the crisis in the provision of affordable housing.[3] The bill passed, but only after a marathon, week-long debate punctuated by the passage of several crucial amendments. Worse for the government, when it came to article 17 of its bill, concerning the responsibilities of local authorities to provide fixed levels of social housing, left and right rallied to reject the proposals by an impressive 314 votes to 21.[4]

Other legislation faced the same challenge. In January 2009, the Senate made a significant amendment to an organic law completing Article 13 of the constitution, concerning the appointment by the President of the Republic of the heads of France Télévision, Radio France and the company responsible for broadcasting overseas. The government's text simply stated that nominations would be vetted by the cultural affairs committee of each chamber. Deputies added the stipulation that the appointment would only come into effect after ratification by the commissions. True to their own traditions, senators appended an extra condition, that the commissions could only ratify (or reject) the appointment after hearing the candidate in public. Deputies agreed at the second reading. Premier Fillon took a rather different view and exercised his right to refer the matter to the Constitutional Council.

Part of the problem for the government has been its own insistence on using the *urgence* procedure, a natural enough response by an administration that wants to be seen to be pushing on with its programme, but a risky strategy nevertheless, because it reduces the number of readings and enhances parliament's leverage. Senators on either side of the chamber have certainly seized the opportunity with both hands, encouraged by a speaker determined to raise his assembly's profile and its autonomy. Larcher is not, however, the only reason for the government's discomfort. Without the support of the Union Centriste there is no majority, which means that any bill that cannot go through on the National Assembly's last word, in particular any organic law affecting the Senate, and there are still a lot of them to be passed before the July 2008 revision is complete, will fail. Michel Mercier is, therefore, in a strong bargaining position, but he also needs to make sure he knows where to draw the line: to obtain what his group wants and still be in a position to negotiate in 2011. One suggestion that was floated to deal with Mercier if he became too difficult was to make him a minister. [5]

By the turn of 2009, both the Elysée and Matignon had come to regard the Senate as 'la chambre de tous les dangers' - even more dangerous and unpredictable terrain than the UMP majority in the lower house and its maverick chair, Jean-François Copé. Like Monnerville before him, Larcher's Senate is pushing the political envelope in ways the executive does not altogether appreciate and the revision of July 2008 gives it weapons with which to do this. With Edouard Balladur about to publish the findings of his enquiry into local government, the Elysée was, according to one insider, expecting 'un rude moment de virilité avec le Sénat' - stiff opposition. [6]

However rough and virile the encounter, it is certain that the Senate faces an eventful short- and long-term future. At the time of writing, it remains unclear whether Larcher will invite Jean-Jacques Hyest and the legislation commission to take the Raincourt proposal down from the shelf and revisit the question of restructuring the electoral colleges so that communes elect one municipal delegate per 700 inhabitants. If this is to happen, then time is of the essence: it cannot be enacted less than a year before the elections it will affect, so it must be passed by September 2010. The UMP's electoral analysts will need to do their sums very carefully to check that this will work in their party's favour. Nor is it clear whether or not the Constitutional Council will accept such a change without an amendment of Article 24-3, although the Council's recent declarations regarding the *découpage* of the constituency boundaries for the National Assembly suggests that the present *sages* are in a serious mood to correct inequalities of representation: the ruling in January 2009 that there was no case to be made for every department having two deputies reverses the existing jurisprudence.

What will the left do with the Senate if it wins a majority there in 2011 and then secures the Elysée and Bourbon Palaces in 2012? Abolition would be self-defeating. On the other hand, stripping out the existing edifice and replacing it with an assembly elected directly by PR on a regional basis, as Arnaud Montebourg and Bastien François suggested in their blueprint for a Sixth Republic, would create an institution that would, in time, come to contest the National Assembly's pre-eminence.[7] The more legitimate one makes a second chamber, the greater the risks to the first. The left might abolish Article 39-2. Restructuring the electoral colleges, if it has not already been done, would be a more likely outcome, as well as lowering the threshold for PR back to the 2001 level of three seats, assuming their electoral analysts think that will be profitable for the PS.

Another issue that may have to be tackled, by either left or right after 2014, is the distribution of seats. The *loi Poncelet* was out of date before it passed. Something along the lines of the proposals drafted by Patrice Gélard, recalibrating the *clé de répartition*, will need to be adopted, if the constitutional limit of 348 seats is not to be raised and disparity between departments corrected. If the Balladur report does lead to a radical redrawing of region and departmental boundaries (and advance leaks have even suggested the division and disappearance of some departments) and redefining their relationships, perhaps the time will come to think again of electing a group of regional senators, as Marcel Prélot suggested 40 years ago. Or even to create *ex officio* senators, the presidents of regional assemblies, for example. One can always be much more creative imagining the Senate than the National Assembly. People will continue to ask, notwithstanding, what it is for.

Notes

Introduction

1. Régis Debray in Hubert Dubost, *Genèse et enjeux de la laïcité*, (Montpellier: Labor et fides, 1990), p. 208
2. Gérard Longuet and Roger Karoutchi were among Sarkozy's inner circle of advisors, while Alain Lambert and Jean-Claude Gaudin worked the notables.
3. Unlike Raffarin in 2002, Fillon stood in the general election in June 2007, along with a dozen other members of his cabinet.
4. *Le Point*, 17 May 2007, p. 43.
5. Gaudin, mayor of Marseille, had returned to the Senate in 1998.
6. *Le Monde*, 21 April 1998.
7. Yves Weber, 'La crise du bicaméralisme', *Revue du droit public*, 88, 1972, pp. 573-602, p. 575
8. Pierre Mazet, 'Portrait du sénateur: La contribution de la doctrine et des acteurs à la production de l'image instituée de sénateur de la République', in Yves Poirmeur and Pierre Mazet, *Le métier politique en représentations*, (Paris: L'Harmattan, 1999), pp. 263-92, p. 265.
9. Pascal Jan, 'La place, le rôle constitutionnel et l'influence du Sénat', *Pouvoirs locaux*, 67, 4/2005, pp. 48-53, p. 50.
10. 'Dans cette maison... on a le temps de se haïr' - *Le Monde*, 3 octobre 1998.
11. Jean Mastias, *Le Sénat de la Cinquième République. Réforme et Renouveau*, (Paris: Economica, 1980), p. 78.
12. *Journal Officiel, Documents, Sénat*, session 2006-2007, no.43. The authors were Patrice Gélard (UMP, Seine-Maritime) and Jean-Claude Peyronnet (PS, Haute-Vienne).
13. Jean Grangé, 'Les déformations de la représentation des collectivités territoriales et de la population au Sénat', *Revue française de science politique*, 40(1), pp. 5-45, p. 41.
14. *Le Monde*, 12 June 2008.
15. 'Royal met le Sénat en émoi', *Le Nouvel observateur*, 15 September 2005, <tempsreel.nouvelobs.com/actualites/ 20050915.OBS9294> (23 February 2009).

1 - Bicameralism and political culture in the French Republic

1. Charles Chesnelong, in Joseph Barthélemy, 'La mise en accusation devant le Sénat du Président et des ministres', *Revue du droit public*, 3-4, (July-December 1918), p. 90.
2. Cf. Sudhir Hazareesingh, 'Defining the Republican Good Life: Second Empire Municipalism and the Emergence of the Third Republic', *French History*, 11, 3, (Oxford 1997), pp. 310-337.
3. Quoted in Max Ginovès, 'Le Sénat: grand conseil des communes de France ? Etude comparative des assemblées parlementaires de la Vème République', (Aix-Marseille Law thesis 1987), p. 15.
4. Joseph Barthélemy, 'Les résistances du Sénat', *Revue du droit public*, 30, (1913), pp. 371-410, p. 401.
5. Peter Campbell, *French Electoral Systems since 1789*, (London: Faber and Faber, 1958), p. 91.
6. Paul Smith, *A History of the French Senate* I *The Third Republic 1870-1940*, (Lampeter: Edwin Mellen Press, 2005), p. 356.
7. *Le Monde*, 25 April 1946.
8. Jean-Eric Callon, *Les projets constitutionnels de la Résistance*, (Paris: La documentation française, 1998), pp. 102-21.
9. Campbell, *op.cit.*, p. 135.
10. Franck Laffaille, *Le Président du Sénat depuis 1875*, (Paris: L'Harmattan, 2003), p. 68.
11. Jean-Paul Brunet, *Gaston Monnerville. Le Républicain qui défia de Gaulle*, (Paris: Albin Michel 1997), p. 137.
12. Laffaille, *op. cit.*, p. 313.
13. Jean-Dominique Lassaigne, 'La compétence législative du Conseil de la République', *Politique*, 45-48, 1969, pp. 157-167, p. 159.
14. Jean-Pierre Rioux, *La France de la Quatrième République,* I *L'ardeur et la nécessité*, (Paris: Seuil, 1980), p. 153.
15. *Le Figaro*, 8 November 1948.
16. Gaston Monnerville, 'Une remontée continue', *Politique*, 45-48, 1969, pp. 169-181.

2 - De Gaulle and the Senate

1. Marcel Prélot, *Pour comprendre la constitution*, (Paris: Editions du Centurion, 1959), p. 51.
2. Jean-Charles Maout and Raymond Muzellec, *Le Parlement sous la Ve République*, (Paris: Armand Colin 1971), p. 12.
3. Jean Gicquel, 'Le rôle des ministres d'Etat' in Didier Maus, Ludovic Favoreu and Jean-Luc Parodi, *L'Ecriture de la constitution de 1958*, (Aix-en-Provence: Presses universitaires d'Aix-Marseille, 1992), pp. 777-84, p. 784.
4. Paul Smith, *A History of the French Senate* II *The Fourth and Fifth Republics 1946-2004*, (Lampeter: Edwin Mellen Press, 2006), p. 136ff.
5. Didier Maus, 'Le Sénat', in Maus, Favoreu and Parodi, *op.cit.*, pp. 415- 57, p. 433.
6. Ibid., pp. 420-9.
7. Pierre Martin, *Les élections municipales en France depuis 1945*, (Paris: La documentation française, 2000), pp. 60-1.
8. *Le Monde*, 28 April 1959.
9. Carole Enfert, *Le règlement du Sénat sous la Ve République*, (Paris: Economica, 1999), p. 3 ; Hélène Ponceau, 'La crise réglementaire', *Politique*, 12 (45-48), 1969, pp.239-47.
10. Pierre Viansson-Ponté, *Histoire de la République gaullienne*. II - *Le temps des orphelins, août 1962-avril 1969*, (Paris: Seuil, 1971), p. 23.
11. *Année politique 1962*, (Paris: Presses universitaires de France, 1963), p. 105.
12. Pierre Avril, 'Georges Pompidou et le Parlement', Jean-Paul Cointet, *et al*, *Un politique: Georges Pompidou*, (Paris: Presses universitaires de France, 2001), pp. 139-68, p. 142.
13. William Safran, *The French Polity*, (New York, Harlow: Longman, fifth edition, 1998), p. 258.
14. Ibid., *p.* 147.
15. Jean Garrigues (ed.), *Histoire du parlement de 1789 à nos jours*, (Paris: Armand Colin, 2007), p. 453.
16. Jean-Marcel Jeanneney, *Une mémoire républicaine. Entretiens avec Jean Lacouture*, (Paris: Seuil, 1997), p. 260.
17. *Revue des deux mondes*, May 1969, p. 421.

3 - The parliamentary other 1969-1997

1. The term was coined by Jean Mastias in his magisterial account *Le Sénat de la Cinquième République*.
2. Pierre Lefranc, *Avec qui vous savez. Vingt-cinq ans avec de Gaulle* (Paris: Plon 1979), p. 291.
3. Gilles Le Béguec and Frédéric Turpin (eds), *Georges Pompidou et les institutions de la Ve République*, (Brussels: Peter Lang 2006), p. 172.
4. Avril, *op.cit.*, p. 149.
5. Smith, *A History*, II, p. 185.
6. Andrew Knapp and Vincent Wright, *The Government and Politics of France* (London: Routledge, 2006) p. 63.
7. Catherine Maynial, 'Le contrôle de l'application des lois exercé par le Sénat', *Contrôle parlementaire et évaluation*, (Paris: La documentation française, 1995), pp. 33-47.
8. Andrew Knapp, *Parties and the Political System in France. A Disconnected Democracy ?* (Basingstoke: Palgrave, 2004).
9. Charles Pasqua, *Ce que je sais... 1. Les Atrides 1974-1988* (Paris: Seuil, 2007), p. 121.
10. *Année politique 1986,* (1987), p. 107
11. Jean Mastias, 'La place du Sénat dans le système politique français', in Alain Delcamp (ed.), *Le bicamérisme* (Paris: Economica, 1997), p. 27.
12. Marie-France Verdier, 'Le Sénat dans les institutions de la Ve République 1958-1990', (Law thesis, Université de Bordeaux I, 1991), p. 173.
13. Mastias, 'La place', p. 25.
14. *Année politique 1986*, (1987), p. 136
15. *Année Politique 1987*, (1988), p. 95.
16. Knapp and Wright, *op.cit.*, p. 155.
17. On the Senate, decentralisation and the *rénovateurs*, see Alain Delcamp, *Le Sénat et la décentralisation* (Paris: Economica, 1991).
18. Jean Grangé, 'Attitudes et vicissitudes du Sénat', *Revue française de science politique,* 31 (1), 1981, pp. 32-84 ; *id.*, 'L'Efficacité normative du Sénat', *Revue française de science politique*, 34 (4-5), 1984, pp. 955-87.
19. *Id.*, 'Le système d'élection des sénateurs et ses effets', *Pouvoirs*, 44, 1988, pp. 35-57.
20. See Introduction note 13 above.

21. Sénat, *Recueil des Analyses des discussions législatives et des scrutins publics (et textes des résolutions portant sur des propositions d'actes communautaires)*, 1991-1992, 1, pp. 371-3.

22. On the Senate and the Balladur government see Jean-Eric Gicquel, 'Le Sénat sous la seconde cohabitation', *Revue du droit public et de la science politique en France et à l'étranger*, July-August 1996, pp. 1069-94.

4 - Anomaly and apotheosis 1998-2009

1. *Le Monde*, 21 April 1998.

2. Chirac established the Observatoire de la Parité in October 1995.

3. On the origins of the amendment to Article 39-2 see: François Robbe, 'Le Sénat défenseur des collectivités locale: histoire d'une "appropriation"', *Pouvoirs locaux*, 67, 4, 2005, 54-8 ; Paul Smith, '300 senators in search of a role: the French Senate as *chambre de la décentralisation*', *Nottingham French Studies*, 44, 1, pp. 82-95.

4. Smith, *A History,* II, p. 400.

5. Jack Lang, *Changer*, (Paris: Plon, 2005).

6. Fillon aired the possibility of the Fifth Republic evolving towards a 'real' presidential regime on the Hôtel Matignon website.<lemonde.fr/web/imprimer_element/0,40-0@2-24,50-931715,0.html> (5 July 2007). Two years later, however, he was concerned to create a clearer balance between the roles of President and prime minister.

7. <www.elysee.fr/download/?mode=press&filename=Disc-Epinal-12_07-07.pdf> (22 February 2009).

8. See note 5 above.

9. Edouard Balladur, *Une Ve République plus démocratique*, (Paris: Fayard/La documentation française, 2008).

10. <www.assemblee-nationale.fr/13/projets/pl0820.asp> (22 February 2009).

11. The progress of the reform can be followed via the Senate web pages at: <www.senat.fr/dossierleg/pjl07-365.html> (22 February 2009).

12. Patrick Roger, 'Pour Didier Maus, le pouvoir de blocage du Sénat est anormal', *Le Monde* 13 June 2008 ; *id.*, 'Réforme des institutions : le Sénat pose ses verrous', *loc cit.*

13. *Le Monde*, 16 July 2008.
14. Ibid., 17 July 2008.
15. Jacques Attali, *300 décisions pour change la France*, (Paris: XO Editions/La documentation française, 2008), p. 201.
16. <www.senat.fr/presse/cp20080121a.html> (5 February 2008).
17. <carrefourlocal.senat.fr/breves/breve4050.html> (14 February 2008).
18. *Le Figaro*, 22 October 2008.
19. Pascal Jan, 'Comité Balladur: réforme des collectivités territoriales', 23 October 2008 : <www.droitpublic.net/spip. php?article2471> (22 February 2009).
20. <carrefourlocal.senat.fr/breves/breve4752.html> (29 October 2008).
21. Xavier Ternisien, 'Le projet de réforme des collectivités locales sème la pagaille à l'UMP', <www.lemondefr/web /imprimer_element/0,40-0@2-823448,50-1102484,0.html> (6 October 2008).
22. The commission's proceedings can be consulted at: <www. reformedescollectiviteslocales.fr/home/index.php>, (22 February 2009).
23. Pascal Jan, 'Rapport Balladur. Réforme des collectivités territoriales', 15 December 2008, <www.droitpublic.net/spip. php?article2535> (22 February 2009).
24. <senat.fr/noticerap/2007/r07-262-notice.html> (22 February 2009).
25. Larcher made his contribution to the committee 7 January 2009
26. Pascal Jan, 'Comité Balladur: 15 régions au lieu des 22 et autres propositions', 13 February 2009, <www.droitpublic.net/spip.php?article2573> (22 February 2009). In the event, the report proposed a new status for 11 cities: Bordeaux, Lille, Lyon, Marseille, Nantes, Nice, Rennes, Rouen, Strasbourg, Toulon and Toulouse, as well as the creation of a Greater Paris unitary authority.

5 - Departments, seats and colleges

1. Ministère de l'Intérieur, de la Sécurité Sociale et des Libertés Locales, *Les Collectivités locales en chiffres 2005*, (Paris: La documentation française, 2005), p. 114.
2. Ginovès, *op.cit.*, p. 334.

3. Gilles Le Béguec, 'Les socialistes et le Sénat', *Parlements. Histoire et Politique*, no.6, 2006, pp. 57-72.
4. Sénat, *Bulletin Quotidien de la Presse*, 24 Novembre 1997, pp. 11-12.
5. Conseil Constitutionnel, Décision 2000-431, 6 July 2000.
6. On the eve of the 1980 *renouvellement*, François Goguel suggested a redistribution package that would have created an extra 17 one-seat departments: *Le Monde*, 25, 26, 27 September 1980.
7. *Journal Officiel, Sénat, Documents*, 2000-2001, no.142.
8. The electoral code introduces a deliberate discrepancy here at the 9,000 inhabitant watershed.
9. Jan, 'La place', p. 53.
10. Smith, *A History* II, pp. 342-5.
11. Balladur, *op. cit.*, p. 139.
12. *Journal Officiel, Sénat, Documents,* 2006-2007, no.386.
13. *Le Monde*, 17 July 2008.
14. <www.senat.fr/presidence/discours/larcher_14_10.html> (22 February 2009).
15. *Le Monde*, 25 September 1998.
16. Ibid., 10 January 2009.

6 - *Les élus des élus*

1. Michel Rocard in Rocard and Georges-Marc Benamou, *Si la gauche savait*, (Paris: Robert Laffont 2005), p. 152.
2. Only two departments elected their senators by PR in series A in 1998, but by 2008 the number had risen to seven.
3. *Le Parisien*, 16 September 2004.
4. *Le Monde*, 23 September 2008.
5. The new seat was for the overseas *collectivité* of Wallis et Futuna.
6. Jean-Luc Parodi, 'Des élections sénatoriales pas tout à fait comme les autres', *Revue politique et parlementaire,* 79 (870), 1977, pp. 36-41.
7. *Le Point*, 25 September 2008
8. *L'Express,* 12 February 2007
9. Charasse was replaced by Gérard Miquel (Lot). One of his most trusted advisors in his second septennate, Charasse acted as messenger between Mitterrand and Chirac during the 1993-5 cohabitation. After backing Laurent Fabius for the PS

nomination in 2006, during the campaign proper Charasse ostentatiously welcomed Sarkozy to Puy-Guillaume, where he was mayor. On Charasse, Mitterrand and the right, see Franz-Oliver Giesbert, *La tragédie du président. Scènes de la vie politique 1986-2006*, (Paris ; Flammarion 2006), pp. 121, 123.

10. Conseil Constitutionnel, DC-2008-572; *Le Monde*, 10 January 2009

11. Smith, '300 senators', pp. 88-90.

12. François Chevalier, *Le Sénateur français 1875-1995. Essai sur le recrutement et la représentativité des membres de la seconde chambre*, (Paris: LGDJ, 1998), p. 281.

13. *Le Monde*, 28 September 1998.

14. Vigouroux also took a seat in the upper house.

15. Fillon stood in the general election. He was elected in the first round in the 4th district of the Sarthe.

16. Trailing Sarkozy by 2 per cent (27 to 25) in Dieppe in the first round, in the second Royal turned the result on its head, polling 54.5 per cent. The Union de la Gauche secured the same vote in the first round in March 2008.

17. Claude Lévy, *La bulle de la République. Enquête sur le Sénat* (Paris: Calmann-Lévy, 2006), pp. 196-7

18. Chevalier, *op.cit.*, pp. 320-1.

19. Smith, *A History* I, p. 105

20. Chevalier, *op.cit.*, p. 311.

21. 'Opération « têtes neuves » au PS', *Le Point*, 25 September 2008, p. 66.

22. Compte rendu analytique, séance du 17 octobre 2006 - <http://www.senat.fr/cra/s20061017/s20061017H10.html > (31 October 2006)

23. Roland du Luart succeeded to his father's title in 1980. In order to comply with the limit on the *cumul* of offices, Luart is presently second assistant mayor of Le Luart.

24. The Dominati dynasty (father Jacques, and son Philippe, as well as his brother Laurent) was associated, unfortunately, with allegations of falsifying electoral lists in the third *arrondissement* of Paris in the late 1980s. The case reached the courts in 2006. Jacques and Laurent Dominati were acquitted, but the senator received a suspended sentence and a fine.

25. <http://robertdelpicchia.typepad.com/about.html> (29 October 2006).

26. *Le Monde*, 21 September 2001

27.   Pierre Favier and Michel Martin-Roland, *La décennie Mitterrand*, I *Les ruptures (1981-1984)*, (Paris: Seuil 1990), p. 329

28.   *Le Monde*, 23 September 2008

29.   <www.conseilconstitutionnel.fr/dossier/senatoriales/2004/documents/contant.htm>, (7 May 2007).

30.   In the absence of a manageable majority, the chair reverted to the *doyen d'âge*. In 2001 the regional Court of Audit published a highly critical report of Bergelin's use of public funds.

31.   Members of the electoral college must produce a verified, *bona fide* excuse for their absence.

32.   Hoeffel's list received 321 votes, while the UMP took the seat with 323.5 on the highest average.

33.   The imminence of the next *renouvellement* of series B, in September 1983, made finding a replacement less urgent

34.   Lévy, *op.cit.*, pp. 27-8.

35.   Ibid., p. 37.

7 - Being a senator

1.   <www.senat.fr/seances/s200110/s20011001/sc20011001004.html>, (25 February 2009)

2.   <www.senat.fr/seances/s200810/s20081001/s20081001001.html#Niv1_SOM7, (25 February 2009)

3.   Arnaud Martin, *Le président des assemblées parlementaires sous la Ve République*, Paris: LGDJ, 1996, p. 23

4.   Laffaille, *op.cit.*, pp. 62-3.

5.   Smith, *A History,* II, pp. 166-8.

6.   *Le Monde*, 4 October 1992.

7.   'Les rôles du Sénat selon René Monory', *Le Courrier du Parlement*, no. 813, novembre 1992, pp. 14-18, p. 16.

8.   *Le Monde*, 16 June 1998

9.   Ibid., 11 September 1998.

10.   Ibid., 3 October 1998. See also Franck Laffaille, 'L'élection d'octobre 1998: l'éviction historique du président du Sénat par ses pairs', *Petites Affiches*, no. 150, 29 juillet 1999, pp. 23-29.

11.   Smith, *A History,* II, p. 324.

12.   Hervé Gattegno, 'M. Poncelet, actionnaire masqué d'une banque en Floride', *Le Monde*, 14 July 2005; *Les "Gaymard" de la République – Les dossiers du Canard enchaîné*, (2005), p. 26.

13. Didier Hassoux and Vanessa Schneider, 'Au Sénat, l'âge du capitaine commence à faire jaser', *Libération*, 11 October 2005.
14. Ibid. Poncelet later nominated Méar to the Conseil Supérieur de l'Audiovisuel.
15. Patrick Roger, 'Au Palais du Luxembourg, atmosphère de fin de règne et règlements de comptes feutrés', *Le Monde*, 14 July 2005.
16. Hassoux and Schneider, *op,cit.*.
17. Patrick Roger, 'La guerre de succession pour la présidence du Sénat est ouverte', *Le Monde*, 7 June 2007.
18. Robert Colonna d'Istria and Yvan Stefanovitch, *Le Sénat - Enquête sur les superprivilégiés de la République*, (Paris: Editions du Rocher 2008), pp. 67-9.
19. Patrick Roger, 'Christian Poncelet s'efface sans gloire', *Le Monde*, 3 October 2008.
20. Ibid., 11 September 2008.
21. *Le Point*, 25 September 2008.
22. *Le Parisien*, 25 September 2008.
23. *Le Monde*, 17 January 2008
24. *Le Figaro*, 23 October 2008.
25. See note 19 above.
26. Anna Bitton, 'Le "bon Gérard" de Sarkozy', *Le Point*, 5 February 2009, pp. 47-8.
27. *Le Parisien*, 25 September 2008.
28. *Le Figaro*, 25 September 2008.
29. Smith, *A History*, I, p. 121.
30. The Ecologists in the Senate, for example, are all *rattachés* of the Socialist group.
31. Centre Républicain d'Action Rurale et Sociale *and* Républicains Indépendants d'Action Sociale.
32. Pierre Martin, *op.cit.*, p. 121
33. After Mélenchon's defection from the Socialists, the CRC became the Groupe Communiste, Républicain et Citoyen et des Sénateurs du Parti de la Gauche. Curiously, Jean-Pierre Chevènement, founder of the Mouvement des Citoyens, whose members had previously joined the CRC, joined the RDSE on his election in 2008.

8 - Conclusion

1. <www.senat.fr/presidence/discours/larcher_14_10.html.> (25 February 2009).

2. Béatrice Gurrey, 'Gérard Larcher: chasse gardée', *Le Monde*, 3 October 2008.

3. In 1983 Larcher defeated Boutin, then of the UDF, in a particularly robust primary to become mayor of Rambouillet. His introduction into politics was thanks to another senator-mayor of the town, the Radical Jacqueline Thome-Patenôtre, who was mayor for 36 years before Larcher, *sénatrice* (before the term existed) under the Fourth Republic (1946-1958), *députée* (1958-1978) and then an MEP (1984-1989).

4. The 'opposition' comprised two Centrist, two RDSE and 17 UMP senators.

5. Anna Bitton, *loc.cit.,* pp. 47-8.

6. Ibid., p. 47

7. Guy Carcassonne, 'La VIe République au banc d'essai', *Le Point*, 15 September 2005, pp. 38-9, p. 38. See also Arnaud Montebourg and Bastien François, *La Constitution de la 6e République. Reconcilier les Français avec la démocratie*, Paris: Odile Jacob, 2005, pp. 76-8.

Select Bibliography

Alexander, G., 'France: Reform Mongering Between Majority Runoff and Proportionality' in Colomer, J. M. (ed.), *Handbook of Electoral System Choice*, Basingstoke: Palgrave Macmillan, 2004, pp. 209-21.

Alliès, P., 'Les effets du cumul des mandats sur le personnel politique', in *Le cumul des mandats et des fonctions*, Paris: La documentation française, 1999, pp. 63-76.

Alliès, P., 'Sénat : pour en finir avec l'anachronisme', *Pouvoirs locaux*, 67, 4, 2005, pp. 87-92.

Attali, J., *300 décisions pour change la France*, Paris: XO Editions - La documentation française, 2008.

Avril, P., 'Georges Pompidou et le Parlement' in Cointet, J.-P. *et al*, *Un politique : Georges Pompidou*, Paris: Presses Universitaires de France, 2001, pp. 139-68.

Balladur, E., *Une Ve République plus démocratique*, Paris, Fayard/La documentation française, 2008.

Baroli, M. and Robert, D., *Du Conseil de la République au Sénat 1946-1958*, Paris: Presses universitaires de France, 2002.

Bellamy, D., *Geoffroy de Montalembert (1898-1993) : Un aristocrate en République*, Rennes: Presses universitaire de Rennes, 2006.

Bon, F., 'Le référendum du 27 avril 1969: suicide politique ou nécessité stratégique?', *Revue française de science politique*, 20(2), 1970, pp. 205-23.

Bruyas, J., 'L'évolution du Conseil de la République', *Revue du droit public*, 1949, pp. 541-78.

Callon, J.-E., *Les projets constitutionnels de la Résistance*, Paris: La documentation française, 1998.

Campbell, P., *French Electoral Systems and Elections 1789-1957*, London: Faber and Faber, 1958.

Chazelle, R., 'Continuité et tradition juridique au sein de la seconde chambre: le Sénat et le droit parlementaire coutumier', *Revue du droit public*, 103, 1987, pp. 711-33.

Chevalier, F., *Le Sénateur français 1875-1995. Essai sur le recrutement et la représentativité des membres de la seconde chambre,* Paris: LGDJ, 1998.

Cluzel, J., *Le Sénat dans la société française*, Paris: Economica, 1990.

Cluzel, J., 'Le Sénat, ses pouvoirs, ses missions', *Revue des sciences morales et politiques*, 1, 1992, pp. 57-94.

Cluzel, J., *L'Indispensable Sénat*, Paris: Economica, 1998.

Cluzel, J., *A propos du Sénat et de ceux qui voudraient en finir avec lui*, Paris: Archipel, 1999.

Colonna d'Istria, R., and Stefanovitch, Y., *Le Sénat. Enquête sur les superprivilegiés des la République*, Paris: Rocher, 2008.

Delcamp, A., 'Le rôle législatif du Sénat', *Revue du droit public*, 88, 1972, pp. 1175-228.

Delcamp, A., *Le Sénat et la décentralisation*, Paris: Economica, 1991.

Delcamp, A., (ed.), *Le bicamérisme*, Paris: Economica, 1997.

Fondraz, L., *Les groupes parlementaires au Sénat sous la Ve République*, Paris: Economica, 2000.

Enfert, C., *Le règlement du Sénat sous la Ve République*, Paris: Economica, 1999.

Garrigues, Jean (ed.), *Histoire du parlement de 1789 à nos jours*, Paris: Armand Colin, 2007.

Georgel, J., *Le Sénat dans l'adversité (1962-1966)*, Paris: Editions Cujas, 1968.

Gicquel, J.-E., 'Le Sénat sous la seconde cohabitation', *Revue du droit public et de la science politique en France et à l'étranger*, juillet-août, 1996, pp. 1069-94.

Grangé, J., 'Attitudes et vicissitudes du Sénat (1958-1980)', *Revue française de science politique*, 31 (1), 1981, pp. 32-84.

Grangé, J., 'L'efficacité normative du Sénat', *Revue française de science politique*, 34 (4-5), 1984, pp. 955-87.

Grangé, J., 'Le système d'élection des sénateurs et ses effets', *Pouvoirs*, 44, 1984, pp. 35-57.

Grangé, J., 'Les déformations de la représentation des collectivités territoriales et de la population au Sénat', *Revue française de science politique*, 40(1), 1990, pp. 5-45.

Grofman, B. and Lewis-Beck, M.S., 'Elections under the French Double-Ballot System: An Introduction', *French Politics*, 3, 2, 2005, pp. 93-7.

Hérin, J.-L., *Le Sénat en devenir*, Paris: Montchrestien, 2001.

Huber, J.D., *Rationalizing Parliament. Legislative Institutions and Party Politics in France*, Cambridge: Cambridge University Press, 1996.

Jan, P., *Les assemblées parlementaires françaises*, Paris: La documentation française, 2005.

Knapp, A., *Gaullism since de Gaulle*, Aldershot: Dartmouth Publishing Company, 1994.

Knapp, A., *Parties and the Political System in France. A Disconnected Democracy?* Basingstoke: Palgrave Macmillan, 2004.

Laffaille F., *Le Président du Sénat depuis 1875*, Paris: L'Harmattan, 2003.

Lassaigne, J.-D., 'Le Sénat et son avenir', *Revue politique et parlementaire*, 68 (764), 1966, pp. 14-22.

Lassaigne, J.-D., 'Le bicamérisme incomplet', *Politique*, 45-48, 1969, pp. 145-55.

Lassaigne, J.-D., 'La compétence législative du Conseil de la République', *Politique*, 45-48, 1969, pp. 157-67.

Le Béguec, G., 'Les socialistes et le Sénat', *Parlements. Histoire et Politique*, 6, 2006, pp. 57-72.

Le Béguec, G., and Turpin, B., *Georges Pompidou et les institutions de la Ve République*, Brussels: Peter Lang, 2006.

Le Gall, G., 'Sénatoriales: la fin de la "discipline républicaine"?', *Revue politique et parlementaire*, 82 (888), 1980, 9-15.

Le Gall, G., 'Sénatoriales 1983: avantage accru de l'opposition au sein d'une assemblée immuable', *Revue politique et parlementaire*, 85 (906), 1983, pp. 19-29.

Lévy, C., *La bulle de la République. Enquête sur le Sénat*, Paris: Calmann-Lévy, 2006

Lijphart, A., *Electoral Systems and Party Systems: A Study of Twenty-Seven Democracies 1945-1990*, Oxford: Oxford University Press, 1994.

Maout, J.-Ch. and Muzellec, R., *Le Parlement sous la Ve République*, Paris: Armand Colin, 1971.

Martin, A., *Le président des assemblées parlementaires sous la Ve République*, Paris: LGDJ, 1996.

Martin, P., *Les élections municipales en France depuis 1945*, Paris: La documentation française, 2000.

Mastias, J., *Le Sénat de la Cinquième République. Réforme et renouveau*, Paris: Economica, 1980.

Mastias, J., and Grangé, J. *Les secondes chambres du parlement en Europe occidentale*, Paris: Economica, 1987.

Mastias, J., 'Histoire des tentations du Sénat sous la Ve République', *Pouvoirs*, 1988, pp. 15-34.

Maynial, C., 'Le contrôle de l'application des lois exercé par le Sénat', in Delcamp, A., Bergel, J.-L. and Dupas, A., (eds)

Contrôle parlementaire et évaluation, pp. 33-47, Paris: La documentation française, 1995.

Maus, D., 'Le Sénat', in Maus, D., Favoreu, L. and Parodi, J.-L., (eds) *L'Ecriture de la constitution de 1958*, pp. 415-66, Aix-en-Provence: Presses universitaires d'Aix-Marseille, 1992.

Maus, D., 'Le Sénat, l'Assemblée nationale et le gouvernement', *Pouvoirs*, 44, 1988, pp. 122-30.

Mazet, Pierre, 'Portrait de sénateur: La contribution de la doctrine et des acteurs à la production de l'image instituée du sénateur de la République', in Poirmeur, Y. and Mazet, P., *Le métier politique en représentations*, pp. 263-92, Paris: L'Harmattan, 1999.

Ministère de l'Intérieur, de la Sécurité Sociale et des Libertés Locales, *Les Collectivités locales en chiffres 2005*, (Paris : La documentation française, 2005).

Monnerville, G., 'Une révision constitutionnelle, est-elle nécessaire?', *Revue politique et parlementaire*, 63 (711), 1961, pp. 3-22.

Monnerville, G., *Le Sénat, institution fondamentale d'une république démocratique*, Paris: Serpic., 1965.

Monnerville, G., *Vingt-deux ans de présidence*, (revised edition) Paris: Le cherche midi 2003.

Moutet, M., 'Le Sénat dans la Ve République', *Revue socialiste*, mai 1959, pp. 149-71.

Parodi, J.-L., 'Le conflit entre l'exécutif et président du Sénat', *Revue française de science politique*, 13(2), 1963, pp. 454-59.

Parodi, J.-L., 'Des élections sénatoriales pas tout à fait comme les autres', *Revue politique et parlementaire,* 79 (870), 1977, pp. 36-41.

Pascaud, G., 'La crise présidentielle', *Politique*, 12 (45-8), 1969, pp. 249-59.

Pasqua, C., *Ce que je sais... 1. Les Atrides*, Paris: Seuil, 2007.

Perrineau, P., 'Les élections sénatoriales: une majorité renforcée et modifiée', *Revue politique et parlementaire*, 88 (925), 1986, pp. 19-26.

Ponceau, H., 'La crise réglementaire', *Politique*, 12 (45-48), 1969, pp. 239-47.

Poncelet, C., 'La Ve: Une répartition claire des pouvoirs et des responsabilités', *Revue politique et parlementaire*, 997, novembre-décembre, 1998, pp. 47-53.

Poncelet, C., 'La Ve République d'aujourd'hui: un régime qui manque de contre-pouvoirs', *Revue du droit public et de la science politique en France et a l'étranger*, numéro spécial, 'La VIe République?', 1 and 2, 2002, pp. 99-104.

Ponceyri, R., *Gaullisme électoral et Ve République*, Toulouse: Presses de l'Institut d'Etudes Politiques de Toulouse, 1985.

Prélot, M., *Pour comprendre la constitution*, Paris: Editions du Centurion, second edition, 1959.

Prélot, M., 'La République sénatoriale', *Politique*, 12 (45-48), 1969, pp. 197-214.

'Pour un vrai Sénat des territoires', *Pouvoirs locaux*, 67, 4, 2005.

Robbe, F., *La représentation des collectivités territoriales par le Sénat. Etude sur l'article 24 alinéa 3 de la constitution française du 4 octobre 1958*, Paris: LGDJ, 2001.

Rocard, M. and Benamou, G.-M. *Si la gauche savait*, Paris: Robert Laffont, 2005.

Roche, J., 'Le Sénat de la République dans la constitution de 1958', *Revue du droit public*, 75, 1959, pp. 1126-54.

Russell, M., *Reforming the House of Lords. Lessons from Overseas*, Oxford: Oxford University Press, 2000.

Safran, W., *The French Polity*, Harlow: Longman, fifth edition, 1998.

Smith, P., '300 senators in search of a role: the French Senate as *chambre de la décentralisation*', *Nottingham French Studies*, 44, 1, 2005, pp. 82-95.

Smith, P., *A History of the French Senate*. Volume 1 - *The Third Republic 1870-1945*, Lampeter: Edwin Mellen Press, 2005.

Smith, P., *A History of the French Senate*. Volume 2 - *The Fourth and Fifth Republics 1945-2004*, Lampeter: Edwin Mellen Press, 2006.

Verdier, M.-F., 'Le Sénat dans les institutions de la Ve République 1958-1992', thèse de droit, Université de Bordeaux I, 1991.

Verdier, M.-F., 'La IIIe cohabitation ou le retour aux sources du Sénat ?', *Revue politique et parlementaire*, 100 (997), 1998, pp. 74-88.

Weber, Y., 'La crise du bicaméralisme', *Revue du droit public*, 88, 1972, pp. 573-602.

Zimmermann, M.-J., 'Parité et moyenne d'âge aux sénatoriales 2004: des progrès limités', Paris: Observatoire de la parité entre les hommes et les femmes, 2004.

Index

Accoyer, Bernard, 87, 89
Afars et Issas (former overseas territory), 102
Ain (department), 47, 98, 107, 112, 114, 126-7, 133
Aisne (department), 111, 116, 133, 150
Alduy, Jacqueline, 149
Alduy, Jean-Paul, 149
Alduy, Paul, 149
Algeria, 38, 46, 96
Algiers, 38
Alliance pour la France, 77
Allier (department), 112, 116, 133
Alpes, Hautes- (department), 17, 113, 115, 133
Alpes-de-Haute-Provence (department), 113, 115
Alpes-Maritimes (department), 111, 114, 119, 127, 133, 146
Alsace (region), 13, 95, 99
alternance, 63, 69, 77, 129, 139, 142, 182
Amélie-les-Bains (Pyrénées-Orientales), 149
Angels, Bernard, 145
Antony (Hauts-de-Seine), 120
apparentés, 182, 188
Ardèche (department), 112, 115, 133, 154
Ardennes (department), 112, 116, 133, 150
Ariège (department), 100, 113, 116, 132-3
Arthuis, Jean, 66, 69, 82, 90, 165, 173, 180, 192
Assemblée de Corse (regional assembly), 110

Assemblée des Départements de France (ADF), 90
Assemblée des Français de l'Étranger (AFE), 122, 152-4; see also Conseil Supérieur des Français de l'Étranger
Association des Maires de France (AMF), 81, 90
Association des Maires de Grandes Villes de France (AMGVF), 90, 144
Association des Régions de France (ARF), 89-90
Association Nationale des Ecoles Françaises de l'Étranger, 153
Attali, Jacques, 84, 88-90, 202
Attilio, Henri d', 156
Aube (department), 112, 115, 133, 154
Aude (department), 112, 116, 133, 149
Audiffret-Pasquier, Duc d', 18
Auriol, Vincent, 28, 30, 35, 38
autoréforme, 50, 103, 119, 163
Aveyron (department), 112, 116, 133
avis conforme (Senate of the Third Republic), 13, 27

Badinter, Elisabeth, 145
Badinter, Robert, 7, 143, 145
Bailly, Jean, 134
Balkany, Patrick 120
Balladur, Edouard, 3, 6, 72-3, 83, 84, 88- 92, 118, 140, 161, 167, 178, 185, 192
Barre, Raymond, 61-3, 66-7, 141, 150, 167

215